# RENEWING HOPE
# WITHIN
# NEIGHBORHOODS
# OF DESPAIR

To Jim,
whose discussion
of "jelly-rolls"
made it all click.

thanks

Herb R.

SUNY series in Urban Public Policy
James Bohland and Patricia Edwards, editors

# Renewing Hope within Neighborhoods of Despair

## The Community-Based Development Model

Herbert J. Rubin

STATE UNIVERSITY OF NEW YORK PRESS

Published by
State University of New York Press, Albany

© 2000 State University of New York

For information, address State University of New York Press,
State University Plaza, Albany, N.Y., 12246

Production by Cathleen Collins
Marketing by Dana E. Yanulavich

**Library of Congress Cataloging in Publication Data**

Rubin, Herbert J.
    Renewing hope within neighborhoods of despair : the community-
based development model / Herbert J. Rubin.
        p.   cm. — (SUNY series in urban public policy)
    Includes bibliographical references and index.
        ISBN 0-7914-4553-4 (alk. paper). — ISBN 0-7914-4554-2 (pbk. :
alk. paper)
        1. Community development, Urban—United States.   2. Community
organization—United States.   3. Economic development projects—
United States.   4. Inner cities—United States.   5. Urban poor—
United States.   6. Neighborhood—United States.   7. Urban renewal—
United States.   I. Title.   II. Series : SUNY series in urban public
policy.
HN90.C6R735   2000
307.1'416'0973—dc21
                                                                    99-39478
                                                                    CIP

10 9 8 7 6 5 4 3 2 1

# Contents

# Tables

# Preface

I know there are times when I come [to] the street and have my rose
colored glasses on and I see things developing and evolve and that
keeps me going and I also see the reality of what is there.
　　　　　　　　—Director of CBDO in a community still not repaired
　　　　　　　　　　　　　from the urban unrest of the sixties

*R*enewing Hope shares the story of those in the community-based development
movement who struggle to recreate hope within neighborhoods of economic
and social despair. These *developmental activists* lead *community-based development
organizations*—*CBDOs*—in uphill battles to bring about affordable, quality housing, commercial opportunities, and employment within poor areas. To gain the
resources needed, CBDOs combine support from government, financial intermediaries, and, foundations with investments from the private sector. In attempting renewal efforts in communities that others have abandoned, developmental
activists, in their own words, remain "profoundly ignorant of the impossible."

Renewing Hope blends together my observations of the community development movement with the narratives of the development activists of how they
accomplish these projects and the organic theories that explain why they do so.
It describes how small non-profit community-based development organizations
are able to build homes and create jobs within poor communities. It also explores
the guiding ideologies of the developmental activists, and how these ideologies
enable CBDOs to integrate the separate agendas of government, foundations,
and intermediaries for community change.

Doing the study took half a decade. I visited six dozen community-based
development organizations, each multiple times, attended meetings of coalitions
and trade associations, read hundreds of separate documents, and mulled over the
millions of words developmental activists shared with me in in-depth interviews.
I observed and audio recorded activists at meetings, walked through projects with
them, took tours along with the practitioners, and read reports written by the
activists, ranging from philosophical discussions of how CBDOs differed from for-
profit firms, to technical documents explaining laboriously prepared spread sheets.

As I better understood how the broader organizational environment influenced development work, I extended my interviewing to include those from foundations, intermediaries, and government.

My initial impressions of what community development was about came through observations made of the physical neighborhoods in which CBDOs work. Within these communities the physical signs of neglect were palpable—potholes in the streets, boarded-up apartments, rows of vacated storefronts, empty lots now cleared of derelict buildings, broken pay telephones, and, in densely settled cities, block after block without a restaurant, grocery store, or place to purchase ordinary goods. I saw bullet holes in the walls of a day-care center developed by a CBDO and shared the sense of violation with a developmental activist, as we viewed gang graffiti on the wall of a new restaurant whose opening was intended to communicate the renewal of the neighborhood. I cried as I held a baby with AIDS who was being cared for in a day-care center build by a CBDO.

I learned of the frustrations felt by developmental activists in "doing the deals" as they

> struggle with the same alligators. . . . Short money. Some days, man I wake up in the morning and I ask myself, . . . "Why the hell I keep doing this?" You take these problems home with you.

And I heard the dismay of the long-time community developer who fretted that

> [development work] is the nature of swimming up stream, it makes you tired. . . . Like salmon you get to swim upstream. . . . You think it's hard because you're not a good swimmer. . . . You're swimming upstream, it's hard, there's no reflection on [how] good a swimmer you are or not. And then the finale is . . . when you get to the top of the stream? . . . You get fucked and then you die!

These first visits put face and texture to the cold social statistics describing high unemployment, escalated crime rates, or abandoned or substandard housing. They also made clear the frustrations felt by those who chose to combat these problems. These were the images of despair.

But within these neighborhoods I saw the hopes and possibilities—new stores, apartments, homes, day-care centers—brought to fruition by the CBDOs. Within blocks, still pockmarked by the upheavals of the sixties, next to vacant lots and boarded-up buildings, I visited newly built bungalows or town homes, owned or rented, thanks to CBDOs, by families with low or very low incomes. I examined numerous gutted apartment buildings being rebuilt into affordable, subsidized units and nervously walked over an open beam to view the construction, where a community-based development organization was converting an abandoned neighborhood school into a care facility for the elderly on Medicaid.

Elsewhere I saw homes rebuilt by professional carpenters who were teaching neighborhood teenagers their craft. In a downwardly mobile, ethnic neighborhood I watched as a convent, too expensive for the archdiocese to maintain, was reconstructed to provide affordable housing for the community elderly. I visited refurbished homes now occupied by those who had moved from public housing homes, made affordable through the sweat-equity contributions of future owners and the deep subsidies packaged by the community-based development organizations. In a gang-dominated neighborhood, I visited an abandoned car dealership that a CBDO had converted into an auto-repair and body shop to provide job training for the immigrant young. I ate a meal in a multi-ethnic food court attached to a new supermarket, co-owned by a CBDO, that provided quality food and household goods in one of the nation's poorest neighborhoods that a year before had no other affordable shopping.

I heard the enthusiasms and dedications of the developmental activists. One person described the excitement of doing the projects themselves:

> I could build things. I could take a dumpy building and change it around or a dumpy area and have an impact on it. . . . This is tangible, bricks and boards and it is concrete and it is steel and I can see those things. And, I love it. I really enjoy taking the risks.

Another talked on the satisfaction in creating jobs that end up "increasing people's income and self-esteem." Others explained the human reasons for building homes, in this case an affordable apartment for the elderly:

> Let me tell . . . the part of the story, the human part. . . . [What] we got in this neighborhood here are a ton of people . . . low-income working-class blue collar workers. . . . These people don't have pensions. . . . Every extra dime they had went to pay for college tuition, for seven kids, or whatever it was. . . .
>
> And, now by virtual of retirement they've become poor people. They are existing on $7,000 worth of social security a year. . . . People who live in a bungalow . . . they are paying the taxes. And, they are just praying that the boiler doesn't break down because they don't have the cash flow to make any structural repairs. . . . That's the kind of people we are dealing with.

Most important, though, I heard the moral obligation felt by the developmental activists to renew communities, as one described

> all the problems I am having in [a particularly deteriorated block] **But that is the point: I mean if we don't do it, nobody's going to do it.** . . . It is not our point to suck up profits that other groups could do. It is my

point to try to encourage as many other people in as possible. **I want to take on the worst of the worst of the worst** and pave the way for the guys who want to make some money at this.

And meeting that moral obligation provides

> the satisfaction to see people become homeowners. Seeing a piece of property that looked like it was only fit for termites, turn around and become something very nice. . . . A piece of property has been saved. One more piece of housing stock hasn't bit the dust.

This moral obligation to renew is part of a broader ideology, an organic theory, about restoring and empowering communities. Developmental activists explained that the goal of community-based development is not simply about building, but rather it is about enabling the poor to gain the personal dignity, pride, empowerment, as well as responsibility, that comes from being socially and economically rooted. One CBDO placed on its organization's masthead "the philosophy of [the CBDO] is that people in our communities can do something about our economic conditions, instead of waiting for and depending on government assistance." John M. Perkins, the founder of the Christian Community Development Association, echoed these sentiments:

> The motto of community development in the 1960s could have been this: "Give people a fish and they'll eat for a day." The 1970s motto could have been: "Teach people to fish and they'll eat for a lifetime."
> . . . The 1990s (and beyond) approach to development needs to ask the question: "Who owns the pond?" (Perkins 1993, p. 119)

The answer for those in the community development movement is that it should either be the poor themselves or organizations responsive to the communities.

I learned about the technicalities of doing deals, as well as the philosophies for why and how these deals should be done. But I also heard of the conflicts that came about as foundations, government, and investors tried to impose their own views of what development should be about. For instance, the CBDO that turned the old convent into housing for the community elderly, did so against the advice of funders, who felt it would have been cheaper to tear down the convent and build anew. Yet, to the developmental activist doing so would destroy a central symbol of the community. The activist, described her encounter with the funder:

> **Yes, it would be cheaper to build new, but we're asking you to invest in a neighborhood. Not in bricks and mortar.** I said, "Look at this building. This thing's built like a Sherman tank—it's got 12" walls, for God's sake. . . . I mean, they don't build buildings like this anymore." So beyond the fact that it was a quality building that needed to be pre-

served, what about the message to the neighborhood? Oh, I'm sorry, just go in and bulldoze it and start new.

Gaining funds for projects can be difficult, requiring constant effort and attention to local politics:

> You're an advocate for the area. And, a lot of times the person who yells the loudest is the one that gets the oil. . . . We try to make friends in the departments, find out who has the power, who has the influence, what does it take, what is hot on their agenda and push the right buttons and get our programs through. We are always competing for these grants, especially the local grants.

To complicate matters, funding for development can change over night as new administrations come into office or, worse yet, the Department of Housing and Urban Development once again has to reinvent itself.

Community-based development organizations must package investment capital from the private sector along with support from government and foundations to pay social costs, but do so in an environment in which few fully trust community groups to be effective. To help CBDOs bridge the gap between the private and public sectors, a set of organizations, the financial *intermediaries*, have come into being. These organizations such as Enterprise, LISC—the Local Initiatives Support Corporation, and several dozen city-wide intermediaries, combine money from businesses, government, and foundations, assure funders on the viability of the projects, and then pass the funds to the CBDOs.

Foundations and intermediaries, and often governments, support community renewal. Yet the images of what must be done held by these larger entities can conflict with those of the developmental activists. Developmental activists appreciate and require the financial and technical support from government and the intermediaries, yet as one commented, "I don't like the idea that LISC speaks for me." Part of work of the developmental activists becomes that of shaping the goals of the broader societal sector (Scott and Meyer 1991) to encourage funders to accept the agendas that emerge from the community groups, rather than impose ideas from above.

To examine the influence process between funders and CBDOs, I selectively studied interactions between CBDOs and their funders over time and in a number of distinct locales. These case studies show the vulnerabilities of the CBDOs to changes in the support environment, but also indicate that small organizations can themselves shape the beliefs that guide what is to be done. To do so, CBDOs create a counterstructure of coalitions and trade associations that collectively push for the agendas preferred by the CBDOs. These agendas emerge as developmental activists reflect on their development experiences, from these experiences formulate an organic theory of social change, and then at conferences, meetings with one another, and discussions with funders provide narratives of success that communicate these agendas. By doing so, developmental activists frame an image of what development ought to be about and encourage the larger agencies to accept this image.

## THE FLOW OF THE STORY

I present my argument in four steps. In the first stage, I suggest the core intellectual questions of how environmental factors affect the way in which community-based organizations go about their work. In chapter 1, I describe exemplary projects and hint at the broader model of how projects emerge as a result of interorganizational contentions. Chapter 2 examines how the volatile organizational and social environment influences what CBDOs can accomplish. The new institutionalism literature suggests that to survive within an unstable environmental, CBDOs would end having to be responsive to the agendas of the larger, wealthier organizations.

The second stage of the argument, presented in chapters 3–5, describes the environmental pressures CBDOs face. Chapter 3 examines the tensions CBDOs confront as they try at one and the same time to accomplish possibly contradictory ends—building projects that are economically viable, providing services for neighborhoods in need, all the while sustaining themselves as viable organizations. Chapter 4 examines how CBDOs respond to changes in government policies, while chapter 5 details interactions with intermediaries and foundations. Without public funding and support from foundations and intermediaries most efforts of the CBDOs would be still-born. Yet obtaining this funding can force CBDOs to follow agendas not their own. Case studies of these tensions are presented, each illustrating suggestions from the new institutionalism literature.

In the third stage of my argument, I suggest that CBDOs, though fiscally dependent, are still able to partially shape their own work environment. First, in the world of social change, ideas do count. By reflecting on their community renewal efforts, developmental activists have worked out an organic theory that indicates rationales—an organic theory—for why their projects are about more than simply physically improving neighborhoods. Chapter 6 describes the organic theory, detailing ways in which projects empower both individuals and communities as a whole. Next by publicizing the successes that come about in following these models, developmental activists persuade others to buy into their approaches to social change. Then developmental activists master the art of fiscal leveraging that enables CBDOs to combine funds from government, foundations, and intermediaries in ways that accomplish the agendas put forth by the smaller organizations. How this is done is described in chapter 7. Finally, to amplify their voices, CBDOs have set up numerous coalitions and trade associations that create a shared framing of their mission that leads to pressureful efforts to convince recalcitrant agencies to adopt community-focused agendas. This process is described in chapters 8–10.

The core finding of this study is that small social change organizations, contrary to what new institutionalism literature suggests, need not simply reflect the beliefs imposed by funders. In chapter 11, I build upon the descriptive material and present a model of how small and weaker organizations can influence larger and wealthier ones. In a methodological appendix I describe the who, how, and what of the research.

*Renewing Hope* is intended to communicate the sense of the possible and the hope for change that motivates the developmental activists. To do so much of what I present is in the words of the developmental activists in which they share their narratives, opinions, experiences, and anecdotes, replete with their enthusiasms as well as the vivid, colorful, and, at times, profane vocabulary with which they communicate with one another. In presenting material in this way, I build upon the ideas of Rob Mier and other activist planners (Giloth 1996; Mier and Bingham 1993; Nichols 1997; Throgmorton 1996 ) who argue that people persuade one another through stories and metaphors. As such, the stories that I quote are not simply incidental chatter, but are intentional efforts by the developmental activists to frame understandings about community development to convince others to buy into their approaches to social change.

The stories make for a livelier tale. But more important they are the central tool that those in weaker positions use to frame the understandings that in turn persuade richer and more powerful entities to accept agendas that emerge from below. These stories are meant to change prevailing views on how to renew hope within poor communities.

## SOME THANKS AND A PERSONAL NOTE

I am grateful for the help I received from the hundreds in the community development movement who shared their accomplishments, hopes, and frustrations with me. Local government officials and senior officials in foundations and intermediaries also spoke to me in impressively candid ways. I cannot thank my conversational partners by name—listing several hundred would be a bit much—and, in most circumstances, I had promised anonymity. I have thanked my conversational partners personally.

During academic conferences, colleagues such as Edward Goetz, Gordana Rabrenovic, Randy Stoecker, and, Avis Vidal commented on my work. Norman Krumholz and Dennis Keating, both knowledgeable about community work, pointed me in a productive direction. Irene Rubin and Jim Thomas patiently listened and questioned me as I tested out numerous ideas. Three reviewers for SUNY Press were quite helpful by forcing me to make explicit the theoretical implications of a descriptive study. Zina Lawrence provided helpful comments, while Cathleen Collins guided this body through production.

The research was started during a sabbatical for which thanks are given to Northern Illinois University. I received no other financial support. The work continued during several academic years during which my chair, Gian Sarup, helped set up a teaching schedule that allowed for travel. I remain grateful.

Thanks are owed to Marcie Early, Deborah Lambert, and Susan Barkman, who transcribed about half the interviews; I did the rest myself.

Finally, I talked over much of what I observed with my mother-in-law, who at the age of seventy-seven moved from metropolitan Boston to rural DeKalb. She passed away before I could complete this book. I dedicate it to her in loving memory, and wish I could have handed her a copy.

# CHAPTER 1

# Working in the Niche

## *The Community-Based Development Model*

There's an old story about a wise woman. . . . [who] went down to the beach and all the villagers were there and all the fish had washed up on shore. And they were all crying and bemoaning the fate of this community without their fish and the wise woman started taking the fish, the live fish, and throwing them back into the ocean, and one of the people in the community said to the wise woman, "Why are you wasting your time? You can't save these fish by throwing them back."

And, the wise woman picked up a fish and threw him back in the ocean and said, "I saved that one."

So, I just keep throwing fish back into the ocean, one at a time in the hope that something will come of that one particular fish. . . . I don't diminish the small gain. I think that a lot of times that's all we got.

—told by a developer while leading a tour
in a de-industrialized neighborhood

You can't get paralyzed by the fact that you can't see how to get there. So if I've learned anything in the last seven years it is that you don't quit and you hang in there.

—an organic theorist

*Renewing Hope* describes how community-based development organizations—CBDOs—toil against Sisyphean obstacles to develop homes, commercial sites, and industrial buildings in their efforts to rejuvenate neighborhoods from which the private sector has fled and that government woefully neglects.[1] By building homes and creating jobs within these locales of extreme deprivation, *developmental activists* work to help the poor gain an economic and material stake in society.

Community-based development organizations own, rent, sell, and develop housing and commercial property, run businesses, and, invest money within the nation's poorest communities. CBDOs establish profit-making subsidiaries, provide entrepreneurial training, teach people job skills, help set up micro-enterprises, and broker economic development deals. As members of advocacy coalitions, CBDOs help pressure banks to live up to the commitments mandated by the Community Reinvestment Act, the federal legislation that sanctions banks that disinvest from

1

communities of need. Collectively those in the community development movement push for the "community option in urban policy" (Clavel et al. 1997), in
which those living and working in the poor neighborhoods initiate redevelopment efforts rather than simply carrying out ideas imposed from above.

In some locales, CBDOs work with government as officially designated agencies to implement public programs of housing and economic renewal. As such,
CBDOs become part of a *contracting regime* (Smith and Lipsky 1993) in which the
public sector "hires" nonprofits to provide a public service, though one determined
by elected or bureaucratic officials. Within the contracting regime, CBDOs as

> nonprofit agencies find that they must remain on good terms with gov-
> ernment, even though they can sometimes mobilize political support
> to fight unfavorable decisions. The result is a complex relationship of
> unbalanced reciprocity. Government and nonprofit contractors may be
> interdependent, but government dominates the relationship; in contrast
> to nonprofits, its survival and stability do not depend upon contracts.
> (Smith and Lipsky 1992, p. 172)

CBDOs are dependent on public funding. Government provides money through
community development block grants, or federal HOME programs, among other
efforts to fund affordable housing, or in a handful of programs run out of the
Office of Community Services set up to stimulate economic development in poor
communities.

But most community-based development organizations are far more than
part of a delivery system for government programs. Instead, CBDOs are *niche
organizations* that shape redevelopment policy by combining the separate agendas
of for-profit entities, government, social service agencies, and community activists.
To carry out complicated housing, commercial, and industrial projects, developmental activists master the tools of capitalism—preparing business plans and pro
formas, making equity investments, leveraging capital, supporting marketing studies, and ensuring that the organizations run in the black. Yet, at the same time,
CBDOs go beyond market logic to integrate physical development efforts within
broader programs to bring about social repair. Developmental activists argue that
their purpose is to promote economic equality and social justice, not simply bring
capitalist efficiency to poor neighborhoods.

Community-based development organizations intermediate between the empa-
thetic world of social service providers and the dog-eat-dog, bottom-line mentality
of for-profit developers. To bring about a housing project, for instance, might
require the CBDO to piece together contributions from foundations and churches
to lower interest charges, obtain government grants for a land purchase, locate
tenants with Section 8 subsidies, negotiate mortgages from banks, and encourage
private sector equity investments. Equity can be obtained from corporations that
invest in these projects to obtain the tax write-offs allowed by the Low Income

Housing Investment Tax Credit (LIHTC), a federal tax subsidy available to encourage private-sector participation in affordable housing efforts.

CBDOs must respond to local need and the realities of community politics, accomplish projects, yet at the same time assure their own survival as ongoing organizations. Observers claim that they succeed. As Robert Halpern summarizes,

> one is struck by the creativity and flexibility [CBDOs] have demon-
> strated . . . by [CBDO]'s balance: between activism and pragmatism,
> between profit and community reinvestment . . . they embody some
> key principles that create a middle ground between laissez-faire and
> radical reform. (Halpern 1995, p. 148)

A former social worker turned developmental activist notes that community developers "are having to deal with both worlds . . . and often being the mediator and communicator to get so that this side sees the issue and this side sees the issue."

To help CBDOs bridge the gap between the world of social change and that of capitalism, an array of support organizations, especially funding intermediaries, have come into being. These large, nonprofit organizations—the Local Initia-tives Support Corporation (LISC), Enterprise, among others—act as *intermedi-aries* that funnel subsidies, equity capital, and information from government, foundations, and for-profit investors to CBDOs, while, at the same time, assuring capitalist investors that it is safe to invest within poor communities. In addition, intermediaries help CBDOs gain the technical expertise for doing projects, both training staff and hiring conultants that aid the smaller organizations in their missions.

But support from both government and intermediaries comes with a cost, since agendas do differ and a cultural gap occurs in how different participants understand what renewal is about. A developmental activist described the deal-ings with a government funder,

> the housing authority[, which] doesn't understand how to talk to non-
> profits. And we've got to somehow find a link between these nonprofits
> . . . the people who have the passion are the people who are going to
> make it happen. . . . The production of affordable housing rests with
> those people. . . . It's the people who say, "You know, I'm not going to
> put up with this crap in my neighborhood anymore. We're going to do
> something about this. We're going to reclaim this territory." It's those
> people who are going to make it happen, but you've got to get the
> bureaucrats to be able to speak the language.

Similarly, intermediaries are seen by the developmental activists as reward-ing those CBDOs who produce the most rather than for the broader efforts at community change. Developmental activists complain that intermediaries like LISC . . . really don't understand the politics of communities. They only base the end of production. They're not interested in capacity buildings, or . . . helping a group make a strong administration to run the program. They're basing it on production.

But the contest over setting agendas involves more than responding to or rejecting pressures from government agencies or intermediaries. Developmental activists are themselves caught up in the multiple roles their organizations play within the neighborhoods. CBDOs have been criticized for being so focused on physical redevelopment work and so fearful of alienating their funders that they ignore efforts to encourage community participation, social empowerment, and community advocacy (Stoecker 1997). Further, CBDOs must decide how much attention to pay to social service efforts. To ignore social service needs in poor communities is to doom physical development projects to rapid destruction; housing people who have no jobs destroys any chance of tenants paying sufficient rent to maintain the apartments. But doing social services, such as job-training programs, can take both time and money away from physical development work.

Community-based development organizations are organizations in the middle, intermediating between the public and private sector, community needs and capitalist demands, balancing out their agendas with those of their funders, all the while trying to remain fiscally afloat. Their work as niche organizations involves piecing together adequate funding for a project, while at the same time reconciling their own agendas for social change with the goals of their funders. This book examines the extent to which these niche organizations are able to determine their own agendas, while responding to pressures from a complicated, evolving, interorganizational environment.

## THE VARIETY OF THE SPECIES

The National Congress for Community Economic Development (NCCED), the trade association for the community development movement, estimates that there are over two thousand formally organized community-based development organizations (NCCED 1995, p. 7). More are found in the East and in the Midwest than elsewhere. Most are located in inner-city neighborhoods, but some are have been set up in Native American reservations, as well as in more isolated rural areas. Most concentrate their efforts within small, bounded neighborhoods, though with exceptions. As an example, Chicanos Por la Causa works throughout the entire state of Arizona.

Overall, CBDOs are small; a 1992 study of the nation's most successful and larger CBDOs still found their median staff size only seven, and a mean of nineteen (Vidal 1992).[2] Further, the budget size and bottom-line worth of these larger community-based development organizations is small, with the average ones operating on a budget of but $700,000 (Vidal 1992, p. 43). The nation's largest CBDO—New Communities Corporation (NCC) in Newark, New Jersey—employs hundreds, owns property worth hundreds of millions, and undertakes a wide array of programs that vary from building apartments to starting community enterprises, providing medical services to helping with job training, but NCC is clearly an exception. Emerging community-based development organizations are often staffed by but a single individual who ends up doing everything from answering the telephone to bargaining with the funders. In many groups, a single part-timer, on loan from a church or social service agency, runs the entire effort. Several CBDOs I studied operated on less than $100,000 a year, had no material assets, and were desperately trying to package the funds to refurbish a single, small building.

Community-based development organizations take on a wide variety of legal forms. Many begin as volunteer organizations with no corporate charter or affiliation, while others are spun off of churches, as the religious institutions attempt housing programs, only to discover that development requires full-time work. Most CBDOs incorporate as 501c3 nonprofit organizations. A few are actually community action agencies, usually considered as social service agencies, but often acting as housing developers. About about 20 percent of the development organizations that are members of NCCED are community action agencies.

Most CBDOs are incorporated as community development corporations (CDCs), a hybrid legal form encompassing features of a competitive business and those of a nonprofit. As nonprofits, CDCs can receive grants from foundations and government, are eligible recipients of property that government might want to give away, and are explicitly mentioned in federal law as designated recipients of fixed percentages of money intended for affordable housing or other redevelopment programs. The supervisory boards of CDCs are composed of community members, frequently those from the poorer sectors of the society, though many professionals also volunteer. However, to be eligible for federal grants for affordable housing the boards must be primarily composed of poorer community members.

By charter, CDCs are set up to undertake capital-intensive physical development projects that require large infusions of equity funds and as such act very much like for-profit businesses. CDCs can make investments and own property, become stockholders or partners in commercial ventures, and accumulate equity capital for later investment in income-producing projects. For-profit investors will partner with CDCs to help fund affordable housing projects, since by doing so the for-profit receives significant tax advantages from the Low Income Housing Tax Credit—LIHTC.

CDCs require adequate income to employ staff with expertise in housing, commercial, and industrial development, as well as to hire individuals who are knowledgeable in handling investment funds. While many CDCs receive direct subsidies, especially from the federal community development block grant, most of their revenue comes from the rental income from their projects and the receipt of fees for the physical development work. The continued viability of a CDC depends upon their housing or business development projects producing a profit, causing some to question whether concern with organizational survival ends up being more important than accomplishing a social mission.

## WORKING MIRACLES WITHIN
## NEIGHBORHOODS OF DEPRIVATION

Collectively, community-based development organizations have achieved much. By 1991, at the beginning of my project, CBDOs had completed over 320,000 units of affordable housing, brought on line over 17.4 million square feet of commercial or industrial space, and created or saved 90,000 permanent jobs (NCCED 1991a, p. 2). The accomplishments continued, so, for instance, by 1995, at the end of my data collection, CBDOs had constructed or repaired an additional 80,000 units of affordable housing, 6.6 million more square feet of commercial or industrial space, as well as lending $200,000,000 to businesses within poor communities (NCCED 1995). Overall, nonprofits have produced 15.7 percent of all federally assisted affordable housing in the last thirty years (Center for Public Finance and Housing 1994, p. 21).

As a business with a social conscience, a CBDO will work to bring about a tangible product as a response to social injustices. A supermarket in Newark started by a CBDO provides community employment, is a source of a cross subsidy for housing projects, and helps pay for community transportation. In Boston, poor people pitched tents on land from which they were being displaced to make room for an upscale shopping-hotel-entertainment center and stayed until promises were received to develop subsidized housing. Then, rather than rely on the word of politicians, they formed a community-based development organization to construct and manage the project.

Some CBDOs employ neighborhood organizers that set up community associations, and at times, lead Alinsky-style protests; CBDOs help fund or provide offices for community councils, and, on occasion, join in efforts to rid communities of the affliction of drug traffic. Others work to improve neighborhoods through political actions, for example, by lobbying against rezonings that permit tawdry sex shops to open or by joining protests against industrial abandonment. On occasion, CBDOs function like advocacy organizations and organize direct action campaigns to force government to deed housing to those in need. Other CBDOs seem more akin to neighborhood chambers of commerce, working to promote community businesses and keep alive a neighborhood shopping strip, running shopping fairs, and soliciting a modicum of help from local government to maintain the business infrastructure.

The Urban Institute reports that two-thirds of CBDOs do community organizing, about half provide homeowners' or tenants' counseling, and a third do advocacy to support the Community Reinvestment Act, the law that pressures banks to reinvest in communities of the poor (Center for Public Finance and Housing 1994). A recent survey of CBDOs done by the National Congress for Community Economic Development, shows many are involved in community service activities. Two-thirds support advocacy and community building and about a quarter work in job training, while 15-20 percent work to carry out youth programs, child care, or anticrime or antidrug activities (NCCED 1995, p. 13). Most recently, CBDOs have become active in helping people move from welfare to work, providing both job training and linkages to actual jobs (Harrison and Weiss 1998).

Developmental activists take pride in much more than the physical results of their work. They are triumphant when they "save the fish by throwing them back." At meetings and in their publications, developmental activists share with each other the victories that occur by helping one women leave welfare and form a day-care business, or the success when they finesse a grant for a minority community with the help of a conservative senator not known for his multi-cultural concerns. They talk with satisfaction about efforts to help people bypass the social chasms that prevent many from economically succeeding. For instance, CBDOs help immigrants overcome the language barriers that disempower. A development group in Milwaukee that owns a car repair/auto body shop, helped immigrant mechanics from Spanish-speaking countries to hone their job skills while they mastered English. Developmental activists describe the exultation that occurs when they effectively pressure banks to reinvest in poor neighborhoods, using threats made possible by the Community Reinvestment Act to do so. In general, as one developmental activists described, CBDOs "incorporate not only the physical progress and improvement, [but] try to stay conscientious about the psychological, moral and spiritual aspects of a person participation in this."

But doing so is far from easy because of both the social and physical conditions within the neighborhoods in which CBDOs work. These neighborhoods have rundown properties, high crime rates, and deteriorated infrastructure, and they are inhabited by people who are quite poor. Vidal and her team found that CDCs work in census tracts whose income is but 73 percent of that for all the census tracts in the older inner cities whose income figures, in turn, are far lower than that of the suburbs (Vidal et al. 1992, p. 81). A not atypical neighborhood was described by an individual who stated after his neighborhood rapidly declined

> The commercial strip was terrible, I mean it was a very, very blighted two-block neighborhood that had been blighted for thirty-four years

that really now hosted a major portion of the city's illegal drug activity, prostitution crime in general, illegal liquor sale.

A developmental activist whose group was setting up an incubator, inexpensive space to house new businesses, described the problems brought about by the location "sandwiched in between . . . a moderate low-income community and one of the largest [public] housing projects in the city."

Within neighborhoods of deprivation, crime, especially gang crime, is visible, while death and murder are never far away. On the day before I visited one neighborhood a gang shoot-out left six people dead; several CBDOs described deaths of teenagers who had been working in their programs. A CBDO persuaded a bank to fix up a building for the CBDO's headquarters but when "this building was wide open they found three people dead in here."

Work is made more difficult by the ever present threat of arson, often done for profit by absentee landlords (Brady 1982). One activist lamented:

> We had just finished a housing project a few months ago. . . . We bought seven buildings in this neighborhood, did a very substantial rehabilitation spent about $45,000 a unit. . . . [I]t was designed exclusively for low-income people. . . .
>
> And anyway they're done, fully occupied and last week we had an arson in one of our units. Young lady who is twenty years old has a boyfriend who has beat her up numerous times and the police have been at that site. She was gone; somebody entered with a key and started a fire in her bedroom with kerosene.

In another city, a CBDO had convinced Woolworths to refurbish a store rather than shut it down but then "on a Sunday morning . . . the Woolworths store burned to the ground . . . fire of undetermined origin." While elsewhere, a CBDO was assembling a site for a community shopping center, and as the housewife turned CBDO director described:

> Before the site was cleared, one Saturday night some winos were in the basement of one building. Torched it, burnt it, they pulled out a body Monday morning. So that, there were so many things that went wrong. During construction people stole wood, they stole brick, they harassed people. I was down there every night. Finally, got the damn thing built.

Working in communities with social problems increases development costs. CBDOs that promote ownership of homes to the poor or help sponsor community members for business loans must expend incredible energy to teach people how to improve their credit ratings and job histories to be eligible for a subsidized bank loan. Or, in neighborhoods with drugs around, the possibility of violence is always present, requiring extra costs to preserve the housing units. An executive director of a CBDO that had overspent its maintenance budget lamented that

> security is at the point where you need metal doors. You need doors that men mostly can't just kick down when they want to go and see their girlfriend and don't have a key to the front door. That's what happening or the drug people want to get into the hallways and take care of vice activity so they'll kick in these wood doors.

Such problems with security are common and reported in cross-sectional studies (Bratt et al. 1994, p. 139).

In poor communities, physical redevelopment can entail costs not found elsewhere. Refurbishing old homes to match current housing codes can be prohibitively expensive, while working in old buildings that CBDOs are trying to save provides "construction stories that would just curl your tooth." In the inner city, land titles are in doubt (cf. Medoff and Sklar 1994 ). In one of the neighborhoods I studied, a program to build new homes was delayed since the title to a central piece of property had been totally clouded, as it had been passed through several generations of family members who did not bother filling out legal forms.

It is within such neighborhoods that community-based development organizations work and accomplish a wide variety of projects, building affordable homes, putting together economic development deals, and in many ways symbolizing through successful work that neighborhoods can be renewed. To provide an overall flavor of the types of work done, let me present some stories on affordable housing projects, economic development efforts, and a few undertakings done as much to show the possibility for renewal, as to accomplish the project itself.

*Providing Affordable Homes*

Building affordable homes is the major activity of the community-based development movement, with efforts varying from a single home built by volunteers to those of the New Communities Corporation, which owns, rents, and manages several thousand units of housing. In Chicago, energy-efficient bungalow homes are built adjacent to lots still scarred by the demonstrations that occurred after Dr. Martin Luther King's death; in one of the poorest neighborhoods in Cleveland, new, two-story, suburban-style homes cluster together in a cul de sac in a subdivision that sold out immediately to middle-class African-Americans who wanted to move back to communities they had abandoned because of the lack of quality housing.

In the simplest form of rental housing projects, the community-based development organization becomes a benevolent landlord who refurbishes a building, chooses tenants, and provides them with clean, well-maintained, and affordable housing. The equity for such projects, in large part, comes from the Low-Income Housing Tax Credit—LIHTC—supplemented with grants that lower mortgage interest rates sufficient to make the rents affordable. Many of these developments depend for their income streams on their tenants having Section 8 certificates.

With the more complicated, lease-purchase home ownership programs, the CBDO obtains title to single-family homes, either through subsidized purchases or outright gifts; the homes are then repaired and "sold" on a contract to community members. The purchasers pay monthly charges, part of which counts toward the downpayment of the house. When the tenant/owners have contributed a predetermined sum, they take full title to the property. The way the initial leases are often constructed, lessees also receive tax advantages during the buy in period. Lease-purchase programs are often leveraged through sweat equity efforts in which community members contribute their time and labor to refurbishing the homes, with the dollar value of their labor being counted toward a downpayment.

Other CBDOs projects house those with special needs, for instance by providing more bedrooms for the larger, poor families that other housing owners shun or creating special facilities for the disabled, projects done together with social service agencies. The most complicated housing project that I studied was the Harmony House built for the homeless by New Community Corporation. This substantial and well-maintained building housed the homeless and helped them maintain contact with social service providers. A report describes it:

> Harmony House [is] a 102-unit transitional facility for homeless families that combines NCC housing expertise with several of its service ventures. . . . NCC is able to transition residents into employment. As a day care provider, it can work with families to obtain quality child care services. And as a housing developer and manager, it can provide permanent housing placements. Harmony House's holistic package is accomplished at a cost 30 percent less than what the county was paying just to warehouse homeless families in rundown welfare hotels—and has created over 80 new jobs. (NCCED 1992, p. 74)

But to bring about this project it took NCC six years to assemble the land and three more to bring it to fruition. In an internal report, NCC documents the recalcitrance of local government to provide needed help and lambasted the government for slowing the permit and inspection process:

> Is it any wonder that so many would-be community developments do not persevere? Official forms and bureaucratic procedures/technicalities are the number one enemies of any group which needs help from governmental structures and lending institutions. [unpublished internal document NCC]

*Doing the Economic Development Deal*

Though housing is dominant in total dollar values, many community-based development organizations also engage in economic development projects. These, too, vary dramatically in scale, from small microloan funds to help local entrepreneurs get a leg up, to dramatic "sizzle projects."

An economic development project might involve the CBDO's orchestrating efforts to stop stores from leaving the neighborhood. In one community, the CBDO learned that "Sears was going to close," so to preserve the shopping area the CBDO had to

> put together a strategy on how we are going to revitalize the street. . . . If we can make Sears make money, we can win this, you see. . . . Can we get something else in as another anchor that will spill off to Sears. . . . We had to tear buildings down. We had to do all kinds of stuff. This is a story. How to put the Jewel there could last three hours if we went through the whole thing, including exposing the deputy commissioner of the Department of———in the [newspaper] because he was trying to shake us down.
>
> That project is the subject of a UDAG [a federal grant program] a 1.1 million dollar second mortgage over twenty years. Health and Human Services [offered a] grant of $407,000 which brought equity into the project for us. . . . [The investments caused] Sears to stay [and] to put a million dollar addition on the building.

The strategy worked and

> And it caused about $50,000,000 worth of additional revitalization up and down———Avenue. All of a sudden we had Walgreens across the street in a vacant furniture store. We had McDonald's across the street in a vacant Jack in the Box. Taco Bell and Wendy's, where there was a burned-out auto dealership. The cable company came in and took over a vacant automobile dealership.

The work though had far more than economic impact, as it helped slow down the racial divisions in the neighborhood:

> If you went into Sears, you would see black, white, and Spanish people both shopping there and working there together. And with working there comes other benefits like people playing on the softball team together and going to each other's birthday parties for their kids.

By bootstrapping one project on top of the other, the commercial area was preserved, the CBDO ended up as partial owner of several income-producing buildings and created 250 new jobs for the community.

Economic development projects complement broader community-development efforts. A CBDO might open a laundromat to serve people in rental apartments it has refurbished, while reintroducing a business presence to a partially deserted street front. Some CBDOs own small stores—a card shop, for instance, or a food cooperative—that employ community members. In an African-American community, a CBDO built a small office building, housed itself there, rented space to two small community businesses, and then convinced the city library to open a branch in the remaining space. The project improved the local economy, but also served as a message to the city that we are still here and we do count.

Economic development is about helping individuals. For instance, CBDOs run revolving loan funds (Parzen and Kieschnick 1992) that lend up to a few thousand dollars to start up a community business, or they act to package Small Business Administration loans for small companies. When asked about his favorite project, the head of a larger, successful CBDO preferred to talk about a micro-enterprise loan fund rather than any of the major commercial or housing developments his organization had put together.

> [The project] was interesting . . . for social issues, not because it was a complicated deal. We had a low-income woman, with a couple of kids . . . she's got this excellent word-processing capacity. . . . [We used] . . . [the] city's micro-loan program and a bank to put together $10,000 so she could buy state-of-the-art computer equipment. . . . She's operating her business now. . . . It is a very successful business. . . . I liked it because here we took a low-income woman with kids who people really didn't think of as being an entrepreneur . . . and she is a very successful entrepreneur. . . . She is about to move into a bigger space. . . . It's just neat. I like deals like that.

CBDOs have set up job networks to introduce workers from communities of deprivation to local manufacturers and studies indicate these programs, though small scale, have been successful (Harrison 1995). One successful program in Chicago used Job Training Partnership Act (JTPA) money to teach the literacy and numeracy needed for the specific jobs that local businesses required. Bethel New Life in Chicago has linked an employment training program for community residents to a day-care service it set up to provide social and medical services to the frail elderly in the community. Another CBDO helped community members acquire the social assets, training and certification, as well as the material assets, to establish their own home-based day-care businesses to serve other poor families within the community. But to bring this project to completion the CBDO had to master a complicated array of funding sources as this national known innovator of development projects explained:

> The day care project ended up with sixteen different funding sources. . . . Sometimes people come in here and say, "Well, it seems to me that you

just chase money." And that is really fucking stupid. If it takes sixteen different sources to put together a project, it is not exactly chasing money, unless you are a masochist.

According to an outside evaluation, the project was succeeding economically as well as bringing about social changes. The evaluation showed that the participants

felt good about themselves and . . . they seemed to be closer as family members. And there was a paradigm that was beginning to emerge and the paradigm was "I am less in my children's face, but I am more in my children's face." And, what that meant was that we yell at each other less but we are in each other's face more. . . . And, then the third area was community. That the members of the co-op felt a stronger sense of their place with other peers in this community and linkage to their contributions as leaders in this community.

In addition, the project helped empower participants:

[T]hose who had been part of this endeavor now see opportunities to move on the next step of the ladder. And what I mean by that is that some of them want to someday operate their own center. I mean not a day-care home but a day-care center. So they want to own a business more than a day-care home. . . . So more and more I think the business, the economic development side, is really taking hold. And there is real pride in the value of what they contribute to this community.

Economic development efforts can be as much about creating empowerment as they are about jobs and income. For instance, at a cost of little over a million dollars, a CBDO refurbished a 20,000 square foot building that had housed a defunct supermarket into a Mercado that would provide stall space for around three dozen local entrepreneurs. Getting funding was difficult. In part, the CBDO provided equity from money set aside from depreciation from the housing it owned. And, then, "we got capital . . . from HHS. . . . We are losing serious money here every month. . . . [The money,] it comes from [the core CBDO's] development fund which we committed to this project."

The CBDO was putting its bucks where its beliefs were, in part because the project was consistent with the ideological mission of the organization, not simply to create jobs but to encourage community participation in its own economic renewal:

Community people have been involved . . . people talking in a progressive sense of how to create real jobs, livable wage jobs, and stuff like that. And out of that grew the idea that we were going to do this project. . . . We now have a group that includes both businesses, representatives from other groups and churches, some of our tenants, some of our poor people. . . . We have tenants on our board to help make sure that board doesn't take control away from that steering committee. . . .

On this Mercado, . . . every decision including which site to pick . . . this Mercado committee . . . [from the community] . . . [they] are going to select the contractor. . . . That is a form of empowerment. . . . We are going to select venders in Mercado by the same principle.

When it opened, the Mercado contained fifteen booths, primarily owned by local Hispanic and black entrepreneurs. The CBDO working with the community decided who should benefit from the new facility:

We . . . worked with our committee and we reached consensus . . . that we shouldn't be about providing business opportunities for assholes that oppose our housing over here in [gentrifying the neighborhood] and give them an opportunity to have a flower shop over here. I'm sorry. Some low-income, Puerto Rican woman, black person who wants to get off aid, she can open a flower shop.

Balancing off its role as a community organization and its ownership of the Mercado, however, became quite tricky for the CBDO. For instance, the executive director feared that stall prices could inflate. In Baltimore, the development activist noted, it cost $100,000 for a new merchant to enter a similar project, a fee prohibitive to low-income people. To prevent this from happening, rules about the net worth of tenants were set up, yet these rules immediately created friction with potential stall owners who did not want to share their financial data. Or the CBDO itself felt that it would be inappropriate to act both as landlord and as entrepreneurial funder, so instead of loaning money itself to the merchants it linked them to both a community loan fund and the Women's Self Employment Project as potential funders.

Other CBDOs set up industrial or commercial incubators to provide affordable space for startup industrial and commercial enterprises. Some incubators simply make space available, others set aside a common area, with a shared photocopy or fax machine, still others help startup firms obtain funding and mentoring, others promote sharing of skills and resources between the firms. For instance, to be licensed, food preparation businesses must have kitchens that are often too expensive for new firms to afford, but that can be shared if built within the incubator.

In the Roxbury section of Boston, an old brewery was converted into an incubator that now included the offices of the Sam Adams beer company and a Hispanic food distributor. In the south side of Chicago, an incubator housed both new pizza firms and a clean assembly room for high-tech communication equipment. Two blocks away, an artists' incubator provided space for a noted African-American texture painter, as well as numerous less-known artists. In northwest

Milwaukee, an CBDO took out a master lease on large empty warehouses, subletting over a 149,000 square feet of space and in so doing helped over sixty businesses. One incubator housed firms that together set up flexible manufacturing schemes, a system that helps smaller entrepreneurs share equipment and join together in projects too large or complicated for any one of them to pursue. For instance, work was done to manufacture products to aid wheelchair-bound people to be able work in their own kitchens.

Other CBDOs themselves become owners or investors in community businesses. One of the best-known examples is the Pathmark Supermarket build in the devastated central ward of Newark. Together the CBDO and the private grocery company built a 43,000 square foot $12 million shopping center including a supermarket, a restaurant emporium, and a donut shop in an area of the city that had been totally devoid of food shopping, except for expensive mini-marts. The initial work on the project began in 1979, though the supermarket did not open until 1990; once completed it immediately turned a profit with the donut shop drawing in over a million a year, while the supermarket was doing over four million. The profit was impressive given the several hundred thousand dollars of extra security expenses required by the location, though the presence of the donut shop and the promise of free coffee to police officers reduced some of the security costs.

Elsewhere, a small CBDO became a virtual mini-conglomerate starting with an auto repair and training center that, at the time of this study, employed 40 people and had in the past provided 150 other individuals, mostly Hispanic, with sufficient skills to gain employment in conventional auto repair work. The initial project came about in response to the disinvestment of the larger metal-bending factories in the neighborhood. At that time, the founder of the CBDO was working as an employee advocate and

> we started getting people . . . who had given us hundred bucks at Christmas time, successful people from the Hispanic community who were at . . . some of the foundries. These are guys who had worked twenty years and now they were dislocated; it was right in that period of de-industrialization. And they were coming in the office and saying that they are losing their cars and their houses and "what do I do?"
>
> We said, "this is the successful part of the Hispanic community and if we can't help them what the hell use are we as an organization?" . . . So we just figured we gotta do something and to create jobs for those people and to create a vehicle for them to get jobs.

These individuals decided to form a car repair business, looked for an appropriate facility, and found an unoccupied building that had been a car dealership:

> Well, we just came over here and sort of moved in the back and the lawyer from the owner came down and said "what are doing here?"

Well, we are going to help fix up the building and he said, "great" and it never had been vandalized and nobody was in it. They gave us the first year free . . . we ended up buying it from him over a period of four years. . . . And, then we started reclaiming it piece by piece.

To fund the project, the CBDO relied on federal job-training money to set up apprenticeships in auto repair for youngsters in the community who would be taught by more experienced workers. An additional goal was to expand employment for those left behind because of racial or ethnic prejudice.

We like mine the community. We find people who nobody wants who have incredible talents. . . . Our tow truck driver Bill, he's an elderly black gentleman. . . . He came in here three years ago under the welfare. . . . He was in our mechanic shop and all of a sudden we found out that he had been working in a junk yard for twenty years. He drove a tow truck, he could memorize, he knows every car we got in our lot down there. He knows which fender is good shape, which isn't. . . . So after three weeks in our training we just hired him and put him in our tow truck and he is in charge of our reclamation project back there now. . . . He is a diamond. And, yet, the system had him as useless and no one wanted him because his yard is closed down and he was getting to be sixty, there is racism, too.

And the other thing here now that we are lucky, especially people who come from Mexico or Puerto Rico they gravitate here. If a good mechanic comes into the community, they come over here. Everybody speaks Spanish, community atmosphere, helping someone. You know, in that sense, . . . if the person only speaks Spanish they can't get a job out there.

Some of our mechanics have been people who didn't speak English but were crack mechanics, real good foreign car specialists and stuff from Puerto Rico. They were on welfare, here, no one would hire them, they couldn't speak English. We put them to work for $12 an hour and made them an instructor right away.

That is the benefit, the beauty of having this kind of program, [it is] that somebody like that the system considers useless until they learn English, they can not only be productive but they can be instructors and be teaching in the same language, at the same time, and, gradually learning English.

As the auto-repair business succeeded, other enterprises were added altogether including

Seven different projects. The first was the rehab project to develop this [shop] area. . . . We didn't contract anything out. Everything was done in there was run by people from the community. The heating, electric, the air conditioning, everything was done by community people. It took longer, but money that went in there, stayed, changed hands a few times in the community before it went out. . . . We have a welding shop where we make waste barrel containers in the back.

The expansion of the CBDO's effort followed a bootstrapping model:

We started with a JTPA grant, three of us, and moved into an abandoned auto dealership with the idea that we're going to train in auto repair but the first day we opened up our shop we charged 29 bucks for the tuneup and that money starting coming in and we've gradually generated more and more to revenue and programs. . . .

You get twice the value for your training dollar if you show somebody how to weld but they're also building a lugger box that Waste Management is going to buy for $1,200. Then you've accomplished two things—you've covered your overhead by fixing that box and you've trained a person and you've given them a skill.

Other spinoff businesses came about in response to the evolving interests of the workers. For instance, after the car repair business appeared to be working, several skilled employees decided that they wanted to learn home rehabilitation skills and began a housing rehab project. While working to repair these buildings, asbestos was found and had to be removed. Rather than hire others to do it, the CBDO got a grant to train its employees and later spun off a specialized asbestos-removal business. And here the CBDO enabled those in the community to take those risks needed to become self-supporting entrepreneurs:

Our manager went out and underbid his first job by . . . $1,000. So alright we have a little meeting we get some of the guys from the housing rehab who are certified as removal people they go over, they bail him out, he gets out of the contract. If we'd set him up as a for-profit company he would have been dead; that would have been the end of his company so he won't make that same mistake again. . . .

But if it was the son of a person with a lot of money he could do those things, daddy would bail him out or the family would bail him out. . . . We don't have that resource. What we do now his truck breaks down we run it in our shop. It's a $500–$1,000 bill, we give it back to him, and he charges it to the business, but he didn't have to go borrow that money he didn't have to stop working because of it.

After that business got underway, the women in the community complained that all the jobs were for the men, so "we did start the day care because we wanted to address jobs for women in the community." The day-care center was expanded to become a home day-care service with certified, Spanish-speaking providers. The women running the service then

> said they wanted a cooperative that they would run. . . . Now before they were just individual women out there powerless in their houses locked in on welfare. And now their starting what amounts to a business. They're going to have a loan fund and they're going to have a fund that will take care of insurance health insurance, which was a big issue for them, and will be able to get it at real reduced rate because it will come through the co-op.

### Symbolizing Hope

Community-based development organizations build homes and supermarkets, projects that satisfy obvious material needs. In addition, developmental activist want their projects to symbolize to community members and outsiders that hope remains. Clean apartments built by the CBDOs provide visible contrasts to the decaying buildings owned by slumlords or the neglected properties of public housing authorities, while successful businesses demonstrate that profits can still be found in neighborhoods of the poor. Part of what a CBDO is about is improving the image of the neighborhood.

One purpose in building homes like this is to allow the poor to avoid the stigmatization of living in institutionalized housing. An executive director described it thus:

> We spent, no doubt, quite a bit of extra money to make these [homes] blend in the community. . . . we could have elected to build a simple sort of ranch on a slab . . . [but] you know our commitment to the dignity to the individual. . . . I wouldn't want to live in a small single-story slab. . . . Why would the Smith family that makes $12,000 a year, are they any different than me? No, fundamentally . . . they don't want to be stigmatized as poor. You drive past these houses you don't see the word poverty. But there are people living here whose incomes aren't $6,000 a year.

Building or refurbishing homes provides a visible sign that the neighborhood is coming back. A developmental activist explained what happened after the CBDO built unattached single-family homes:

> Now the people begin to move back because of the housing conditions changing and they began to have better jobs. Better connection with the government, better voice at city hall. With those things [we] begin to sell a neighborhood.

Renewing an old abandoned building is an important symbolic action, as explained by one developmental activist:

> Over here is our first building. . . . We have 17, 18 companies in there. . . . We believe you work in the worst buildings, not the best. That is the worst building that God has created in this neighborhood. It is 100 years old.

A CBDO ran a small loan program to upgrade store-front facades on a business strip and by doing so "[business people] see that the city is committed to reinvestment in the neighborhood. That will almost subliminally affect their strategic planning on things that we can have some control over."

To expand the catalytic effect of their work, the CBDO tries to "focus on a lot on things that are as visible as possible." Visible successes become a direct, dramatic challenge to the image of community decay, though such projects can be risky. A minority community developer explained the reasoning for building a mall in the worst section of a mid-sized city:

> I had to put down a big enough footprint to influence the community. And I just refused to do little bitty things because I know you are just pissing money down a rat hole that way. And, [you see] the psychological implications of putting a lot of glass back in the neighborhood [the mall being described was built with large glass windows] would have on people's appreciation of what you did.

He continued with pride:

> If you brought your people to town, your relatives and your friends, and say, "Come on let me go show you something. This is something we got in [city name]. Man do you know this is all controlled by African-Americans?" That's something African-Americans feel proud about. And there's nothing like this around anymore, and you come to town, and it's like, "What's happening?"
>
> So from my point of view, I think that we have to hold on for the historical value of what we've done and for the inspirational value to people, so that people have something that they can say, "This is ours."

Projects to save old buildings take on broader symbolic value by providing a center for the neighborhood. In one city, an old school was converted to be both a community center and a home to nonprofits, many with a focus on community arts. In another locale, the center of the neighborhood was marred by a large, unused and deteriorating former middle school. The building was deeded to a CBDO by the school district, and the CBDO obtained a large federal grant. Working with help from others in the community development movement, this CBDO converted the old school to a room and board project for the Medicaid elderly. The project tapped a community need and constructively recycled the largest, dominant but unused building in the neighborhood.

## THINKING ABOUT BEING IN THE NICHE

In this chapter and in the preface, I have tried to give an overall impression of the fervor and potentials of the community development movement. I have intentionally presented stories of the projects that succeeded to indicate that the possibilities for community renewal are not pipe dreams. Still, developmental activists recognize that what they do is but a drop in the bucket. Julia Koschinsky has calculated that at their best "community development corporations were able . . . to meet 0.7% of worst-case housing needs in 1993" (Koschinsky 1998, p. 127).

Further, success is far from easy, as projects must take into account both physical needs as well as social concerns. To do both, developmental activists recognize that someone has to pick up the financial losses endemic to accomplishing economic and social redress. To gain these resources requires the CBDO to learn to work within a complicated web of funders, technical assistance providers, government and other community agencies, each with agendas of their own. In the next chapter, I'll elaborate on the difficulties that are faced in bringing about community-based renewal projects.

CHAPTER 2

# Negotiating an Environment for Community Renewal

Have you ever talked to [a CBDO] that wasn't in the frying pan? . . .
It is always the hot seat. . . . But it always seems that nonprofits never
have a rest period . . . you don't have the revenues and you have to
deal with your venders and your creditors and all that. . . . you know
you speculate a lot on where your money come in. . . . So it is very risky
business.

> —director of nieghborhood group now building homes

Well, the funder said to me, "Lois, that was a really bad business decision 'cause that house you could have made money . . ." and I said, "I
know that. And if I were in this to do business. . . . I could make a lot
of money for the organization. . . ." But, I said, "That's not what we're
here for."

> —A religious activist turned developer

When we go to talk to tenants [and say], "Would you like to relocate to
the [incubator]?" What are we telling them? We are telling them
wouldn't you like to [move] into a high-crime area in the inner city, in
an old building with a developer who doesn't have enough capital to
do all the repairs in an efficient way.

> —an incubator developer speaking at a conference

Community-based development organizations attempt to solve complicated
problems of physical and economic decline within defined geographic areas.
Implicit in each physical redevelopment effort is a series of questions that developmental activists ask themselves:

- *Is the project simply meant to accomplish a narrow purpose or does it
  have implications beyond the immediate physical building or opening of
  the business?* Is success in housing measured by the number of units
  produced or its effectiveness in creating social capital? Should new
  stores only be judged by their bottom line or can they be seen as a
  source of ethnic affirmation?

21

- *Who decides on the purpose?* The CBDO? Community members? The funders? Or does the quasi-invisible hand of the market really determine what will come about?
- *Do the projects speak to broader concerns about community change?* Are projects part of a plan at all, or are they simply undertaken opportunistically in accordance with the whims of funders? Is the project an end in and of itself or is it a means toward broader efforts at economic and social reform?
- *Does the environment of poverty pile obstacle on top of obstacle, handicapping the physical development work?* Are the sites so contaminated or the buildings so derelict that renewal becomes overwhelmingly expensive? Do the people within the neighborhood have the economic and social assets to maintain new property or support new stores?
- *What are the consequences of the particular project for the CBDO as an organization?* Is the CBDO economically and technically capable of handling the economic risk or does it increase dependence upon the funder? Are developmental activists so concerned about the survival of the CBDO that the organization only attempts low-risk, profitable endeavors in spite of community need?

As these questions imply, doing deals is far more than a mechanical process of obtaining funding, constructing property, and then renting it out. Projects are not decontextualized activities—building this house, or setting up that laundromat—but rather represent the success (or failure) of developmental activists to reconcile numerous forces and to accomplish sometimes quite antagonistic goals.

In this chapter, I will first present a pastiche of stories to show the variety of troubles, tensions, and problems developmental activists face as they attempt community projects. These stories are meant to illustrate the cross-pressures developmental activists face, as they balance off accomplishing what they feel is right with what they are allowed to do by their funders and what their communities permit.

In the second half of this chapter, I step back, change tone, and suggest how these cross-pressures, many created by the needs of the CBDOs for economic resources, speak to issues suggested within the literature on new institutionalism. Particular attention will be paid to the new institutionalism models that describe how wealthier and more powerful organizations dominate the task environments in which smaller nonprofits seek to work. I argue that these mechanisms, in part, help create the tensions that the developmental activists seek to reconcile.

I conclude this chapter by suggesting a model of how those in smaller nonprofits do reconcile these tensions, but do so according to their own agendas. Chapters 3–10 provide empirical evidence of both the cross-pressures the CBDOs face, and then their various ways of responding. In the concluding chapter I suggest a model that indicates how smaller organizations can gain power over their funders.

## PROJECTS EMERGE WITHIN AND REFLECT
## DISTINCT AND UNSTABLE ENVIRONMENTS

Development projects are not isolated happenings to be counted, aggregated, and examined devoid of their broader context. A nine-flat affordable housing project with a floor space of 10,800 square feet in one community provides the same housing as does a nine-flat affordable housing project built elsewhere. But beyond that, the similarity of the projects ends; each comes about in a separate environment and each reflects both the needs in the immediate communities as well as the pressures from the funders, inputs that differ from place to place and from time to time.

Was the building constructed anew on an empty lot, to provide housing, or did it replace a derelict building used for the drug trade? Did the project result from a routine city-sponsored program to construct affordable housing in which the CBDO was just part of the "delivery system," or was the city compelled to participate because the project answered a crying neighborhood need made politically salient by the CBDO? Once completed, is the project sold to lower-middle-class owners, or is it set up as a cooperative for the quite poor? In doing this project, did the CBDO feel pressure to quickly sell new homes in order to meet production quotas assigned by the funders, or could it take the time to teach the working poor needed skills in homeownership?

Funders often want development projects to be carried out in regimented fashion, that is in an efficient and economically viable manner. Yet developmental activists understand that their work requires learning and adjustment, as projects emerge and are then reframed to fit in with local realities that change as the projects are underway. For instance, a developmental activist working in a rural CBDO initially felt that the poor could be helped by forming worker-owned cooperatives. Her organization set up a cooperatively owned restaurant that was run democratically, stayed fiscally afloat, but rarely paid its workers much above minimum wage.

Being dissatisfied with the outcome, the CBDO changed its tact, and following the new funding fashion to quickly move the poor into business, set up small niche enterprises owned by the poor. The first effort was a cleaning services firm that

> when it started it had mostly minorities, two black folks who were still
> in the business and a Native American women. . . . But you know it

was a horrible business I mean incredible turnover, people have the bad things about cleaning.

From this experience, the CBDO learned that by working only with the poor, no one had any business experience to share, while personal lives of the owner/employees were often in disarray. Based on this learning, the CBDO altered its mission to that of setting up networks of firms that brought together individuals from a wide array of sectors. As a result of this reflection, the mission of the CBDO evolved, from that of setting up businesses to catalyzing others to work together. In their next project the CBDO designed and organized a system of flexible and networked manufacturing that brought together skilled local inventors who designed products that would be manufactured by small established community businesses that employed people at living wages. Throughout this changing agenda, the CBDO had defined its mission as experimenting to learn what would work with the poor in its community, rather then simply applying a model from above. Convincing funders that the learning process was as important as the outcomes was far from an easy task.

More common are the tensions CBDOs feel as they try to reconcile physical redevelopment projects with demonstrable outcomes, with complementary programs of social repair. To fund such projects is difficult since few government agencies, foundations, or intermediaries provide support for both physical redevelopment work and social services. Yet these projects must come about since social service needs are implicit within the physical redevelopment efforts. A developmental activist whose organization had converted World War II emergency housing into tenant-owned cooperatives explained:

> [W]e have an interest broader than just being a landlord. We have an interest in the people that are housed there. I think initially we looked at housing as a way to transform peoples' lives. . . . People who move to one of the coops that we have developed, also bring up a history with them of either abuse, or lack of education, or lack of job skills, or employment history . . . and housing alone is not going to change that.

This individual described how social services were implicit within the redevelopment effort:

> We sort of waded into the social service area. . . . Two years ago we said, "Jeez we've got all of these kids during the summer, what are they going to do?" And we need to provide them with some structured activities so they are not raising hell and destroying the property. . . . So we said, let's put together a summer program where we will have some sort of structured activities and we'll do a little remedial education and activities and mostly we will have some supervision for these kids. So we started out with a summer program.

To maintain such programs, the CBDO that had to that point received most of its funding from a city-sponsored housing program, now had to reach out to educational funders, as well as seek out money from a crime-control program set up to keep teenagers occupied during the summer.

Similarly, concerns with crime, social decay, or a moral imperative to help those most in need, force CBDOs to simultaneously work with an array of other agencies whose approaches and understandings differ dramatically. Efforts to stamp out the drug trade can involve cooperation with the very authorities that many community members fear.

Projects need support of neighborhood organizations but such support might be antagonistic to the goals that the CBDOs wish to achieve. In some communities, the neighborhood groups reject the affordable housing CBDOs build, for fear the new tenants will disrupt the community. In other locales, quite progressive neighborhood groups want the CBDO to only house the very poorest of people, not recognizing that the CBDO cannot possible obtain the deep subsidies needed to do so. Community groups legitimately demand that the physical development projects done by the CBDOs employ community members at (comparatively) well-paid wages. Again, the CBDO wants to respond, but training community members as construction workers involves time and money that the funders won't provide, and can delay work as the negotiations with construction unions to train new workers can be involved.

Sometimes the deteriorated physical environments within many inner-city communities makes work nearly impossible. Environmental condemnation can be so heavy that developmental activists joke about setting up mining operations, then more seriously detail the technical problems involved in removing toxic chemicals or the difficulties caused by asbestos, endemic to old properties in inner cities. Lead condemnation can add incredible expenses even to simple home repair projects, as a CBDO director running a city-sponsored home repair program noted:

> If you go into a property where there's a child under the age of seven, you have to get a lead testing. . . . [If] you're using federal money through HUD and get caught, you can be required to totally delead that property, so you know fixing the flush mechanism could end up with a $40,000 deleading of that house.

And environmental problems appear when least expected, as the developer of a commercial property narrated. After convincing funders on the need to repair a building and obtaining what appeared to be an adequate budget for so doing,

> we found that when we went into the building, the interior wall that had asbestos was actually insulated in between two layers of brick. Once it was discovered, unfortunately, you had to remove it. We had to

remove all of the woodwork, interior, and that was also the building that we decided to give the historic [preservation] tax credit on. Which meant that when we removed all the woodwork, we had to turn around and remill all the woodwork in order to sustain the tax credit. Needless to say that was about half million dollars.

Complying with laws on the environment were hard enough, but the CBDO had to do so in ways that preserved the building so the (commercial) investors in the project would receive the benefits from the historic preservation tax credit.

Sometimes, though, CBDOs simply bluff their ways out of such problems. A developer of an inner-city incubator described it thus:

Environmental issues are a big deal. . . . I have two oil tanks on the back of our site. Two 50,000 gallon oil tanks. . . . The fire department. showed up one day and said you have to have this oil out within twenty-four hours. I can tell you what the estimates were. The first one that came was $65,000. I turned to the fire department and said, "Here is the keys to the [building] You now own it. Its yours."

At that point you start working with them as you do in all other things. . . . We solved the environmental problem.

Surviving means knowing how to manipulate a broader environment.

To simultaneously carry out both a social and physical redevelopment agenda, or to handle the problems created by the physical neglect of poor communities, costs money. Piecing together funds for any project can be quite problematic, as there are multiple sources and each source imposes its own conditions. Sometimes the problems are technical: to expend funds received from the federal historic tax credit requires that no substantial alterations be done to the appearance of the building.

To further complicate matters, redevelopment work done within the inner city is surprising expensive, often exceeding that for suburban projects. Money is required to clear away burnt-out lots, to abate environmental hazards, or to pay the extra insurance costs for inner-city work. In a detailed study of the costs of fifteen affordable housing projects, a team from Abt Associates found that refurbishing affordable apartments ran a total of $76,706 a unit, with the legal, organizational and consultant fees that were special to affordable housing work running 6.4 percent of the expenditures, or about $6,203 an apartment unit (Hebert 1993).

In addition, expenses for managing affordable rental projects are often higher than for conventional projects. Tenants are more likely to fall behind in rent, create expenses because of their inexperience in living in quality housing, while the older buildings themselves, especially those donated to nonprofits by HUD, often have structural defects that require more routine maintenance.

Further, income streams from rent are far from stable. Rachel Bratt and her team found that only three of the dozen housing developments they studied had been able to put aside the recommended capital or operating reserves from the rent (Bratt et al. 1994, p. 110); many organizations had no reserves whatsoever while many had more than 5 percent of the tenants in arrears in rent (Bratt et al. 1994, p. 105).

To make projects affordable for the poor, community-based development organizations must find subsidy money. In commercial ventures, upfront risk capital is required, even just to explore the feasibility of the effort. Further, as ongoing organizations CBDOs need cash for operating expenses—salaries of a staff, heat, light, and rent for their own offices.

To obtain these funds, a wide variety of sources from government, the foundations, and the intermediaries must be approached; but piecing together funding remains problematic. The very dependence on external funding sources can entangle a CBDO within a rippling web of interorganizational pressures and obligations. Obtaining equity capital as well as expertise, for example, in managing a supermarket, requires partnering with for-profit firms. Yet, by doing so, the development organization adds the vagaries of the capitalist economy to the many other uncertainties nonprofits face.

To package the financing for housing or economic development deal necessitates working with many other organizations. Doing so, requires the CBDO to respond to contradictory agendas—the goal of churches or foundations to do social good, that of the city to maximize the number of units built, and the concerns with assuring debt repayment that comes from the LIHTC investors.

To obtain equity funding for affordable housing, most CBDOS rely upon the Low Income Housing Tax Credit—LIHTC—that in turn thoroughly embeds the CBDO in a series of relationships and obligations. First, the CBDO must form a subsidiary for-profit partnership with a capitalist investor who signs up primarily to obtain an incredibly generous tax benefit. But for a project to be eligible for the tax credits, it must follow numerous federal requirements that mandate who can live in the buildings, how long the building must be used for low-income tenants, as well as setting specified rental limits. If the rules are violated, the for-profit partner can lose its tax-benefits retroactively. Because of these complexities, most such deals are brokered by a financial intermediary such as LISC. Lease-purchase housing deals, as described in the previous chapter, can be even more cumbersome. Since lease-purchase projects are intended to house families on the economic margins, deep subsidies are needed, and funds for training renter-owners needed, while at the same time satisfying the many conditions for LIHTC projects.

Physical and funding problems can reinforce one another. In a housing project, environmental problems were found after construction had begun, increasing the costs of the work. To get approval for the new work required renegotiating a grant from the state housing agency, that then in turned necessitated redoing all the paper work for the associated LIHTC. The developmental activist described the endless stream of problems:

> I think of how many road blocks have been in the way . . . at this point there is probably a hundred. . . . We have come this far, there's no way all this work is going to be wasted. Just looking like this [she points out two large book shelves of binders of reports and applications to funders]. . . . There were twenty some studies related to doing it before you even start, then now that we are underway you are dealing with the city, the state, the architects, the federal, the tax credit whole deal, the property management, the lawyers, you know, the whole.
>
> Also once a month, if the community council agenda is too busy and keeping community support as the program changes is very difficult. First of all getting a community to accept forty-seven units of low-income housing is difficult. Once you find one, you best get the units in there because they could say no at any point. Yes, our project is more complicated because we are using an abandoned school building, and the other things is federal guidelines have changed since we started the project. The whole lead abatement is totally different now than it was. . . . The accessibility, we were committed to accessible units, what have you, but now the laws have changed and require additional . . .
>
> So, the whole prior year of nursing this project along, rules are changing around you that you have no control over but you have to abide by them. The rules changes and you find the money to change with it and at the same time you are being daily criticized for the cost. . . . Every time you think you are moving forward, you're starting over again. Everytime you think you are almost there, something else falls out.

She estimated as a private developer she could have done a similar sized project for 20 percent less.

Worse yet, the CBDO is dependent upon the capitalist climate, as mortgage rates rise and fall or commercial businesses fail or prosper. In one project, a CBDO received city money to clear land to rebuild a large mall, only to find its partnership with the experienced commercial developer Trammel Crow collapse as this large firm was in severe financial trouble. In another case, a CBDO was about to start work on a small mall that would provide a needed supermarket to the city's poorest community when the anchor tenant pulled out and, as a result, the Federal EDA grant that had taken years to obtain and from which the nonprofit was to pay its share was lost.

Delays are common in for-profit development work, but for CBDOs that are skating close to the financial edge delays can prove financially disastrous, especially when the development organization has borrowed money to purchase property. One organization whose operating budget ran about $300,000 a year ended up holding property for almost two years at an out-of-pocket interest cost of almost $8,000 a month. The longer it takes to get each piece of money, the greater the chance that the initial source of funding will back out or that costs will escalate. For commercial projects, conventional funding will not be provided unless a building is [largely] preleased. Yet the initial foundation or government grantees might lose patience before the lease-up process can be completed. A minority developer who was trying to restore an abandoned business strip complained:

> [T]hat project took three years to get that project from concept to construction . . . and then your deadline[s] on these grants are running out, but you're not ready to build the building yet and . . . there always seems to be a new and different wrinkle. We call those new and different wrinkle hoops to have to jump through, but that's part of the game.

Further, trying to coordinate the actions of commercial businesses with the erratic timing of public grants necessitates that the developmental activist play a game of financial pickup. One reflected on the first major project her startup group attempted, as it sought to provide stability to a neighborhood known for transiency:

> EDA was horrible to work with. We lost that grant four different times, through no fault of our own. The [shopping] center had to be 80% or 70% leased before they release the funds but [the anchor wouldn't] sign a lease until they knew I had the funds. I mean it was just was awful. The city won't come into the land until they knew I had the money.

An established community developer who headed a community action agency in a small city described how the CBDO had pieced together city funding, Section 8 commitments, and money from a state housing trust fund, and was just about to start construction:

> And [then] . . . there was a change in administration within the city and the person that had originally committed about $8,000 or $10,000 per unit for the rehab . . . wasn't there anymore and there was a new person there. . . . That was the first thing that fell through and then the Housing Authority started talking iffy, saying, "Oh, we already have a waiting list of all these people on Section 8 and your people are going to have to go on that waiting list, and maybe they'll . . ." and all of a sudden all of the money that we though we had in this project completely fell down.

Getting banks to commit seems even more difficult than convincing the public sector. One of the nation's most successful developers described the problem:

> Bankers are notorious for almost saying yes. They can drag transactions out for years. And one of the most precarious things about these transactions

is that you have what is called quilt financing here. You may have CDBG grant, you have a first mortgage from one party, you have a second mortgage here . . . you have balance housing funds and you are balancing all of these parts during your marketing. You have to keep these together so that the tax credit equity is the last part. And if its not done in a timely fashion where your momentum for the project won't be gone, your other parts can start falling apart.

The supermarket built as a partnership between Pathmart and the New Communities Corporation in Newark illustrates these numerous hurdles. The original planning began in 1979 with construction intended for 1984, with the first five years devoted to land assembly. Unfortunately, the next half a decade was spent in litigation over the land, as well as in repeated negotiations of grants from the city development authority that was so recalcitrant in releasing the promised money that a mass protest at city hall was required. The construction finally began in 1989 and the complex opened in 1990 after eleven years of arduous effort.

When a CBDO acts as a bridge between capitalist investors and the government a nightmare can occur, as shown in the following case in which a CBDO partnered with a city to acquire and upgrade a neighborhood plaza. The CBDO wanted to improve the plaza both to reintroduce needed stores while discouraging the slumlord who had let the mall property deteriorate. The development activist explained:

> We acquired the land ourselves. We went first to the owner of each of the properties . . . and said we want to fix up your property. And, they said "Forget it." And, then we offered them some incentives, low-interest loans, store-front renovation funds, and they said we are not interested. And, we said to them, "Well we'll buy it from you." And, they said they didn't want to. They were happy to run this slum building. And we said, "We are not going to allow this neighborhood to be run down by slum landlords, we are going to turn that around."

He continued:

> We asked the city to acquire the property, which they did. And then we borrowed some money. . . . We worked with a private developer to co-venture the deal. . . . So that project, that I spend two minutes telling you about took ten years to do.

But why the ten years?

First, the city incorrectly filed condemnation. Then the CBDO had to ride herd on the city's legal department to make sure the case did not slip into the nether land of unfinished public business. During this time, the city administration changed, creating further delays as all neighborhood projects were again reviewed. To further complicate matters, some of the money was to be borrowed from LISC, but with the delays,

> LISC, which had originally committed a half million dollars reduced the amount to $200,000 because it was six years later and they didn't have the money available, they had before, so we had to scale back the project.

The CBDO was able to obtain the missing funds from a responsive neighborhood bank, whose president was also on the CBDO's board, but the city was still

> arguing over the cost of the property with [owners of the plaza]. They said "we are not going [to give] these guys $800,000 for this property. We think it is only worth $600,000." And, we said, "You know, you are going to get $240,000 back in the first year, alright, so let's not argue over 50,000 bucks and take a year and half to do that. . . . We had to spell it out and then threaten to embarrass people [chuckle] until we could get the deal through.

Two years later, the project was finished.

In another case, a CBDO spearheaded an effort to coordinate local, federal, and private actions to reopen a factory that a conglomerate had abandoned. Midstream,

> the whole deal fell apart. Our [for-profit] partner walked away, we lost the public subsidies. . . . All of that fell apart just at the time that OCS [the Office of Community Services the major source of federal funding for community economic development] was giving us a favorable reaction. . . . We were trying to keep [the corporation] interested in donating the factory to us but because . . . the tax law had changed and it was more beneficial for them to sell it outright than to donate it. . . . The city pulled it's CDBG commitment out of the deal and the state pulled it's Development Action Grant out of the deal. . . . So here I was trying to hold OCS at bay, saying there had been some changes in our deal we would like to keep the grant, "What do you need in order for us to keep the grant?" and they said, "Show us that the same public benefits are being leveraged the same private dollar is being leveraged" and so I had to do in effect a reapplication.
>
> We had to go out and solicit another partner; we had to show OCS that even though the state and city monies were not there and even though the plant wasn't being donated, we had none the less leveraged this and that and the other thing and we succeeded we got them to reconsider.

## PACKAGING PROJECTS IN ENTANGLED ENVIRONMENTS

The narratives just presented are intended to communicate the complicated evolving environments in which community-based development organizations orchestrate redevelopment projects. The work of the developmental activist is very much akin to that of painting a moving train, which moves over rough tracks, while working with a palette whose colors are changing.

The environment can be seen in several embedded layers. Most visible is the physical environment of the deteriorated buildings and the communities in which they are located. Looking within the neighborhoods in which they work, CBDOs see deteriorated properties, societal neglect, and racial tensions. In trying to work in these communities, CBDOs can be caught between the realities of what funders allow and the pressures from neighborhood groups. To protest against banks that disinvest or government that seems indifferent, CBDOs work with neighborhood coalitions, sometimes in direct action campaigns. Yet, if CBDOs appear to be too close to protesters, dealing with banks or local government becomes quite problematic.

The next layer of environmental complexity comes about as CBDOs try to piece together funding, facing both technical complexities as well as the need to satisfy often contradictory agendas. Funders offer a wide array of programs, from the federal government's virtual alphabet soup of programs, to the ever reinvented grant programs of the foundation. Grants come with their own contingencies, on when and how they are to be used. A veritable juggling act must take place, to assure each piece of funding arrives at an appropriate time, and then remains in place while other funds are obtained. A delay, or a removal of one piece, and the whole pyramid of cards crumble. Yet the purposes and requirements of separate granting programs often do not mesh.

Packaging money from a variety of sources or acting as capitalist and protester simultaneously is difficult enough. But more is involved, as money usually comes with ideological strings attached. Government wants housing to provide social uplift, but some programs favor housing that reach the very poorest, the homeless, while other government efforts are meant to refurbish poor neighborhoods to lure back a middle class.

The requirements imposed by intermediaries are tautologically in between. Intermediaries speak for those in need and support the goals of community renewal. But they also speak for the capitalists who provide the wealth and want to see more hammering for the development buck, while looking askance at physical development efforts that morph into programs of social amelioration. Further, intermediaries are staffed by both bankers and former community developers, people who have strong beliefs about what programs will work and what is now appropriate to try. Such values can be imposed upon the CBDOs simply by threatening to withhold the funds.

Still, intermediaries, and many agencies of government, do not want to be seen as coercive in their interactions with CBDOs. But they can shape the actions of the CBDO in less direct ways. For instance, funders can insist that the community organization hire technicians with knowledge of financial management, the micro-details of developmental budgeting, and other technical matters. Such individuals are more likely to reflect values from the bottom-line world of for-profits than they are to be motivated by issues of community advocacy and empowerment.

To complicate matters, the political and funding environment for community-development work is in constant flux, while the support CBDOs receive differ from time to time, so that history is less of a teacher. Even during the few years of my project, federal support differed dramatically. The project began right after the major cutbacks brought about by the Reagan-Bush administration, to be replaced by the initial optimism President Clinton inspired. Yet, during much of Clinton's administration, the support for the Department of Housing and Urban Development, the financial mainstay for affordable housing, and that of the Office of Community Services, Department Health and Human Resources, a funder for economic development work, were quite uncertain. Support for the Community Reinvestment Act wavered, and, for a time, the fate of the Low Income Housing Tax Credit was in doubt. The changes in federal welfare legislation have now roiled the environment in which CBDOs work. With money available for job-training efforts, and the fear that those now on welfare and receiving housing assistance will lose both and be unable to afford to live in properties built by CBDOs, some development organizations again are having to refocus their missions.

The agendas promoted by these funders varies greatly. LISC, for instance, has maintained steadfast support for housing development. But depending on time and locale, LISC vacillates on whether or not it accepts a CBDO's having a broad social mission, rather than being merely an efficient producer of homes.

Major foundations have provided support for the most innovative efforts of the CBDOs and continue to be generous funders. But fashion in the foundation world changes rapidly. During the study time alone, the foundation's image of what development should be took a sea-change. As my study began, the foundations were pushing for physical developments, albeit those of a quite innovative nature. By the end of the project, foundation fashion had changed to support programs of holistic programs especially Comprehensive Community-Based Initiatives (Kubisch 1996; Wright 1998 ), rather than efforts emphasizing the physical renewal work done by CDCs. The problem for the CBDO has been determine what is in fashion today.

Trying to build projects that at first blush appear both simple and obvious—a new apartment building, a supermarket, helping people get off welfare and form businesses—end up entangling CBDOs within a complicated, shifting, value-laden interorganizational environment. At first blush, it would appear that the CBDO, as the little guy, can do little other than to capitulate to the agendas others want to impose, rationalizing that any help received does improve the lot of those living in neighborhoods of deprivation. Yet, at the same time, developmental activists experientially learn what works and what doesn't within the particular neighborhoods and want to bring about these agendas. Can developmental activists influence those in more powerful organizations to accept the CBDO's own agendas for change? I shall argue for the possibility of their doing so.

## A PRELUDE TO THE THEORY OF NICHE ORGANIZATIONS

The first half of this chapter suggests the overall flavor of the interorganizational environment in which community redevelopment comes about. Skillful juggling is required to hold a deal together, contending agendas must be reconciled, while an array of financial and technical problems need to be overcome. Deals come apart, while what is supported by whom changes over time and between places.

Stepping back, several conceptual questions about interorganizational relationships and the ability of non profits to negotiate such networks are suggested. Specifically,

1. How within complicated interorganizational systems are goals set and by whom?
2. What strategies are followed as organizations with markedly different resources strive to influence one another?
3. How can and do smaller organizations accommodate to pressures from larger, more powerful entities?
4. What role do values/ideological beliefs play in shaping the interorganizational environment?
5. How do so such values/ideological beliefs emerge and then diffuse?

Such questions have been discussed by theorists of the new institutionalism approaches to organizations, as well as scholars who examine how issues are framed within social movements. In the remainder of this chapter, I briefly summarize some concepts and perspectives from this literature that speak to the questions above. I then sketch out a model that suggests how CBDOs can have influence within the complicated interorganizational environment in which they work. This model provides a scaffolding for the descriptive chapters. In the concluding chapter, I build upon the descriptions, flesh out the model, and suggest how small nonprofit organizations are able to partially set the broader task agenda, even when they are dependent upon powerful funders.

*Perspectives Suggested by the New Institutionalism Literature*

New institutionalism theorists provide a wealth of conceptual and empirical insights on the ways in which organizations influence one another within changing, uncertain, and, turbulent environments. New institutionalism theorists indicate that organizations, especially nonprofits, should be visualized as part of an interdependent social system—a *societal sector*—rather than as isolated entities. A societal sector includes "all organizations . . . supplying a given type of product or service together with their associated organizational sets: suppliers, financiers, regulators, and so forth" (Scott and Meyer 1991, p. 108). Organizations within sectors share meanings and framings about their collective work and are seen as part of an *organizational field* of "organizations that participate in the same meaning systems, are defined by similar symbolic processes, and are subject to common regulatory processes" (Scott 1994, p. 71).

While the core organizations within a societal sector can be identified, the boundaries of the sector are diffuse and changing. Within a societal sector, organizations range from those central to the task, in the case of the material discussed in this book, the community-based development organizations are the focal units, but the sector includes important organizational actors, such as LISC, as well as more peripheral entities, such as academic institutions that occasionally provide technical support.

Within societal sectors, organizations bargain, persuade, coerce, and otherwise interact with one another and, by doing so, end up changing the texture, shape, and purposes of the sector. In turn, the structures of individual organizations are shaped by these ongoing interactions (Meyer, Boli, and Thomas 1994, p. 19). Together the process has been labeled as "structuration."

> "Structuration" consists of four parts: an increase in the extent of interaction among organizations in the field; the emergence of sharply defined interorganizational structures of domination and patterns of coalition; an increase in the information load with which organizations in a field must contend; and the development of a mutual awareness among participants in a set of organizations that they are involved in a common enterprise. (Dimaggio and Powell 1991, p. 65)

Actions taken by a single organization within the sector—its choice of goals, the formal structure it assumes, who it hires and for what purposes—emerge as a consequence of its broader involvement within the societal sector. More powerful organizations set up expectations on how other organizations should behave, but because of the diffuseness of relationships and the multiplicity that exist such expectations cannot be imperiously imposed. Rather, influence on the smaller organizations takes place through ongoing and incremental negotiations, both overt and tacit.

Influence occurs as ideas about values and goals are exchanged, but who influences whom depends in part upon the relative economic or political influence of distinct organizations. Organizations with more material resources tend to dominate, but ideas and values do count, so that those who can better frame what the sector ought to be about, even if economically weaker, might affect the overall direction of the sector. By strategic capturing of symbols, or through the intentional efforts of individuals who occupy crucial communication nodes, redefinitions of what a sector is about can occur, in ways that can favor the smaller and weaker organizations.

Still, financial and political resources are important, especially as richer, politically more central organizations attempt to dominate the weaker, using what DiMaggio and Power have labeled as coercive, mimetic, and normative techniques (Dimaggio and Powell 1991, p. 67ff.). With coercive techniques, the stronger organizations rely upon financial pressures to force compliance, while legislative or bureaucratic pressures from governmental funders also compel actions (Glazier and Hall 1996 ). Smaller organizations have little choice, but to do the projects for which funding is available, a direct form of coercion. More subtly, funders set up requirements that necessitate organizations changing form, and thence mission, but in ways that make the process appear inadvertent. For instance, to obtain Low-Income Housing Tax Credit money, federal agencies require that community-based development organizations establish independent, nonprofit subsidiaries. To manage these subsidiaries necessitates that CBDOs take on specific forms and hire people with particular expertise and by doing so the subsidiary ends up being the tail that wags the larger organizational dog.

Mimetic influence occurs as smaller organizations imitate the form and behaviors of the most successful of their peers, initially for the very reason that these other organizations appear to be successful. For instance, a nationally known organization partners with the police in an antidrug effort and others follow. In one sense, the imitation is quite voluntary; drug problems do pervade the nation. But mimetic influence of the funders is indirect: the successful CBDO took on an antidrug effort because it was paid to do so by its government supporters. In general, mimetic influence is more subtle than direct pressure, but subtle coercion is involved.

In the tacit contention over values, funders, in part, decide which organizations to support by evaluating whether the structures and procedures of the smaller organization are those preferred by the funders. As such, an "environmental congruence" (DiMaggio and Powell 1991, p. 73; Meyer and Rowan 1991) comes about in which organizations survive not because they have better ideas but rather because they taken on organizational forms and pursue goals that give funders sufficient comfort to provide the resources the smaller organizations need to stay afloat. For instance, at first blush, a requirement by a funder to hire an accountant, rather than relying upon community volunteers to manage large grants, seems reasonable enough. But the values of the accountant, for efficiency, production, and the like, are more likely to be compatible with those of the funders, than the values of a community activist who wants to encourage empowerment and neighborhood participation. Segregating housing management from housing development appears to make good sense, especially if a funder is willing to pay. But once management is professionalized, the pressure to treat community members as merely rent paying tenants, not as poor people being helped, becomes overwhelming. As such, *structural isomorphism* comes about since "organizations which adopt the appropriate forms perform well not because they are most efficient, but because these forms are most effective at eliciting resources from other organizations which take them to be legitimate" (Friedland and Alford, 1991, p. 243).

Finally, normative influence occurs as wealthier organizations share ideas about what actions should be about and also the criteria for evaluative the effectiveness of these actions. Further these beliefs are held and transmitted by professionals in the field, professionals whose training is often influenced in programs set up by the more powerful organizations who "create a pool of almost interchangeable individuals who occupy similar positions. . . and possess a similarity of orientation and disposition that may . . . shape organizational behavior" (Dimaggio and Powell 1991, p. 71).

Still such ideational influence can be a two-way process, allowing the weak to influence the strong. For instance, in writings, at meetings, in training workshops, and through dyadic conversations, professionals who work for the smaller organizations discuss among themselves the values and goals that define the sector (DiMaggio and Powell 1991, p. 3) and, by do doing, can enact new meanings of what a sector is about (Dimaggio and Powell, 1991 p. 13). Such shared cultural understandings are then transmitted through a series of repeated stories and iconic symbols that become the guiding myths and definition of the culture of the sector (Scott 1991, p. 169). The question of power can become a question of who can capture the means for propagating these cultural understandings.

### Issue Framing within Multi-Organizational Fields

New institutionalism theorists accept that contentions within a societal sector can be about the values that shape the broader interorganizational culture, but provide fewer insights into how values propagate. In contrast, scholars of new social movements theories explore the ways in which social activists reframe issues to shape perceptions and values (Polletta 1998; Snow and Benford, 1992 p. 137; Snow et al. 1986, p. 464). They argue that in successful social movements activists have a shared interpretive frame (Buechler 1995).

Support for change comes about as those in a movement persuade each other and those in the broader environment what changes should occur by creating shared frames. These "frames combine a *diagnosis* of the social condition in need of remedy, a *prognosis* for how to do that, and a *rationale* for action" (Benford and Hunt 1992; Snow and Benford 1988, from Polletta, p. 139). As new institutionalists also recognize, the values implicit within the interpretive frames are transmitted through "organizational coalitions, overlapping social movement communities, shared personnel, and changes in the external environment" (Meyer 1994, p. 278). Eventually, the frames that are accepted transform into an ideology that creates the shared symbols and indicates what within a movement is valued and why.

Further, as Francesca Polletta (Polletta 1998) describes, frames are transmitted through shared "narratives" that are passed along interorganizational ties. Narratives—that is, "stories, tales, anecdotes, allegories" (Polletta 1998, p. 140)—rather than the more abstract theories are the ways in which ideas are transmitted. Narratives are effective as framing devices since they enable those listening to link their individual experiences to the broader lessons contained within the shared communications. As Polletta explains, "narratives necessitate our interpretive participation, require that we struggle to fill the gaps and resolve the ambiguities. We struggle because the story's end is consequential—not only as the outcome but as the moral of the events which precede it" (Polletta 1998, p. 141). A narrative enables people to draw out lessons of values and of goals, but do so in a concrete fashion that speaks to their own experiences.

New social movement theories also indicate that the ideological direction that shapes a movement results from ongoing, iterative negotiations that take place within loosely linked interorganizational networks. It is both the concrete actions that are taken, protesting injustices, building homes for the welfare poor, as well as the symbols that are imputed to these actions that create political and cultural change (Buechler 1995, p. 442). Such influence proceeds along interorganizational and interpersonal networks rather than being promulgated from one source (Buechler 1995, p. 442).

However, the interorganizational system remains in flux. Ideologies change as new organizations enter into the fray, and as older organizations withdraw. As a result, the accepted definition of the problem might only hold for a brief period of time, though, for that time, participants share a common understanding of what the problems are about and agree on the characteristics of possible solutions (Snow 1992).

But who transmits these ideologies? This is done by organic intellectuals whose organic theories provide a shared understanding of both what change is needed and how change can come about (Carroll and Rattner 1996; Rubin 1994). As Antonio Gramsci, the Marxist intellectual, describes it organic theories emerge as *organic intellectuals* reflect upon their actions to provide an interpretive framework for others. Organic intellectuals create an ideological shape for a movement, not through an appeal to abstract principles or an imposed tradition, but rather by sharing through stories and narratives their grounded understanding of what in daily work has failed and what has succeeded. As Lipsitz explains,

> Organic intellectuals . . . conduct their intellectual inquiries through the practical activities of social contestation. . . . Organic intellectuals generate and circulate oppositional ideas through social action. They create symbols and slogans that disclose the commonalities among seemingly atomized experiences, and they establish principles that unite disparate groups into effective coalitions. (Lipsitz 1995, pp. 9–10)

In creating an organic theory, a multipart conversation takes place, in which organic intellectuals communicate to others in their organizations, to the broader societal sector, to potential supporters, as well as reflexively with themselves. Through contemplation about praxis, they bring forth theories based on experience on what needs to be accomplished. In this way, an

> organic intellectual [is] a manipulator of signs and symbols, an educator and an agitator rationally translating the needs and aspirations of [the] community into effective action. . . . In order to succeed, organic intellectuals rely on collective memory—shared experiences and perceptions about the past that legitimate action in the present—and on social learning—experiences with contestation in the present that transform values and goals for the future. (Lipsitz 1988, p. 228)

## CBDOs as Niche Organizations within a Complicated Interorganizational Environment

When I began this study I had neither the literature on the new institutionalism nor that of social movement framing in mind. As is common in qualitative work, the theoretical concerns emerged afterwards as I tried to understand my observations. In response to the conversations in which the developmental activists described their frustrations with funders and government I examined both the new institutionalism literature as well as the material on government-nonprofit relationships (Smith and Lipsky 1993).

Within this literature some scholars recognize that new institutionalism theory speaks to the world of community-based development organizations. For instance, in a marvelous and detailed study of the financing of nonprofits, Kirsten Groenjberg (1993) shows, consistent with new institutionalism theory, how funders use the financial dependency of community organization to force them to adopt specific organizational and structural features. Funding constraints

shape internal organizational structures, including the locus of control
. . . the nature and intensity of management efforts, and the extent
and nature of planning. They also set parameters for inter-organizational
dependencies and control mechanisms. To the extent that funding
sources reduce internal or external resource uncertainties, organizations
will find them attractive in spite of the control, management difficulties
and work they impose. (Groenjberg 1993, pp. 298–299)

Yet, other literature implies that even in the nonprofit sector mutual influence does occur and some semblance of independence is possible. For instance, during a period of financial cutbacks, in which the dependence of most nonprofits on government increased, Lester Salamon describes that

the one exception is the housing and community development organizations, which started the period with extremely high reliance on government support, experienced sharp reductions in that support, but were nevertheless able to generate alternative sources of support from virtually all other sources. (Salamon 1995, p. 165)

There are indications that small organizations might have some ability to fight back, a perception that was reinforced by what I learned from my interviews, as developmental activists, while complaining about their funders, still vigorously showed me how their organizations could be effective in influencing what was accomplished. They described how their ideas often prevailed, how the coalitions they established could reshape the broader sector, and how by strategically leveraging money they could play off one funder against another.

In addition, my observations and historic reconstructions indicated that several major ideas pushed for by the intermediaries and foundations as their own, in actuality emerged from the experiences of the developmental activists. For instance, developmental activists worked out models of how to keep capital within neighborhoods of the poor, by setting up supermarkets, or linking social service programs such as day care to physical development projects, that later were transformed into endorsed programs of the foundations or intermediaries.

In addition, the developmental activists shared with me, and more importantly with each other, organic theories of why they did what they did. These theories were transmitted as narratives of project success at meetings, in training academies, and through the messages that consultants spread from one organization to another. These evolving theories ended up structuring the broader culture of the community development movement. These observations when interpreted in light of questions posed by new institutionalism theories suggest how developmental activists, behaving as organic theorists, are able to restructure the broader culture of the community development movement to reflect the values of the CBDOs rather than those of the funders.

What I suggest occurs is the following:

To survive within a complicated, interorganizational environment in which resources are at a premium, smaller organizations create a set of strategies that I term the logic of the *niche*. These strategies first allow the smaller organizations to balance off pressures from funders by learning how to skillfully leverage resources and ideas. Next, the organic theorists who gain understandings of what works and why diffuse stories, narratives, and exemplary cases—the organic theory—that reframes for those in the sector what community-development ought to be about.

In addition, to gain needed resources that they themselves control, and, developmental activists build a *support sector* of coalitions, trade associations, training academies that end up counterbalancing to some extent the influence of funders and governmental agencies. These organizations actively speak for the beliefs of the developmental activists, through propagandizing for the movement, doing lobbying, and at times through more aggressive advocacy campaigns. In addition, and probably of greater import, the support organizations provide the shared opportunities—through training programs, meetings, publications, and simply by enabling developmental activists to meet one another—that allow activists to create a common lore on how to solve community problems.

This lore is based upon the organic theory that frames what community-based development ought to be about, a theory that emerges from the daily experiences of the developmental activists, and is shared through the narratives of project success, and, at times, failures. What gives the organic theory the power to persuade is that those hearing it recognize, from their experiences, that the theory reflects actual happenings that resonate with their own experiences rather than being an ideological imposition. Organic theory emerges as the developmental activists reflect upon their concrete experiences that come about in building homes, creating jobs, establishing commercial areas, and in general reconciling the tensions that community developers face.

The organic theory offers lessons on how to balance the cross-pressures that development organizations confront, but builds these lessons on realistic experiences. Many of developmental activists have strong normative (usually left-leaning) beliefs about what is needed to empower the poor. Yet they recognize how their actions are limited by the resources made available from government, intermediaries, and the foundations, as well as being constrained by the social realities that poverty itself creates. Developmental activists cannot delude themselves with some abstract theory; to gain credence among those who work in the field, the organic theory must imply practical actions that can simultaneously balance out social goals with developmental ones, by showing how to help the poor in an environment of severe resource limitations.

But merely formulating an organic theory is not enough. The need is to effectively communicate its values and beliefs to persuade those in government, intermediaries, and the foundations of its worth. This comes about within the forums provided by the meetings sponsored by the coalitions and trade associations, as well as during the conversations that occur along the networks that emerge out of such meetings. Support organizations provide a place at which those who lead CBDOs can meet, share their ideas with others in the field, and communicate narratives of success. These narratives help create a collective framing of what community development ought to be about that influences the larger funders. The counterstructures constitute the agency that enables developmental activists to share with one another and with those in government, intermediaries, and the foundations, a set of values, goals, and directions, of their own, that frames what those involved in development work should accomplish.

The rest of this book builds toward this theory. In the next three chapters I describe the cross-pressures community-based development organizations face, first, because of their multiple missions, then because of the pressures from different governmental agencies, and, last, but far from least, in their complicated relationships with the intermediaries and foundations.

I then explore how developmental activists work to shape the environment in which they work. I discuss the organic theories that guide their work, the strategies followed to obtain resources for projects that enable them to accomplish projects that reflect their visions, and conclude with several chapters on how the support sector enables smaller and weaker organizations, but those that have a vision of what should be done, to shape what a societal sector is about.

# CHAPTER 3

# Confronting Ideological Tensions

> If we have someone that is behind in their rent, and they are truly
> trying to catch up . . . and they face some problem, . . . we can network
> with [an]other agency to help provide that rent. We do not forgive
> rents . . . if we started forgetting rents and clients learn that happens
> then . . . eventually all of them start . . . taking advantage.
>
> —a housing developer

This chapter examines cross-pressures developmental activists feel as they simultaneously try to create economically viable projects and not neglect a social change mission, while maintaining the economic viability of the CBDO itself. The pressures come about, in part, because of the bifurcated origins of the CBDOs, some starting as creatures of the state, with others emerging as part of the neighborhood movement. A core purpose of the organic theory of development is to enable community groups to reconcile these potentially contending missions.

## CONTRADICTORY BEGINNINGS

In part, the tensions developmental activists must reconcile in their daily work stem from the contradictory pressures brought about by the different origins of the CBDOs. Those organizations most dependent upon government funding initially focused more on production than empowerment, while those that emerged from the neighborhoods often were continuations of protest and empowerment efforts. As time passed, each tradition influenced the other.

Federal support for community-based development organizations began as part of Johnson's War on Poverty efforts when federal officials, goaded by civil rights activists, tried unsuccessfully to extend the work of Community Action Agencies to help neighborhoods rather than simply focusing on the poor within neighborhoods (Blaustein and Faux 1972; Goetz 1993; Halpern 1995; Parachini 1980; Peirce and Steinbach 1987; Perry 1987; Zdenek 1990). Major foundations echoed this concern about holistic neighborhood redevelopment and gave voice to these concerns with the Ford Foundation's funding of a "gray areas" programs that coordinated economic and social service programs within defined geographic locales. Building on the lessons learned from the Ford effort, Senators Robert Kennedy and Jacob Jacobs sponsored legislation to establish a Special Impact Program—SIP—to target and coordinate aid to geographic communities that housed large numbers of low-income people and encouraged the Office of Economic Opportunity—the OEO—to fund the Hough Area Development Corporation in Cleveland, as a test program. A successful external evaluation of HADC was bureaucratically parleyed by supporters of the community development corporation idea into Congress' passing Title VII of the Economic Development Act that provided direct funding for several dozen CDCs.

These initial Title VII CDCs were large, bureaucratically sophisticated organizations that took on a multipart mission, but one focusing more on bringing physical change than on pushing for neighborhood empowerment. Still, even these first-generation CDCs had strong roots in advocacy (Halpern 1995, p. 134). An elder statesperson of the CBDO movement who worked for a Title VII CDC described the linkages:

> I came out of college and immediately went to work for an organization, the National Welfare Rights organization, which was a civil rights organization. . . . I was a civil rights activist and a community organizer. And as we start to look at the issues and look at how we could overcome the social problems that existed we looked towards economic development. And all of a sudden there was a new vehicle available from the federal government [the CDCs].

This ex-community activist now heads an organization that is a successful developer of inner-city shopping centers.

The aggregate funding for Title VII organizations was small, with only about a hundred million dollars provided over fifteen years with funds concentrated in grants to few organizations (Halpern 1995, p. 132). However, to provide technical assistance to these thirty-five CDCs, Title VII also funded many support organizations that were also allowed to help other CDCs, even those not receiving federal money. These technical assistance shops were led by individuals such as Stewart Perry (cf. Perry 1987), a former employee of OEO and ideological guru for community-based development, who not only provided technical help to other organizations but helped circulate the idea that CDCs were about more than simply carrying out federal renewal programs.

Voice was given to these alternative interpretations of what CBDOs were about, as a wide array of organizations emerged locally, responding to immediately perceived problems of palpable and visible poverty. In contrast to the federal thrust, these organizations reflected their roots in neighborhood work, in religious missions, or, at times, in advocacy.

Many emerged out of the neighborhood movement itself, starting with little more than as a response to conversations between dissatisfied neighbors, but at some point becoming linked to the larger, national efforts. A developmental activist, whose CBDO now has built a small shopping mall, a business incubator, as well as clearing out derelict stores, described the provenance of her organization:

> [I]t was just six people in my living room saying, "boy, am I sick of look-ing at this stuff!"
>
> "Let's build a factory."
>
> "Okay."
>
> You know, no one had the faintest idea what we were talking about, including us. . . . Well, we ended up not doing a factory. But we started a group of us because we were tired of the conditions here. And, we ended up just as a volunteer group, we all had jobs. . . . And, we did things, we started surveying the neighborhood and we said, . . . if "you are going to do anything big you are going to need the federal govern-ment involved" and we found out to do that we had to get federal funds, we would have to qualify as a distressed neighborhood etc.
>
> So we started statistical gathering in our spare time, we started leafletting the neighborhood. . . . And we had a big community meet-ing and people gave us page after page after page of what they wanted in their neighborhood. They wanted everything that anything else had. They wanted book stores, and clothing stores, and jewelry stores and you know, why isn't the city this? and why do we have all these bars? And why do we have, you know. And that ended up saying shop-ping center.

Another CBDO, the only neighborhood based group in a middle-sized city started as

> residents in this neighborhood really felt like, that they wanted more control over the types of developments that were going to happen in the area, their concern was that since it is a central city neighborhood fairly close to the university and the state capitol and the downtown that gentrification would take place unless they tried to have a more balanced kind of development. So people in the neighborhood wanted . . . some control of it instead of just leaving it in the hands of the city planners.

Others emerged to repair the neighborhoods devastated by street protests. For example, in Miami, the Talcolcy Economic Development Corporation was set up as direct response to the devastation caused by the unrests in Liberty City (Berger 1992, p. 8). The New Communities Corporation, probably the largest CDC in the nation, grew out of the effort of a parish priest to bring food, and later hope for renewal, to the riot-torn area of central Newark. But early days were hard:

We didn't have anyone who wanted to fund us. So we had to go out and raise the money in the local community. We raised it in the suburbs. . . . we created something that was modeled after a kind of a tree in Israel campaign, except we had a square foot of land in [city name] and eventually raised about $100,000, which is [a] significant amount of money. . . . And that got us going. It took us seven years before we walked into our first project too. It didn't come easy.

Some emerge as part of a broader neighborhood movement, but then break off from the neighborhood groups. In a city noted for its progressive neighborhood politics, the CDC was initially set up by the neighborhood association as a tool to achieve neighborhood economic empowerment. As the director described it,

the vision that evolved during those years of struggle . . . was a vision of a neighborhood-based economy where assets would be controlled by the people who lived here. The [ ] CDC was founded . . . to be the technical vehicle to implement that.

But as community members began to squabble, in part reflecting internal social class divisions, the neighborhood association entered a state of administrative and political disarray. As a result,

the staff came to feel besieged here, became less receptive to the neighborhood input. Some board members were elected . . . who clearly had the intent of either disassembling the————CDC or radically changing it. There was a major meeting . . . at which time the decision was made to keep the CDC. But the CDC needed to be restructured.

And while it still reported to the neighborhood group, the CDC now had its own board administered by an executive director rather than a management committee from the neighborhood group, but one that still maintained the thrust of preserving the neighborhood economy.

In Indianapolis, in another common pattern, a CBDO was spun off from several social service organizations in an effort to speak for an ethnic group. As its president described it,

this neighborhood used to be the heart of the African-American community . . . [but] in the '80s this area was targeted for . . . redevelopment because of its close proximity to downtown and the university. . . . In the early '80s the . . . Urban Life Center [one of the social service agencies] . . . purchased the building and began to restore it to use it kind of a public trust, to serve the purposes it served before, as an African-American business and cultural center. . . . But we realized that we had to do more than just focus on the restoration of that building, we had to be concerned about the redevelopment of the neighborhood. . . . Would it be redeveloped with neighborhood and African-American participation?

The Urban Life Center sought out allies and

went to the neighborhood association . . . that . . . had been involved . . . trying to keep the city and the university from just swallowing up the neighborhood and with a bulldozer mentality and wiping out everything.

More help, though was needed, so

we went to . . . a multi-service center, that . . . had one of the nation's first and most successful sweat equity program. . . . and asked them to join us in creating [CBDO] And that is what happened is these three organizations came together with a common purpose.

The CBDO was then set up as an independent organization to be better able to employ its own staff of technical experts.

In another community, a CBDO came about as an old-line Alinsky-style group determined "to build on the organizing and take it to another level." The developmental activist explained:

People were basically pissed off in two ways. We were either ignored, or when downtown did pay attention to the community, bad developments were done. . . . It promised the community no high-rises, ended up building a high rise, tore down all these houses and nobody from the community got one of the new houses. . . . So [CBDO] was created and focused a lot on home ownership.

In Baltimore, the South East Community Organization (SECO), or in Chicago, the Woodlawn Organization, and throughout the nation, ACORN Housing, began as protest groups, though of markedly different degrees of radicalness. The Delta Foundation in the impoverished Delta region of Mississippi grew "out of Mississippi's dramatic civil rights struggles of the sixties" (Berger 1992, p. 4) and is now is a quasicapitalist holding company of small firms. The three major Mexican-American CDCs—the East Los Angeles Community Union, Chicanos por la Causa, and the Mexican American Unity Council—initially were started by student activists inspired by the work in the civil rights era to empower the minority poor (Marquez 1993).

Many community-based development organizations were influenced by ideologies of progressive neighborhood advocacy. Several CBDOs gained a progressive focus, as they sought out help from the highly ideological National Center for Urban Economic Affairs, a support organization set up to help community groups involved in empowerment efforts. The Center for Community Change, an organization set up to train activists, assisted CBDOs by teaching them how to blend together development work with efforts at community empowerment.

Other community-based development organizations emerged with church support, taking on an ideological tilt that combined a soupçon of humanitarian self-help with an ethos of tough love. These organizations refocused the social services programs that had been given support by programs such as the Catholic Campaign for Human Development or the outreach efforts of the Presbyterian Church, and extended them to programs of physical development.

Other efforts, such as Milwaukee's Northwest Side CDC, Cleveland's Midtown Corridor, Indianapolis's Near North, and, Chicago's Lawrence Avenue Development Corporation or Greater Southwest Development Corporation, came about to preserve business and industrial districts. Neighborhood business and industrial districts recognized that government had been focusing primarily on downtown and on the larger companies. In response, as a Chicago activist described, neighborhood businesses set up an "industrial council. . . . Almost sort of Saul Alinsky style of organization, adapted to the needs of small and medium sized manufacturing companies. . . . They are companies that employee twenty-five people or less. They are mostly family-owned businesses. They've been there a long time. . . . There are about a thousand of them."

But these CBDOs learned that business preservation also necessitate broader efforts at community change. Today, these business focused CBDOs are also involved in job-training efforts, incubator management, community anti-crime work, as well as providing affordable housing for families and low-income elderly.

In contrast to the Title VII CDCs, these other organizations were "smaller, more opportunistic, and more pragmatic" (Halpern 1995, p. 138). But they also faced more directly the tensions that came about as physical development work displaced either doing social service or the even more diffuse efforts of neighborhood organizations of running fairs, or of advocating for more city services to the community. Tensions began to appear. A developmental activist whose neighborhood organization had to that time concentrated on running ethnic festivities or fighting to keep a neighborhood library opened, reflected on the consequences for her organization of successfully converting an old convent to housing for the old. She described that the project

> has sort of a certain sex appeal. You know, it's bricks and mortar and it's visible. It was a creative adaptive reuse. . . . I mean, it's like we have done wonderful things in this neighborhood before, on a much smaller scale, but we've had other miracles, and it wasn't until we had this miracle that some of these people wanted to take us seriously.

But she worried how the project took time away from neighborhood organizing and was torn about her responsibilities:

> I really have a love of the bricks and mortar. . . . I've been distracted from much of the organizing. And so it's important that I still do door knocking and it's important that I still go to zoning hearings and that kind of thing, and I made a point that during the construction to occasionally take time off to remember to do that.

In general, developmental activists are well aware of how project success can distract from the ideological purity of the CBDO. At a plenary session of the NCCED, a leading development activist reflected:

> If there is a killer of [a] CDC it is success. Managing success is the most difficult task you can do. . . . You've got all these assets. And all of a sudden, you are like a dog chasing a car, you caught the car now you are part of the traffic problem.
>
> Success is tough. You lose sight of that box or window you set out to address and you have to constantly address your goals. Are you in business to make money? Are you in business to make other people make money? Are you in business to be center stage when the curtain goes up? You have to constantly examine who you are and what your task is. Success will kill you.

Success necessitates hiring technical staff to run projects and once staff are on board the obligation is to keep them employed. There is no guarantee that needed technical people will have a fire-in-the-belly belief in support of empowering neighborhoods.

One activist remembered that when he, his roommate, and a few community members began the CBDO to combat the city's neglect of the housing in the neighborhood, no one had technical skills. He then described that

> we're going to hire two people this next month. One has a CPA-MBA and the other person has been a bank public relations executive for twenty years. And these people are sharp as hell. Our staff needs to be smarter than the local government and smarter than local business community. They have to understand numbers and they have to understand public relations.

Yet, what does this say about the ideological fervor to help those in need?

> Nobody is hiring people who have ideology. You're hiring people who'll do spreadsheets and ultimately that's going to really hurt the movement.

Success can create an organizational dynamic and economic pressure for the CBDOs to do safe and profitable projects that in turn might force the CBDO into acting little different than a for-profit business. But so long as the CBDO continues to service the poor, counterpressures persist, as developers once again rediscover that their work must maintain an empowerment mission. A long-time housing director reflected that after her organization had primarily concentrated on building and managing apartments:

> It is almost like now we are almost coming full circle. We've always had a resident services piece. . . . But what we find now is that there is a tremendous need for the whole family support services piece, given the various rise in drug activity in the city now and just a whole bunch of vary[ing] social issues. We are finding that we really have to actively raise that to the same level as maybe development has been raised, [or] in the past maybe property management [has] been raised.

As both funding opportunities change and as understandings of community needs evolve, community-based development organizations rethink their missions, often at extended retreats or workshops. CBDOs wrestle with moving from programs of renting homes to those of selling them and in doing so ended up with internal discussions "on what constitutes the behavioral manifestations of empowerment. How do you measure empowerment and so forth and so on." Staff and board ask each other: Are renters truly empowered? How do tenant councils compare with programs to purchase homes as a means to enable those in the neighborhood to gain a sense of control and ownership? Missions can be reshaped as a result of these internal conversations.

A leading CBDO had brought a successful industrial park on line and recognized that the organization could easily continue to work on similar programs. But the organization's leadership and board members were not sure that doing so was enough to bring about the neighborhood change that benefited those most in need. The CBDO held a retreat to discuss what the organization ought to be about:

> we were having to face up to the challenges of [a board member] who would say that "this industrial park is great but it is not getting the guy who is unemployed living next door to me a job." So you know, we were also internally going through the struggle of trying to assess what it meant to create jobs for a community and beginning to, I think, have the fundamental discussion about wealth creation.

After several such meetings, the CBDO refocused its efforts to start a series of integrated projects to create self-generating assets within the community. As part of this redirected mission, the executive director encouraged the CBDO's staff to better reach out to the community, discover the social assets already in place, and work out projects that built on these assets. The home-day project described on page 13 resulted.

Community-based development organizations come about for a wide array of reasons and evolve in response to a changing environment. Implicit within this evolution is an ongoing tension over what the overall purpose of a CBDO ought to be about, a process that is affected by the availability of resources. These topics are covered in the next two chapters.

## CHOOSING DIRECTIONS

No matter what the provenance of their organizations, the daily demands of community work create cross-pressures for the developmental activists. They are torn between concentrating the work of CBDOs in repairing the physical damage to the community, the need to maintain the organization as a financially viable entity, and the moral obligation to provide social support for community members. Community-based development organizations confront what has been termed the

> "double bottom line"—the simultaneous need for *financial accountability* and attention to the nonprofit organization's *social goals* . . . many nonprofit housing sponsors have had to struggle mightily with this duality, given the inexorable logic of "the numbers." (Bratt et al. 1994, p. 3)

To be too concerned with bottom-line survival might mitigate against serving the most needy clientele, but to ignore the bottom line dooms the CBDO to collapse.

Other tensions occur, as developmental activists respond to concerns of those on the activist left who argue that development is but a distraction from broader efforts at social empowerment. Can CBDOs engage in advocacy work against the very banks and governmental agencies whose economic support is needed to finance the physical redevelopment work? (Stoecker 1995).

*Tensions between Doing Social Development,*
*Providing Services and Property Management*

Community-based development organizations balance the need to keep costs reasonable in the projects, yet at the same time help potential clients and community members overcome social and personal problems. Cross-sectional studies have shown that when projects are financially marginal, CBDOs pay less attention to social services and more to keeping the project afloat (Bratt et al. 1994; Hebert 1993). But doing so is problematic for the socially concerned developmental activist. A director of a rural community action agency that was also a leading physical developer explained the pressures in running a subsidized day-care center:

It's really a hard balance. . . . The day center . . . and the services it's providing, it's terrific. . . . We're serving a tremendous amount of kids. And we're losing about $100,000 a year. . . . We'd accumulated enough money over the years that we can subsidize this for a period of time, but you reach a point where you have to make a decision that "Hey, that's it."

Or, when acting as landlords, CBDO directors are torn on whether to let an impoverished tenant's delinquent rent ride for a month or two.

[As owners] we have to collect the rent. We're not a social service agency . . . , but in dealing with people [we] realize that there are a lot of folks who live in our units that have multiple problems. We've got babies having babies. . . . We've got people with very low education levels, people who are getting AFDC and towards the end of the month the food stamps run out so that's what I mean, just to empathize, to realize that people have these problems.

The individual is torn, but reluctantly concluded "if people can't pay the rent they still have to go."

In another case, a developmental activist described the difficulties both to fund housing for displaced women and provide these women with a supportive social network. She reflected that

the hardest thing for us as an organization to deal with is the reality [that] we can't both subsidize the housing and subsidize the women. . . . We cannot make the project work and subsidize the women.

She told me of a warning shared with her by a national leader:

When we first took on that project . . . he explained,
"You'd better think really quick and get ourself to an understanding. You know do you want to develop housing or do you want to take care of people, you can't do both."
It was real sobering, it was very good to hear that because the reality is no, you can't, **but I'm still believing that there is a way.**

She continued in her efforts to do both, thereby complicating getting the funding and delaying completion of the housing by an extra year. Other studies, also report, that CBDOs "sometimes 'let the heart overrule the head' and in a compassionate effort not to evict delinquent tenants neglect to collect rents" (Sullivan 1993, p. 28).

The balance between the bottom line and the obligation to help people is compounded by pressure from funders who argue that CBDOs should pay less attention to social service issues and concentrate on building enough homes to create an asset base for the development organizations (Giloth et al. 1992; NCCED

1991b; Rubin 1995a). Government, banks, and even foundations, demand that CBDOs support themselves, in part, from overhead profits from the homes, recognizing that to do so precludes providing social services.

Community-based development organizations try to resist becoming totally immersed in the direct provision of services, lest doing so overwhelm an overworked staff. The director of an organization that set up limited equity cooperatives fretted that

> the more involved you get with families, the more involved you get with social service issues and what we found we are not trained to deal with social services or family issues. . . . We already have three roles that we play. We are the developer, we are the owner, we are the neighborhood organization. And then to be the social worker on top of it is, it's . . . too much.

Yet, he continued, helping people is both a moral and practical necessity:

> the tilt toward helping people is what continues their [CBDO's] credibility to exist and be able to attract the free money. . . . That is one of the good things about the granting sources is that they force you to keep that sensitivity for the people in the deprived aspect of humanity into whatever deal in order to qualify for the money.

This organization became actively involved in summer school programs for at-risk adolescents and anticrime programs, and spent much time teaching people how to be organizers.

Developmental activists recognize that to neglect the social problems of people being helped is to doom the economic projects to failure:

> We have costs in running this venture, this enterprise, the way we do that we wouldn't have if we were just trying to make a profit. We don't see the point, for example, in developing affordable housing and then evicting somebody the first day they're past due on rent because they become unemployed. I mean we want to work with them to get a job and get their family back together and so forth—that's consistent with our mission.
>
> We don't see the point of doing affordable housing and then letting the gangs paint graffiti all over. We've got to paint that stuff over every day. . . .
>
> We want to rent to large families. It's more expensive to rent to large families—the kids tear the place up—but that's why large families can't get apartments in this neighborhood. So because they can't, we are going to. If we were trying to make profit we would also exclude them and go for the one- and two-bedroom units and so forth.

But to work with people with troubled histories, developmental activists need the skills of social workers, skills they lack, while providing services hurts the bottom line. Property management makes quite clear to the community-based development organizations how much they are on the border between being a nonprofit with responsibilities to clients and community and a self-financing organization with concerns with its own bottom line. As landlords, developmental activists recognize that if they do not provide close management, undesirables enter the building and destroy property (Bratt et al. 1994). Too much supervision, though, is demeaning to the tenant. Still, CBDOs that manage property often set up policies of "tough love," requiring routine apartment checks and evicting people quickly for violations such as dope use, or even inadequate maintenance of the apartments.

Still, housing people with problems implies that a CBDO will take on some social mission. Regarding a CBDO-owned home for women with problems, many of them former prostitutes, the developmental activist explained:

> the dilemma that we're looking at . . . [is] if you're going to live in Liz's House [affordable housing for women with social problems] you have to be working towards thinking more future oriented. You have to be working toward education, job training, all that sort of thing. . . . We're really telling people that live in our area and that live in our neighborhood that these are the values that we think are important. And if you don't like it, you can go somewhere else you know and create your own neighborhood.

Similar cross-pressures are felt by developers of commercial property. A leading incubator developer told those at a national conference that

> If your objective is the development and establishment of strong successful companies, there is inherent conflict between the owner of the building and operator [building manager]. If you are perceived simultaneously as landlord and the business assistant specialist, you will always get hit up for more concessions than you can give to tenants. . . . Our staff was getting trapped in sort of cross-fire relationship between the economics of the building and . . . our concern about the success of the compan[ies].

*The Tradeoffs between Doing Development, Joining in to Social Advocacy, and Building Empowerment Neighborhoods*

Another set of ideological tensions comes about as developmental activists wrestle with the responsibilities of whether to join into advocacy work, especially that linked with more activist neighborhood groups (cf. Marquez 1993, Stoecker 1995). Related to this tension is a concern of how much a participatory neighborhood group should set the redevelopment agenda, for in doing so such groups bypass the economic or technical expertise that a CBDO can offer.

Many of the developmental activists began their own careers as community organizers and, as such, are particularly attuned to the value debates involved between developers and advocates. In Chicago, several of the city's leading developmental activists got their own start working for Gale Cincotta's Neighborhood Peoples' Action, a national direct action coalition, but then

> we said to ourselves, "Gee, performing the advocacy work and stopping bad things isn't enough. **Stopping negatives isn't enough. Stopping negatives isn't the same as producing positives. . . .**"

> In those days, there was a lot of controversy about whether you did that. There were kind of two schools of thought among community organizers. There was the Cincotta-Trapp school of thought from NTIC and National Peoples' Action . . . that said, any organization that got involved in development activity was impure. And then there was the other school of thought . . . which said any organization that doesn't get that, ultimately end up in development, is forever immature. And they had these kind of battlelines drawn.

> Well, development is a tactic, a strategy, a line of work that produce[s homes and jobs] that you do to solve a problem and it is appropriate or inappropriate depending upon your need in your community, in your constituency. And it is not a be-all or end-all. And it is also not a cardinal sin. It is somewhere in the middle. It is appropriate when it is appropriate and it is not appropriate when it is not.

Still, the technical work of development can drive out organizing. A former community developer now a city official reflected on his past experience:

> [I] worked as a neighborhood organizer and also developer. When push came to shove and I needed to get something done, I could always put off door knocking—I couldn't always put off something that I needed to get to a bank or something. Development becomes an all-encompassing thing and it's the organizing that always falls flat especially [in] a small organization that doesn't have . . . a large staff to do stuff.

But developmental activists can't escape the tensions, as they are continually chided in no uncertain times by direct-action advocates. A director of a city-wide CBDO coalition described how

> executive directors of these development groups . . . once upon a time they were out there doing organizing or working to organize the groups

[and now activists complain]: "God damn developers. You don't come out when we picket. You don't come out when we picket. You don't come out when we have these press conferences. You don't come out and call the mayor a SOB. But when we go out and do it and shake the apple tree and some apples come down. You are the son of the bitches who get 80 percent of the apples and you didn't do any of the work."

Still, perspectives on when direct action is appropriate have changed. The director of an organization that got its start organizing tenants against landlords and protesting the lack of affordable housing, indicated that

> you don't have the same kind of dynamics you had in the sixties or the seventies. The city is not necessarily the enemy; the enemy is crime and drug houses. So we work a lot with the police, we have hassles but it is more that they are not responding quick enough.

In discussions with developmental activists as well as in the observations made by other scholars of the community movement (Stoecker 1997) the tensions between advocacy and development become conflated with questions of who should set the development agenda: the CBDO or an elected democratic neighborhood organization. In Minneapolis, for instance, one observer described how "CDCs tended to undermine the broader aims of their parent community organizations, however, because of the organizational resources they consumed" (Nickel 1995, p. 366).

Further, a CBDO that enforces behavioral standards in housing can be seen as repressive by left-wing activist organizations. A director of a successful CBDO, itself associated with an activist neighborhood organization, indicated the nature of this tension:

> I mean we are fighting advocates, we are fighting neighborhood groups. . . . You have the advocates who say, "Regardless almost how bad people behave they should be housed. They have an unalienable right to housing. And if people play the music all night or sell drugs or whatever, that you almost have to you know, that's just part of the deal folks."
>
> And then on the other hand you've got neighborhood groups that like are saying, "We don't want any affordable housing, not in my back yard, we've had enough, but we've never had any and we've seen what happens when folks get it and we don't want it." And so there ain't nothing about this job that's inclined to make you very popular.

In other neighborhoods, neighborhood activists fear that, as a result of improvements made by a CBDO, gentrification might occur and the very poor will be displaced. To complicate this perception, the CBDO might believe that it is important to bring back a middle class, particularly a black middle class, that can provide the social infrastructure needed to sustain the neighborhood, while neighborhood groups only want to help those now there.

Agendas differ as those in the neighborhood organization might press the development organization to work on housing rather than commercial development, in part, because housing is more readily understood. An incubator developer complained:

> The neighborhood group was . . . a tight-knit group of about forty folks. . . . This neighborhood only understood housing. And they loved housing and you could talk housing. . . . Somebody comes in and say shopping center, we are going to take out housing—[moaning sound].
>
> I mean I had about a three-year uphill battle. I would go to their meetings, twice a month. We would keep them apprised of what we were doing. We would show them drawings, bring architects, we'd answer questions. It was an education process. And I say, "You know I support housing, we need it, but you can't have a neighborhood with just housing. You have to have your commercial, you have to give your people goods." I mean we did a whole economic education of those people.

Such tensions between CBDOs and neighborhood associations take on crisis proportions when city governments require approval of an elected neighborhood association before funds are released. A developmental activist described what happened when his organization wanted to tear out derelict stores and replace them with a mini-mall, and community members feared they would be harmed by change:

> It generated a very large amount of controversy. It has taken us three years now working on that project back and forth with the city and different neighborhood group meetings . . . because the preservation issue gets so personal with some people. It generated a real hassle with the neighborhood group . . . because the preservations had control.

The battle went on for some time, and the dialogue was embittered since the CBDO had built and sold affordable housing to minority group members, offending some within this lower-middle-class white neighborhood. On my last visit to the city I learned that this CBDO had gone under while awaiting approval from the neighborhood association. In another case, a CBDO complained how the neighborhood organization had cost it many years in its effort to build a major shopping strip anchored by a large supermarket:

> This project took seven years to complete. Approximately a $10,000,000 project and one of the reasons that it took so long to complete was that this project was planned with total community involvement. And what

would happen was you would be working with a group, in about two or three years that group would change, and you'd have to start all over again of informing them of what the other group had already agreed to.

In a similar case, a city government had provided a community council with grant money to design a neighborhood mall that ended being designed on paper as a grandiose 300,000 square foot facility. When no funding could be raised for this large-scale project within the city's poorest neighborhood, the community council devolved the responsibility upon the CBDO, which itself developed a small strip mall with a supermarket, drugstore, laundromat, and a few convenience stores. But, as the head of the CBDO complained,

> people said, "it is ugly." . . . The reality of it is at the time, that was the best, you know, we could get for the money. . . . it is functional. We got 30,000 [feet], 20,000 for the grocery, we got a drugstore, we eventually got a bank in there. We got two clothing stores, a small little restaurant. We got Wendy's. . . . It served the needs of the community. People who before had to drive five miles to get food, now can walk to the store.

Yet, as the table below, from Vidal's studies of the background of the board members of CBDOs (Vidal 1992, p. 39), shows, there is large neighborhood control involved, at least in this formal sense:

| Type of Members | Percentage of Board Members of This Type |
|---|---|
| Residents/clients | 44% |
| Representatives of other community-based organizations | 11% |
| Local religious leaders | 4% |
| Relevant professionals | 20% |
| Local bankers or business people | 12% |
| Local government officials | 3% |
| Donors (funders) | 4% |
| Others | 5% |

In addition, scholars point out that CBDOs speak to the issues of poverty more sincerely than do neighborhood associations:

> Research shows that neighborhood organizations are likely to be dominated by . . . residents with higher incomes. . . . On the other hand, [CBDOs] have led efforts to assist low-income residents . . . when neighborhood groups are captured by conservative property owners. . . . Thus, the suggestion that [CBDOs] are less oppositional than voluntary

neighborhood associations is not supported by the evidence. (Goetz and Sidney 1995, p. 17)

Developmental activists see some of what they are doing as battling this local entrenched community oligarchy, that itself is indifferent to the plight of the poor.

In addition, developmental activists work to create integration within the community in ways that formal neighborhood associations cannot. CBDOs empower people by making them feel like owners of the community. At a national conference, a leading community developer of inner-city shopping centers described how, by reaching out to the churches to get support for a development project, many people ended up feeling part of the overall renewal effort:

> What happens in the real spirit of the movement hit me a few years ago as I stood across the street from the shopping center. I watched them hike our sign up. . . . I felt real good as I looked at the community that had been burned out. . . . And all of a sudden we had a brand new shopping center there getting ready to hire four hundred new people. . . .
>
> And I had a little lady come to me. She was about seventy years old and I was sitting there with my chest out and she said to me, "Young man—you see our shopping center." I said, "Yes, ma'm, I sure do." She said, "We built that. My preacher every Sunday we donated and I put a dollar in every Sunday. And we built that shopping center."

Still, developmental activists worry if their efforts are really about empowering the community or if they are more concerned with carrying out their redevelopment plans. The ambivalence felt can be heard in this story of an CBDO affiliated with the progressive Center for Community Change. The organization hired and paid for a professional organizer to work with community members, still the developmental activist worried that

> one of the things that happened in community organizing is the community will select your agenda as much as you will let them so you have to have an agenda of your own so you can also direct some movement for the neighborhood.

He continued by describing the compromises between the CBDO's goals to replace a blighted shopping area with new shopping and the neighborhood's fear of who would own the shopping:

> The commercial strip was terrible, I mean it was a very, very blighted two-block neighborhood that had been blighted for thirty-four years that really now hosted a major portion of the city's illegal drug activity, prostitution, crime in general, illegal liquor sale. . . .
>
> So we tackled that issue. And we decided after inspecting buildings, after a three-month process of a comprehensive plan, we would going to tear it down. . . .

So Gladys [the community organizer] essentially organized people to get them out to meetings . . . we had as many as two hundred people at these meetings and people were mad, people were excited, people were pessimistic said it would never happen. . . . Someone said to tear this down to get rid of the drug dealers; other people said you are tearing this down so rich white folk could move in.

. . . We think, these strips are a blight on the neighborhood, we got to get rid of them. . . . So we took it down, we are taking it down. And the neighborhood said what we want in its place is affordable housing, alright. . . . Then people look to us and say, you are a developer, let [the CBDO] do the affordable housing because we know who will manage it. . . . As you must know and hear, neighborhood people [starts pounding desk] don't trust any institution. None. None. None. None. Black neighborhood people don't trust white people unless they known them a long time. Prove your worth.

It appeared that the CBDO carried out its goal of tearing down the derelict strip, but reconciled community members who feared outsiders coming in, by building homes owned by the CBDO and made available to community members.

## Surviving as a Business

Developmental activists worry whether a CBDO can afford to provide a social service, at a loss, or charge too little rent for needy tenants. To what extent do CBDOs focus on doing deals that benefit them financially rather than concentrating on a broader mission of social change? Does a CBDO end up work to help lower-middle-class people buy homes, with the CBDO receiving an immediate fee, instead of housing the extremely poor in more marginal projects?

For developmental activists such tension are nuanced, not constituting either/or decisions. Developmental activists recognize that they are running businesses, albeit community-oriented, socially responsible businesses. They understand that the very rationale for having CDCs in the first place is to bring a bottom-line expertise to doing deals that help the poor. Being labeled as a business is not considered as an insult, but rather a compliment to the growing community-based development **industry**.

Still, being seen as both a social service agency and a business leave the CBDO in perpetually awkward situations. For instance, community-based development organizations can appear as both broke and flush with money, depending on whether an outsider examines its operating budget (usually in short supply), its capital budget for an immediate project (sometimes a quite significant figure), or its illiquid asset base. Net worth is hard to determine: How is it possible to provide a realistic value for an apartment complex that primarily houses Section 8 tenants and is located in the worst areas of a city, even if the building's refurbishment cost several million? Or a revolving loan fund, intended as a catalyst for development, not as a money-making endeavor, might appear on the books as a money loser and by auditing standards it is, yet some funders treat the money as an asset:

> If the funding source sees that you have revolving loan fund, lets say of 3 million dollars and that's reflected in your financial [but] it isn't reflected that it's uses are restricted. They're going to think that you are in much better shape than you really are. That's true of perhaps your venture capital pool as well.

Such differences in understanding complicates communications with mainstream charitable funders, such as the United Way, that seem not to understand how organizations can be both nonprofits yet act like businesses. An official of an intermediary described the problem:

> Look at the United Way, which is now getting into housing development. It is also having culture problems [as they expect that] social service [agencies] run deficits, they don't have any money. Development organizations if they are good ones, you want to have a net worth of half a million, million dollars. That kind of freaks out traditional philanthropies.

To complicate matters, many CBDOs are not the best of businesses, either because of lack of technical acumen or because of an intentional decision to take on risky projects. Sometimes failure occurs and community-based development organizations simply disappear or new executive directors are hired to replace failed predecessors. The problems created by the lack of business skill were shown in a small city, in which a neighborhood-based development organization wanted to expand its housing program and fund it from business profits. To do so, it began a program to repair industrial pallets, buoyed by a guarantee from Honda Corporation to purchase the product. At first, the pallet plant seemed to be doing well and the hope was it would provide income to support the housing. The executive director explained that the plant employed about thirty-five people with a payroll of about $300,000 and that how the CBDO wanted to "develop that rascal into a full fledge, well-bred, nicely cared for cash cow."

I returned a year later and asked about the fate of their "cash cow" and was shocked to hear the following:

> Our pallet operation . . . went into the red as of June 30 . . . ended the year about $13,000 in the red I'm talking net worth. . . . We found as a

matter of fact we probably lost tremendous amounts of money. . . .In any event that has had a tremendous impact on our cash flow. I transferred $15,000 from a [housing] project to the pallet side of the equation in January. . . . We reduced staff from approximately 45 to 30 employees.

I asked, what had happened, and learned about problems of nonprofit administration. This community-based development organization stretched its management too thin, both trying to keep producing affordable homes, while earning money through a difficult to manage competitive business. There was inadequate supervision, lack of cost controls, as well as nepotistic hiring.

In general, both income figures and net worth of CBDOs fluctuate dramatically and a CBDO can vanish entirely with but a single failure. Several years before my study, an outside evaluation time described one CBDO as having "no experience, no capital, no staff, and no plans," "poorly structured joint ventureship," "record keeping was incomplete," and "serious tax problems." In response, a new executive director was hired who recruited a whole new team of managers. She restructured the organization, establishing cost centers and creating accounting systems that enabled this organization to build up both a reputation for innovation and to appear financially quite stable. But, three years later, this fiscally healthy organization went bankrupt, leading people to question,

> Where did an organization with a million dollar budget and national reputation as a model affordable housing developer lose its way?
>
> Everyone has different answers to these questions: poor property management, little or no cash flow, the inherent instability of the affordable housing tax credit system, a weak executive board, internal management problems. But most agree it was likely a combination of all those factors. (Caudros 1996, p. 10)

Elsewhere in Chicago, two successful CBDOs—Bethel New Life and Voice of the People—were required by funders to reorganize their managerial and financial control staff as a condition of receiving funding (Sullivan 1993, p. 51).

Developmental activists are profoundly aware of the problem of balancing out the organization's financial success with that of taking needed risks. Rather than reject the idea of profit, however, CBDOs argue that it is their very ability to make a profit that allows them to continue to help the poor. A development activist whose organization had just completed its first economic development project was simply irate when funders denied the CBDOs the profits they needed to survive: "Profit is a four-letter word. Baloney! Baloney! It's no different. We're still gonna do it cheaper than anybody else." Another emoted:

> You know, we just won't do projects without [profit]. . . . Because we work too hard, you know. You work in the poorest neighborhoods with

the lowest rents, the highest crime, the worst politics, and nobody is overpaid in this business, and nobody has fancy digs, so you know we are not going to add additional burden by being total do-gooders. . . . You have to pay your people.

Some CBDOs are skilled enough to support their operating expenses from profits made from project development, yet feel that the public sector wants to deny them this money. One described how as "you write in a developer's fee . . . the powers that be kind of look over your shoulder and they don't want you to make too much."

Still, activists wonder if what they receive is truly "profit." The housing director of big-city CBDO reflected:

> As I sit back there and think, gee, strange definition of profit, when you are going out and beg six different organizations to give you money to make the project work and you beg hard enough and long enough to get enough money so you can stick a little bit of it in your pocket. That is a strange idea of profit, if you ask me.

Further, the "profit" seems small when compared to the effort expended:

> I mean it took three years to pull the thing together. So our develop-ment fee was like $200,000 but we didn't make any money. We proba-bly lost money even with that cause it was the three-year process of doing it.

Another developmental activist described how the unfunded costs of doing the project far exceeded the fee obtained:

> I'm writing the final report for one of the foundations now and one of the things that I say in my report is that the cost to the organization were almost too much. . . . We took a $35,000 development fee and that was helpful. It paid for my salary. It paid for some overhead expenses. It helped us get a decent office. It did all of those things, but [we] went to the board and said, "For the six months that we are going to be in construction you can pretty much bet that 75 percent of my time will be devoted to the project." . . . It was probably about 75 per-cent, that's probably pretty accurate. Of course, what I didn't tell them is that it would be sixty hours a week.

Other organizations hope to make money from rental income, but such income often does not materialize since low-income housing projects rarely pro-duce steady revenue streams. Bratt and her team show that only three of the dozen housing developments they studied had been able to put aside the recom-mended reserves from the rent (Bratt et al. 1994, p. 110), many organizations had no reserves whatsoever and many of those had more than 5 percent of the tenants in arrears in rent (Bratt et al. 1994, p. 105).

Developmental activists point out that expenses are greater in managing affordable rental property then conventional housing, implying that the CBDOs must be better at business than for-profit firms. A housing manager of one of the few CBDOs that claimed to make money from managing its property described the added expenses involved, expenses that don't take into account any auxiliary social service programs: "I would guess that being very very conservative one-third of our work orders are work orders that wouldn't exist . . . in market-rate housing and it might be 50 percent."

Community-based development organizations make money managing affordable housing only when they adopt tight business practices. For instance, an activist in the national trade association and director of a profitable CBDO described:

> We . . . started to earn money when we started managing it: the seventeen refrigerators no longer walk away because the person who has to drive the truck works for me. If I know that I put the seventeen refrigerators on the truck and hired him to drive it, he either has to get those refrigerators there or at least answer to me where they are. . . . It does come on with some headaches because when they come in to pay the rent, . . . and they want to see the owner, not the manager. The owner happens to be me, so I've got to take the time to hear about the welfare check but I've also sent a message that (1) I'm concerned; (2) I'm still not so big that I cannot listen; (3) I clearly understand that they pay my check.

This organization was able to retain $800,000 in management and maintenance fees.

However, making a profit from community investments seemed more the exception than the rule and dreams of profit attenuate as the realities of inner-city redevelopment become apparent. In the initial interview, the executive director of a fiscally solvent CBDO described how his organization obtained a half a million dollar federal grant plus some state and city money for restoring an abandoned plant. He planned to later sell the CBDO's share in the building, legally claim back the half a million grant, and use the money for further community reinvestment. A few years later, the CBDO's annual report described troubles with the project that "at three different times . . . had . . . drop[ped] abruptly to a mere 40 percent occupancy," making it exceeding difficult to take out the invested capital.

Fortunately, for the CBDO, during one of the periods of higher occupancy, the private partner packaged the property as part of a real estate investment trust that was sold. The CBDO was only able to take out $265,000 in equity from its initial grant funded half a million dollar investment. The community benefited from the reopening of the original building and the CBDO had a new investment pool of a quarter of a million dollars for further development work, but the bottom line was that almost $300,000 had vanished from operating losses, though at a cost to the public sector, not the neighborhood or the CBDO.

But the problems circle, as being seen as a responsible business can distract from accomplishing broader ideological goals. For instance, community-based development organizations work with limited-equity cooperatives to help tenant-owners gain the skills and responsibility from running the building. But technically the CBDO remains the owner of record of the cooperative and the development organization's financial reputation depends on how well it handles the debt. The CBDO can be cross-pressured as the executive director of an organization that helped fund and manage cooperatives explained:

> We find that . . . in more complicated financial management and asset management issues that we play . . . a more active role . . . in which the coops would want us to, but they need us to. When you deal, for example, [with] Section 8, HUD will not deal with the coops. HUD is going to deal with the general partners. . . . We . . . have to approve their annual budgets. . . . And that relationship is a source of some tension, at times, because, we have to make sure in part that the coop continues to fulfill its obligations to the various financing authority. . . . And you know that's there's no way out of that trap.

## INHERENT TENSIONS

When seen as part of a governmental "delivery system," a subordinate organization within the larger contracting regime, the manifest tasks of the community-based development organizations are to build homes, restore businesses, and recreate commercial opportunities within communities of deprivation. But, as their histories show, CBDOs are more than delivery agencies. They are community groups that span the niche between government, for-profits, and poor neighborhoods.

Community-based development organizations are nonprofit fish and for-profit fowl undertaking work that requires tradeoffs and balance. Too much attention to finances and a social mission is lost, but too much concern with providing a social service and a project can lose its economic viability. Community-based development organizations are of and for the communities—many emerged out of neighborhood groups, social service agencies, and churches—but end up accomplishing agendas that do not always mesh with those chosen by community groups.

Developmental activists, both as committed community workers and as leaders of the CBDOs, recognize the precarious balancing acts their organizations face. As thoughtful individuals and reflective practitioners—the organic intellectuals of the movement—developmental activists are themselves equivocated by the value chooses entailed. Organizations might begin with an ideological fervor, pushing for empowerment and community participation. As external funds dry up and the only money available is that for efficiently building affordable housing, the mission does change, or else the organizations simply die, as many have. But as some semblance of economic stability returns, the recognition occurs that building homes is not enough, that services are required, as is a more holistic approach to renewal, and once again developmental activists attempt to build, to serve, and to empower.

The problems of reconciling these tensions are compounded because of the economic vulnerabilities of the CBDOs. To obtain the funds for building homes, or providing services, community-based development organizations must respond to an ever-changing set of goals, whims, and priorities of funders, government, and foundations, whose very involvement can tilt the balance on what tasks the CBDOs undertake. I discuss these problems in the next two chapters.

# CHAPTER 4

# Responding to the Public Sector

It's . . . a phenomenon called mission whip. The State puts money out
there for housing and everyone builds housing.
                              —from a conference seminar on funding

I've been executive director since 1980. . . . There's been four mayors,
six commissioners of economic development, three commissioners in
the Department of Planning. . . . If there's any stability to this world,
it's the neighborhood groups rather than in city departments.

What CBDOs can achieve depends on government policies and actions.
Without support from Office of Community Services (OCS), Home Ownership Made Easy (HOME), Community Development Block Grant (CDBG),
Low Income Housing Tax Credit (LIHTC), Community Reinvestment Act
(CRA), and a whole alphabet soup of other government programs, there would
be no way for community-based development organizations to obtain the capital,
operating subsidies, or political endorsement needed to accomplish their missions. But such support comes with a cost, as developmental activists must adjust
what they do to respond to political environments that differ from place to place
and that seem in constant flux. This chapter begins by noting how changes in the
political environment affect community work, examines the impact on the community development movement of threats to core federal programs, and concludes
by detailing how changes in the support environments in Chicago, Cleveland,
and Minneapolis affected CBDOs.

## A WIDE ARRAY OF RESOURCES

Federal, state, and local governments provide CBDOs with a wide array of
resources for their work. Table 4.1 sketches out a variety of programs ranging
from those such as the Community Development Block Grant that provides cash
aid, to enforcement efforts such as the Community Reinvestment Act that pressure banks to reinvest in poor neighborhoods.

Only a few federal programs, such as the economic development efforts sponsored by the Office of Community Services, and a handful of small HUD programs,

**Table 4.1.** Government as Facilitator of Community-Based Development Projects

| Category of Support | Level of Government | Program | Description |
|---|---|---|---|
| Direct Financial aid for Projects | Federal | Projects of Office of Community Services | Competitive grant program that provides equity capital to CBDOs for economic development projects |
| | | McKinney Act | Money for housing the homeless |
| | | Small Business Administration (run through states) | Community-based development organizations package loans for local businesses |
| | State | Housing Trust Funds | Direct project subsidies for low and very low income housing projects |
| | Localities | CDBG (block grant from federal level) | Subsidies that depending on locale can reduce housing costs, help in purchasing properties or pay operating expenses of CBDOs |
| | | HOME Money (block grant from federal level) | Buy down subsidies on housing projects; HOME sets aside a fixed percent of the money that must be expended by not-for-profits |
| | | Land contributions | Providing either vacant land or reclaimed properties to community-based development organizations for redevelopment |
| | | Tax reactivation programs | Enables CBDOs to obtain property on which slumlords have not paid local taxes |
| Facilitators of Private Sector Aid | Federal (though reallocated on a state and local level) | Low income housing tax credit | Enables private investors to gain substantial tax credits for equity investments made in affordable housing |
| | | Historic Preservation Tax Credits | Tax credits for historic restorations of buildings either for housing or commercial use |

Table 4.1 (continued)

| Category of Support | Level of Government | Program | Description |
|---|---|---|---|
| | | Community Reinvestment Act | Provides legal pressures on financial institutions to reinvest funds within communities of the poor |
| | | FIRREA Financial Institutions, Reform, Recovery, and Enforcement Act | The banking "bail-out" bill that reinforced Communuty Reinvestment Act (CRA) requirements. Also created a public authority that sold reclaimed properties to community-based development organizations |
| | | Community Development Finance Institutions | CDFIs are alternative financial institutions that invest in neighborhoods of need |
| | State | Linked bank deposits | Public money deposited in banks with the provision that banks then loan fixed amounts at subsidized interest rates for affordable housing projects |
| Operating expenses for CBDOs | Localities | CDBG | At local option, Community Development Block Grant money can be used for CBDO operating costs |
| | | Delegate Agencies | A city assigns CBDOs responsibilities to provide governmental services, allowing CBDO to obtain needed fees |
| Aid to Individual Client of Project | Federal | Section 8 | Federal payment of rent gaps between what poor can afford and fair market value of property paid to property owner |
| | State /locality | Welfare waivers (usually requires federal permission) | Enables clients to maintain social subsidies while involved in property ownership or job development programs run by the CBDOs |

provide direct grants to nonprofit developers. Instead, crucial financial assistance comes about as part of federal block grants or categorical programs administered by localities. CBDOs are eligible pass-through recipients of Community Development Block Grant (CDBG) money, or the McKinney programs for the homeless, as well as the HOME funds to develop housing. Most of this money is allocated at the discretion of the locality, often on a competitive basis.

CBDOs also receive indirect support because of provisions in the tax code. The Low Income Housing Tax Credit (LIHTC) encourages for-profit investors to partner in affordable housing projects to gain substantial tax benefits. The LIHTC with "the indirect subsidy of tax expenditure . . . represents the largest federal outlay for low-income housing" (Center for Public Finance Public Finance 1994, p. 41), and, for instance, from 1987 and 1991, created "between one and three billion dollars of annual tax subsidies [that] contributed to the production of about 100,000 units per year."

Of equal import, government pressure encourages financial institutions to invest in poor communities. The Community Reinvestment Act—CRA—and the associated Home Mortgage Disclosure Act—HMDA, pressure banks to reinvest capital within their neighborhoods. However, sustaining CRA has required continual lobbying, as well as advocacy efforts. CRA came into being only after a direct action campaign spearheaded by Gale Cincotta's National Peoples' Action coalition. But even when on the books, CRA offered few incentives for banks to comply. Only after the bank bail-out bill in the mid-eighties, FIRREA—Financial Institutions, Reform, Recovery, and Enforcement Act—allowed federal regulatory agencies to refuse permission to merge if banks were not in CRA compliance did the bill have any clout. By threatening to delay a merger by making a CRA appeal, housing advocates and CBDO activists could coerce banks to reinvest in poor communities. In addition, provisions of FIRREA have also encouraged government-sponsored banking enterprises—GSEs—such as FHLB, Freddie Mac, Fannie Mae, to pressure the banks they supervise to support affordable housing, while the GSEs themselves maintain a secondary market for mortgages made on low and moderate income housing. For instance, by the end of 1995, the FHLB's affordable housing program made available over $400 million in funds with a per unit subsidy of $3,772 (NHLIC 9–7).

In contrast to money available for housing, funds for economic development work are quite scarce, though, if a locality allows, CDBG money can be used for these purposes while CBDOs do package federal SBA loans. The small number of grants from the Housing and Human Services Discretionary Fund at the Office of Community Services has funded numerous, innovative economic development projects. OCS can provide CDCs up to $500,000 in equity capital that then is leveraged in community economic renewal projects. Data compiled by NCCED finds that through this program

$26 million in investments created 3,914 jobs and helped to maintain another 446 jobs at an average cost of $6,000 per job. The . . . grant program leveraged $51 million in private and other public funds that otherwise would not have been invested in distressed communities. In total, the program is responsible for the creation of nearly 30,000 jobs. (Development Times Jan 1995, pp. 1, 5)

Community-based development organizations are also eligible recipients of social service grants. CBDOs provide employment training, often in conjunction with economic development projects, while those housed in apartments built by CBDOs are often eligible for Section 8 certificates. Federal support for Community Development Finance Institutions whose charters mandate reinvestments in poor communities, indirectly helps the community development movement.

Unfortunately, during the last several decades, the amount of federal money available, especially for housing, has been in decline, and only in small part compensated for by increases in state and local programs (Goetz 1993, p. 199). Still, local money is available. One study reports that over a third of the CBDOs receive money from local government to pay for operating expenses (NCCED 1991), while another survey found that of 133 cities examined, 59% helped the nonprofits with general administrative funding, 82% with project financing, 52% with predevelopment support, and 56% with technical assistance (Goetz 1992, p. 425).

Contributions from states and localities are also obtained from Housing Trust Funds that provide gap funding or help lower interest rates on mortgages to make projects affordable for the extremely poor. To establish Housing Trust Funds (HTF), activists lobby and on occasion conducted direct-action campaigns, often guided by the Center for Community Change. Still, the total available from trust funds is quite small. In Illinois, for instance,

the trust fund is around, depending on the economy . . . $15 million a year. . . . But the state's budget is $26 billion a year and this trust fund is the *only* state money that goes into low-income housing.

HTF money is intended to be leveraged with other forms of funding, and as such, as a state administrator described, HTF money is

quite flexible. . . . I think that it shows the influence of community organizations in setting it up. . . . It's almost *never* the sole source [of funding]. . . . Usually you seek conventional financing, some form of city, or gap financing for rental housing, syndication, or some other source.

In several cities, CBDOs have become the delegated representatives of local government responsible for programs to retain jobs, repair store facades, and facilitate neighborhood fix-up. Under Mayor Washington, Chicago's economic development office funded neighborhood organizations to help keep industries in their communities (Clavel and Wiewel 1991). In addition, supportive government administrators can play catalytic roles in community projects by using city or CDBG funds to take the least-secure position on a mortgage for a CBDO-sponsored housing or commercial development project.

Government support extends beyond financial aid. For example, local officials have provided administrative waivers of building and inspection fees. Several states allow nonprofits to take possession of tax-delinquent properties that are then refurbished as affordable housing. Cities help fund training programs for CBDO personnel. In a few locales, officials join with CBDOs in campaigns to drive out slumlords, for example, by increasing health and safety inspections of visibly deteriorating properties.

Some public administrators offer strategic and tactical support to CBDOs. In one city, a progressive administrator worked with community groups to pressure the banks to set aside funding for neighborhood development. While negotiating with the banks to help poor neighborhoods, this administrator informed community activists which of the banks were recalcitrant and suggested where direct action efforts might pay off.

Some local governments have formed active public-private partnerships to provide affordable housing. During the study time, Chicago, Cleveland, and the state of Wisconsin all had public-private-nonprofit partnership organizations to support affordable housing (Suchman 1990), while in Michigan local organizations received state support through the Michigan Neighborhood Builder's Alliance. Though few of these programs are large, the money made available is very valuable as it provides the deep subsidies needed to make the projects affordable to low- and very low-income people. Observers of partnership organizations, however, question whether or not they end up co-opting the community development movement into following the agendas of government (Jezierski 1990).

TENSIONS IN THE PUBLIC-NONPROFIT RELATIONSHIP

Though CBDOs receive extensive support from the public sector, the relationship between government and community developers can be tense. Public officials worry about the ephemeral nature of many community groups, and fret about past scandals in neighborhood expenditure of public funds. City officials are aware of stalled production among CBDOs. On a daily basis, public administrators who support the community movement still witness the internecine contention between CBDOs, and shudder as racial and social-class schisms become evident.

Even officials who work in support of the community development movement express concern about the competence of the CBDOs. One mid-ranking city official who had gone on the line to defend CBDOs both with her boss and the city council, complained that "all these nonprofits . . . don't want to follow any rules anyway" while a senior official in another city confided that though the city had increased support for CBDOs "some of the CDCs were very weak."

In turn, developmental activists played back encounters in which local government definitely was not on their side. The director of one the nation's exemplary CBDOs said that

> when we were just getting started . . . we received some block grant money as the first CDC to do so because the expectation was that we would hang ourselves. . . . [The city's] idea was let's kill this idea off; let's let them have some money and you know see what happens. . . . But . . . we did a good job. And, you know, we began to develop a track record of being able to rehab and sell, I would say, a better product, faster, more economical than what the city was doing. And I think they began to change their process.

Developmental activists express frustration with working with public officials who act authoritatively, yet often are ill-informed about community needs. An activist lamented that though his city had greatly increased the funding for community-based development.

> Now the city will come in and tell you what they want done and tell you go do it. Some of us will tell them to go take a jump, some of the times we have to do it, as it is the only way to get enough money in to keep you alive long enough to do something you really want to do. But the direction has been getting slowly turned around again from neighborhood produced goals to city's wanted results coming first. . . . Nothing is happening except for what the city wants done.

CBDO directors complained about the extensive paper work and long delays involved in obtaining public funds, especially pass-through federal grants. A federal audit occurred in one city with the city officials then demanding old records from the funded CBDOs requiring, as a director of a two person organization lamented: "Spend[ing] time going through boxes and files and coming up with information . . . the attitude comes across: we are not partners in this endeavor."

Other developmental activists question why local officials look over their shoulders to assure every rule was punctiliously followed, while at the same time casually providing large sums to commercial developers working downtown. The head of a successful, large-scale housing producer described that "a for-profit person does not have to go through the months of work that we put into to prove to them that we were a professional, viable organization."

Activists are angered when promises government make to help community projects are put on hold and then ignored. One CBDO partnered with the city to renew a large commercial strip. They mayor had approved the CBDO's street-scape improvement programs, but then as the head of the CBDO described, "we met every two weeks for a year and a half with the Department of Planning staff, arguing, cajoling, persuading, the city to put in trees, lights and benches on our shopping street." The city misunderstood the goals of the CBDO to symbolize and publicize neighborhood renewal. According to the developmental activist, the city officials argued:

"We'll put in them nice little pedestrians plazas around the corners and you'll have a nice little plaza there."
We said, "No: this is a signal to the neighborhood that things are getting better. That means it has to be seen by the fifty thousand cars that go through the intersection. . . . Not the fifty cars that go down the side street."

The developmental activist continued to lament the city's lack of follow-through. In another interview, he explained that more than inefficiency was involved, as the CBDO suffered from the lack of aldermanic support. As a community group, the CBDO was involved in more than the streetscape program, in fact, it had been actively against the zoning approval of a X-rated store, for which the alderman would have received a bribe. The director of the development group explained that

If we're not around [the crooked alderman] makes a whole lot more money. We get in the middle of zoning issues, we get in the middle of anything that goes before the city council and we're representing a community on that and we're opening it up to lights to the lights and to public air.

Developmental activists are infuriated when technical incompetence on the part of a city costs the neighborhood and the CBDO both time and money. The same developmental activist with the misadventure with the trees described the problems the CBDO faced in renovating a mall when the

city . . . in its preparation for the court case [to condemn the land] improperly filed it so everything had to be done over, that took an extra six months. The three-month process of doing the designation report, took five months. There was a change in mayoral administrations.

The CBDO, though, was the one that paid the price for the delays:

[The funders] are saying you guys must be incompetent. So we had to bring the [funders] there to the Commissioner of Economic Development of the city who explained to them. . . . We reached the point with the city . . . where corporation council has a stack on their desks of a one hundred different suits and projects and it was always getting put to the bottom. Somehow [downtown] would take priority over [neighborhood shopping area]. . . . Well, we eventually went to the newspapers, had public meetings, met with the commissioner, we met with the mayor.

Delays can cause severe financial problems for CBDOs. In one case, a housing organization had to advance its own capital because promised city money was delayed. The problem was created by the city's law department that

got caught up in an issue of lead-based paint and they couldn't figure out a way to get out of it. . . . Do you scrape and paint, scrape and repaint or completely redo dry wall, and they couldn't understand— and they couldn't figure out the statute and they couldn't figure out what to do.

This technical concern delayed the closing, almost causing a major developer of affordable housing to fold.

Even more extreme, several developmental activists felt that the city government wanted organizations to fail, perhaps because of an underlying racial agenda. In chapter 1, I described a small mall that an African-American CBDO had completed. The city's reluctant and wavering support for the project evoked concerns on the part of the developmental activist.

I am very suspicious about the intent of the city . . . because [the project] had been talked [about] in excess of ten years. And I think that the discussions continued on as a placebo to community interests. . . . So every time the question was raised about we need to generate some economic activity in this area, we need to create a better economic environment here then the discussion would fall on the shopping plaza and all of what we need to do in order to make that thing happen. But no real commitment in terms of dollars was ever made.

I asked him how he got out of this situation. He explained that his organization was

able to go to a bank and get a commitment for a million and a half dollars, that was really pushed it to a point whereas the [city officials] could not say no. . . . The city had agreed to let us develop it and also commit $500,000 cash and $114,000 in land costs if we could go out and find a million and half dollars to finance the rest of the project . . . Because they figured most of the banks would turn us down. But what they did not figure . . . is that . . . I went to the National Coop Bank in Washington.

But the tensions continued and were interpreted in racial terms:

> The city . . . would demand things of me that had nothing to do with the proficiency of the project. They even went so far as to suggest that I put some Caucasians on my board of directors.
>
> [They said,] "You need to expand your board."
>
> I said, "What do you mean expand your board?"
>
> "You know, so you have got a more diverse representation on your board."
>
> Now I got schoolteachers, I got business owners, I got directors of alternative education programs. I got an accountant. You know, all of them African-American. But in his eye, he didn't see shit. All he saw was a bunch of black folk down there and "you need to expand your board."
>
> So I said, "What do you mean expand my board?"
>
> [The city official responded,] "Well, you know it is perceived as being a very closed corporation and you know a lot of people won't trust that situation, the way it is, so if you expanded it, you know, a little more expertise, and what not."
>
> "So you're talking, put some white people on my board?"
>
> "Well that would help, you know, that would help."
>
> I gave him their $50,000 back.

Distrust continued even after the project succeeded and the CBDO ended up with equity in the mall as well as in other developments. Yet, while property-rich, the CBDO had barely enough cash on hand to pay current bills, in fact, it was ducking its creditors. But because of the distrust of government the CBDO refused to touch its equity to pay off its current account debts:

> We have $219,000 left owing on this building and it's appraised value is $655,000. That's a lot of equity. . . . The City [suggests,] "Why don't you go and refinance that, take the equity out of the building and all that?" I'm going to struggle along right now. . . . I've got people on my door, knocking on my door, calling me every five minutes for a payment. But I know that they may be leaner times down the road and I would much rather save that equity. . . .
>
> So my thing is, let's look at how we can maintain this asset, I would be willing to bet you the city . . . would support me taking two or three hundred thousand dollars net out of all these projects, refinance, sell them, and walk away.
>
> That's the ideal, this is their white mentality. . . . Because they figure $200,000 or $300,000 [is] not going to last very long, but then you're through. You never get back into the ball game again. You have no assets, you don't have anything, by the time you get through spend-

ing that money, you won't even have anything that you can invest back into anything. And so I've been very cautious with that strategy. Not to fall into that trap.

See, the way things stand now, this is the largest ethnic-owned controlled area in this whole city. There's no where else like this in the entire city . . . for people who have been excluded and oppressed, and have not had an opportunity to really share or glorify and full participation.

Symbolism, community pride, and ethnic fear all were confounded as part of the meaning of these financial assets.

## PROGRAMMATIC CUMBERSOMENESS

Though vicious struggles do occur, more often the frustrations are simply over the difficulties of dealing with a complicated array of ever-changing public sector programs. Even learning what public funds are available, can prove troublesome. A ranking official in a city known for its support of community-based development movement described that:

the city had at least three different [funding] windows. . . . And also the state had about twelve windows. . . . The problem for the CDCs though is that they were all administered by separate, either agencies, or subagencies. . . . So you have at least six city-state agencies, within those agencies some of them probably have four or five different programs. . . . There are all these different [programs]. The problem is that for CDC to get a project done, . . . with limited staff resources and trying to do all these other things at the same time.

Understanding the arcane rules that govern some programs can overwhelm both community developer and government official alike. Equally irksome is the frequency with which rules for one government program that supports community work are inconsistent with another vital sources of financial aid. A city official explained how the difficulties created when city program had requirements that did not mesh with those of IRS. To obtain a city grant, CBDOs require

cash equity. . . . It can't be cash raised through tax credit deals. So you can't really use this stuff with tax credit deals. . . . So it throws it out of those deals, so even though the tax credit deals might seem a logical match as far as the income of the tenant and the rent structure.

Or, under the initial regulations for HOME, CBDOs were not allowed to use any HOME funds to pay for operating support, guaranteeing that each HOME project would be a money loser for the CBDO, as overhead expenses had to be met somehow. Further, HOME money could not be used in a LIHTC deal (Cohen

1992, p. 15) until HUD changed the rules after lobbying efforts by nonprofits and housing advocates. A similar problem occurred with the Financial Institutions, Reform, Recovery, and Enforcement Act, which "mandated that moderately priced property be reserved for sale to low- and moderate-income households or [for] organizations that would return units to qualified households" (MacDonald, 1995, p. 559), and would only allow such sales under quite rigorous conditions that the poor could rarely achieve (MacDonald 1995, p. 565).

To receive federal money that passes through another level of government, CBDOs must master a cascading set of complexities. The rules about tax credits are spelled out in endless detail in federal regulations, but since tax credits are allocated first to states and then often passed through to localities, three levels of rules apply. Some rules involve complicated interpretations. For instance, federal standards allowed money to be spent in any neighborhood that is poor when compared to the entire metropolitan area, thereby often including virtually the entire central city as an eligible area. But poverty advocates feel that such money should only be spent in the poorest neighborhoods of the inner city and fear that central cities will spend the money to house the elderly in moderate-income neighborhoods. Still, activists felt they couldn't protest with HUD since to complain involved a

> two-edged sword. . . . You go to HUD and you raise hell about the [city] plan . . . and HUD disapproves the plan. . . . Then there's no HOME funds whatsoever. You don't go to HUD and don't complain about the program, the city gets its money, then you get a little piece of the pie. You really have [to] weigh, is getting some of the pie better than getting none of the pie or with the possibility of getting all of the pie down the road.

Other complexities occur. For instance, the ordinances cities establish to combat slumlords can end up handicapping the work of the CBDO, as a construction manager explained. To battle slumlords,

> there's some legislation in the books about condemned houses. Once a house becomes condemned, you no longer can meet the rehab codes, you have to meet all new construction codes . . . as if you're building a house from the ground up. . . . [But] there's significant cost to having those codes enforced as new construction codes. That if you want us to do it, either put the money up or modify the code.

Or, while CBDOs do not like to evict tenants, doing so sometimes is a necessity, but a problematic one when tenants have Section 8 certificates (Bratt et al., p. 6). As the homelessness crisis evolved,

> legal aid changed their strategy, . . . and that is "we want to keep folks in the units at all cost, because otherwise they could be homeless." So

what legal aid does with us is they ask for jury trials, which is their right to do it, but they're going to try to expense it to death. And a jury trial would take about a year, depositions, discovery, motions for postponement, . . . and then the longer people stay in, the more potential for damage. Now you can trash a unit in a day.

Other federal rules create a bind for progressive CBDOs. Under the federal Davis-Bacon Act, builders who receive governmental funds are required to pay construction workers the prevailing wage, usually interpreted as the top-end union rates. But for CBDOs working in central cities "if it has prevailing wage on it, it's not worth applying for in many cases anymore." Yet ignoring prevailing wages brings developmental activists into conflict with the unionized building trades, who otherwise are good allies. A coalition activist described the problems that occurred when her organization lobbied at the state level against prevailing wage legislation:

We have spent a fair amount of time protecting ourselves from being covered by [prevailing] wage on the housing sites . . . and it cost us dearly for . . . our Democratic supporters who thought that we were like rabble. The Republicans . . . weren't interested in giving us any money, but they just thought it was wonderful we were taking the building trades on. It was really an awkward situation. We used up lots of political capital . . . but we were not going to have them put a prevailing wage on these affordable housing projects.

## UNSTABLE POLITICAL AND PROGRAM ENVIRONMENTS

Nonprofits accommodate to the funding and support environment; almost all the executive directors have a reasonable understanding of the minute technicalities of the Low Income Housing Tax Credit. But learning the ins and out of one program is not enough, as what has been learned quickly becomes irrelevant. An unstable political environment, whether at the federal level, or as I shall later describe locally in Chicago, Cleveland, and Minneapolis, requires financially dependent organizations to be constantly accommodating to the directions chosen by government officials. In the dance with public funders, CBDOs discover that the cadence changes midstream.

### The Changing Environment of Federal Support

Federal support for redevelopment and housing programs has been always quite volatile, while programmatic support for the community development movement is inconsistent.[1] Whole programs on which community-based development organizations were dependent simply have vanished, while changes in bureaucratic rules dramatically alter what projects could be done and how.

By 1974 the initial support for Title VII programs ended, as the Nixon Republicans completed the dismantling of the Office of Economic Opportunity and moved responsibility for CDCs to the Community Services Administration. Though direct support was reduced, CDCs were now allowed to seek funding from federal social service programs, such as CETA, encouraging the more skillful groups to package together social service with housing programs, though in doing so altering their missions.

During the Ford administration and the early Carter years, changes in regulations enabled CBDOs to better pressure the private sector for support. With the passage of HMDA, the Home Mortgage Disclosure Act of 1975, which mandated that banks make public where they lent mortgage money and CRA, the Community Reinvestment Act of 1977, which required banks to reinvest within their own communities, CBDOs gained a lever to use to pressure the private sector. Other programs initiated during the Carter administration also helped an expanding community development movement. Carter established the Office of Neighborhoods in HUD run by Father Gino Baroni, a community activist, which catalyzed neighborhood organizing and community development by providing strategic grants and supporting training programs. In addition, Carter increased funding for housing.

During the Reagan administration federal support for CBDOs quickly and dramatically reversed. Reagan reduced federal funding for housing programs, while at the same time eliminating the targeted neighborhood development efforts set up under Carter. The impact on the community development movement was traumatic, as a developmental activist who had been working on some innovative housing program in a small city recalled:

> On September 29th, 1982 at 2:30 in the afternoon, I remember it, I got a phone call from the local HUD office saying you may no longer market your houses with FHA 235 mortgages. FHA 235 was dead. . . . In early October, 1982, I had the dubious pleasure of letting everybody off including myself.

The community-based development movement, though, was resilient. As this conversational partner continued:

> I stayed close to the organization while ostensibly I was looking for other work. I was collecting unemployment benefits, see, [nervous titter] and I was supposed to be available for other work. . . . Well, I was able to bring myself back on in March of '83.

However, the change in environment brought about by the Reagan cutbacks forced the entire community development movement to recognize the dangers of relying primarily on federal funding while concentrating on housing. As a national leader of the movement reflected:

> In hindsight Reagan was probably a good thing for [CBDO] . . . because we were 95% federally supported in 1982. . . . We were a Title VII from the Office of Economic Opportunity. So by 1983 that money was gone. And, what it meant for us . . . we had to pare back staff and we had to get pretty lean, first of all to survive and then . . . we had to begin to think about [ways] to diversify the funding base. . . . The lesson learned was . . . if you become too dependent upon any one source you are creating problems for yourself.

Other changes during the Reagan administration affected the present-day movement. Title VII was officially eliminated and replaced by the Secretary's Discretionary Fund housed in the Office of Community Services. Tax incentives for syndicated real estate investments were also eliminated, a blow to those community-based development organizations who had been funding housing projects through these elaborate tax dodges for the rich. In response, the community development movement persuaded Congress to set up the Low-Income Housing Tax Credit, a temporary provision in the tax code that provided major tax advantages to corporations that invest equity capital in housing projects for low-income tenants.

During the Bush administration funding again became available for housing. In addition, as part of the legislation that helped bail out the banking industry from its speculative lending, banks were required to become more responsive to CRA pressure; many actually set aside mortgage money for building affordable housing. Housing got a further boost when Congress passed the National Affordable Housing Act (Cranston-Gonzales Bill) with the HOME legislation, a housing block grant that provided localities with housing money and required that a minimum of 15 percent be allocated to nonprofits. While the 15 percent minimum set-aside was appreciated, a development activist noted that

> 60 percent of the deals that are done in the city are done by nonprofits. . . . So we initially proposed 60 percent of the funds should go to nonprofits right off the bat. . . . [The city] totally rejected that out of hand.

HOME legislation included funds to help localities and community groups pay for so-called "expiring use mortgages." What had happened was that in the seventies during a period of very high interest rates, the federal government offered mortgage support for for-profit developers who built apartments, so long as a certain percentage of the units were rented out at affordable rates. But as part of the agreement, after twenty years developers were allowed to pay off the mortgages and convert the properties to full market rates. These contracts were beginning to expire, and supporters of affordable housing feared that affordable housing, especially those projects adjacent to newly vibrant central business districts, would be lost to the poor.

Many CBDOs redirected their work to respond to this problem. I followed one case in a mixed-income residential neighborhood a few minutes from downtown, in which 640 units would have been converted to full market rates. The executive director of the CDC remarked that:

> these buildings were built under a federal program that was established twenty years ago that had a forty-year mortgage that allowed owners to [take title after twenty years]. . . . So three and half years ago, four years ago, we started worrying about this because its prepayment date was coming up and we knew that the owner, most likely was going to . . . convert it to market rate. . . . This was 640 units.
>
> The city, of course, is concerned about, are we [the city] going to have to put any money into the deal? . . . Does it fit with our priorities?

The developmental activist continued describing how she brought city people together with the tenants as well as a citywide housing advocacy organization:

> What I did, some people had called me the quarterback, is I assembled the team of people. . . . Each of those people around the table was really, really critical to the deal. They each brought stuff that no one else brought. . . . It was a real collaborative effort, we had to be incredibly creative. We looked at six different financing schemes.

But political action was required to make the mix come together.

> We were seeking the council's support in terms of directing its staff . . . to make [project] a priority; we got that. But we were also seeking approval for a financing plan, which we didn't get. And the reason we didn't get it [is] because the city council directed us to go back to HUD and say we needed twenty-year Section 8 contracts. Well, HUD [said] . . . "only five years and that is all you can get, forget it."

At this point, the CBDO

> used the residents . . . to write letters, saying that please give us twenty year Section 8s. Well we never got twenty-year Section 8. . . . And, what they gave us was five-year Section 8 with the guarantee that those five-year Section 8 would be renewed if the money was available or replaced by some other program. . . . So that give the city the comfort it needed to go forward with the project.

The project was completed with financing backed by the city and no displacement took place. The CBDO spun off a subsidiary to manage the property in conjunction with a tenants' board.

The Clinton administration began on a hopeful note for the community development movement. As governor, Clinton had been friendly to the community development movement, while during the transition his staff requested developmental activists, including several of my conversational partners, to present their views on poverty policies. As his Secretary of Housing, Clinton appointed Henry Cisneros, a person supportive of community-based housing, who in turned appointed several activists to ranking positions.

Under Clinton, virtually all categorical social service and development programs, such as Youth Build, had explicit provisions allowing, and at times mandating, that community-based development organizations be eligible recipients. HOME established set-asides for nonprofits and funded technical assistance programs for community-based developers. With the support of Clinton administration, the community development movement convinced Congress to make the Low-Income Housing Tax Credit a permanent part of the tax code. Clinton pushed for empowerment zone legislation that would provide a handful of competitively chosen areas $100,000,000 over ten years, guarantee recipients priority on money from other federal programs, and set up tax advantages for companies that relocated and employed individuals within them. The application process that localities had to follow required them to involve community groups and nonprofits. In addition, the legislation included tax credits to companies that economically helped twenty designated CDCs (Development Times, April 1994, p. 1).

However, with public sector programs, hopes quickly arise, only to be dashed. HUD was beset with a series of scandals, its overall budget declined dramatically, and the agency's very existence was threatened. The number of Section 8 certificates dropped precipitously, making it difficult to house the lowest of low-income people. After the 1994 congressional elections, attacks occurred against virtually all programs that benefited the poor, and, though the community movement fought back, the amount of money continued to drop. The overall budget for HUD dropped by more than $7 billion, while individual programs were in chaos; thirty-three major HUD programs (as of July 1995) had been terminated, while the Community Development Block Grant declined in real terms and was but a quarter of what it had been a decade ago.[2]

Further, as the homeless crisis came apparent and McKinney money was made available, CBDOs driven by mission whip, refocused work to shelter the homeless. But doing so taught many that they were not geared up to handle the poorest of the poor, unless they were willing to expand their social mission. Similarly, the availability of federal funds for crime prevention (when combined with the lack of other funds) convinced many CBDOs to get involved in crime-fighting programs. One organization that had a year before vigorously rejected any ideas that it reduce its efforts to restore jobs to the community, now secretly housed in its headquarters the police official working on an antidrug program, while NCCED, the trade association, was partnering with the Department of Justice to train developmental activists in anticrime work.

**Instability in Two Iconic Programs.** Changes in two federal efforts—the special grants program from the Office of Community Services, OCS; and the Low Income Housing Tax Credit, LIHTC—illustrate how instability in federal funding affects CBDOs. Though neither program involves large expenditures of federal money, each is crucial to the community development movement.

Grants from the Secretary's Discretionary Fund at the Office of Community Services enable CBDOs to undertake some of their most innovative economic development projects. This program provides the recipient development organization with up to $500,000 in equity capital that the CBDO then owns and if the project is sold can reinvest in other efforts. The entire history of the OCS program illustrates the volatility and bureaucratic fragility of federal programs.

The financial instability of the OCS program creates immense bureaucratic obstacles. For instance, during the early Reagan years, "the program . . . from the fiscal year 81 on was zero funded (although) every year Congress puts money in," a problem that still occurs. As a result, OCS grants are announced on the last day of the fiscal year, the only time that the bureaucrats are certain that money is in place, making planning quite difficult. Further, as a consultant described it,

> every project that had to be submitted could only be [for] a one-year grant period. [OCS] . . . didn't want to admit that it would be around for more than a year. So as a result you had projects that were being proposed like the development of 200,000 square foot shopping center . . . where you were going to acquire the property, get the tenants, get the financing, build the property and have the people employed in one year.

Major recipients eventually hired a lobbyist to try to keep OCS running, but the battle continues.

The Low Income Housing Tax Credit—LIHTC—is a federal tax expenditure that encourages for-profit capitalists to invest in affordable housing. Today it is the dominant source of equity funding for affordable housing. Still carrying out an LIHTC project can be quite complicated. As a nonprofit, a CBDO itself cannot benefit from tax credits, so it has to form a housing development partnership with for-profit entities that then "purchase" the "tax" credits by providing equity investments. Most for-profit investors are totally unconcerned with constructing affordable housing, participating only because of the tax advantages. As such, the partnership agreements are complicated ones making the CBDO as owner of record, though often having but a nominal equity investment. Further, by law, tax credit are paid in over a matter of years, forcing the CBDO to scrounge for bridge money to pay expenses until the credits are received.

LIHTC projects must comply with numerous federally mandated rules describing who can live in what building, how long the building must be used for low-income tenants, as well as the rental limits. The for-profit investor has to be assured that all rules are followed, lest the investing corporation end up paying a penalty and potentially lose the entire credit retroactively. Because of this complexity, much of the LIHTC money is passed through intermediaries such as LISC that have expertise in carrying out such projects.

During the entire research, the fate of the LIHTC was up in the air. As a "temporary" provision, LIHTC had to be renewed each and every year, though fortunately no opposition appeared. Still, the renewal often took place late in the fiscal year, putting on hold all development work depending on this funding. After lobbying by affordable housing advocates working in a coalition with those in the community development movement, LIHTC was made a "permanent" part of the tax code, apparently stabilizing the support environment for a while.

But "permanence" can be a doubtful thing. Just after LIHTC became permanent, the Philadelphia office of the IRS audited the program and pointed out the obvious: LIHTC credit was given for derelict buildings, precisely the sort that CBDOs refurbish. On prodding by housing activists, IRS rejected the negative tone of this ill-informed study. But damage had been done, as the uncorrected report was picked up by staff of conservative Congress people who then tried once again to terminate the tax credit.

### Separate Local Realities

Political support for community-based development differs from city to city and seems in perpetual flux. High points exist, for instance, in Burlington, Vermont, where the city government itself set up a land trust to support affordable housing, while CBDOs in Boston received transfer payments from the city's housing linkage program (Dreier and Ehlrich 1991). Support can be found in many other places, though, as Vidal points out: in numerous cities, CBDOs are virtually invisible to governmental agencies involved in the development business (Vidal 1992, p. 15).

Local environments change, at times, dramatically. In Pittsburgh, CDCs were set up to be community partners with the city and corporations within an encompassing governing corporatist regime (Ferman 1997), but more recently CDCs have acted more like service providers than innovators of community renewal (Metzger 1998, p. 27). In Los Angeles, over the course of a generation, public officials moved from active opposition to CBDOs to most recently being willing to provide them "ongoing administrative support and technical assistance" (Goetz

1993, p. 161), initiating a housing trust fund and appointing developmental activists to high-level city positions.

During the research, I examined changes in the overall political environment for CBDOs in Chicago and Cleveland. I also examined how in Minneapolis the advent of the Neighborhood Revitalization Program, a city effort to establish community-based, community-controlled planning, dramatically altered the relationships between CBDOs, community members, and the local government.

### *Cleveland's Community-Based Development Organizations as Part of the Corporate-Foundation Hegemony*

During the last generation, the corporate-foundation regime that has governed Cleveland has redirected the community development movement away from activism and protest (Yin 1994, p. 3). Initially, community-development groups formed after the unrest of the sixties, such as the Hough Area Development Corporation, were activist organizations, advocating for empowerment and supported in so doing by activist city officials (Krumholz and Forester 1990). However, by the late 1980s the combined housing and community development movement was "largely apolitical" (Keating 1989, p. 26).

The withdrawal of the CBDO from activism came about under pressure from the major foundations and the corporate sector, who felt that community activists were too aggressively pushing for neighborhood control. For a time after the sixties, the corporate community and the powerful foundations had funded programs of social remediation that were seen by activists as too little, too late. Being frustrated at the unwillingness of the corporate/foundation sector to listen to their complaints, activists physically invaded a meeting at the exclusive Hunt Club during which leaders of the major corporations and foundations were making plans for the future shape of the city and made their case through direct action. The ploy backfired. Using this outburst as an excuse, both foundations and the corporate sector stopped funding neighborhood-advocacy organizations and redirected money only to those organizations concentrating on physical redevelopment work.

Still, the corporate and foundation sector recognized that the economic and social deterioration of Cleveland was real and harmful to business; to try to reverse the decline, these wealthier interests formed a regionwide public-private redevelopment corporation, Cleveland Tomorrow, to promote redevelopment. Cleveland Tomorrow's efforts, however, focused on programs to renew the downtown area or to promote suburban growth. This combined downtown/suburban focus appeared to receive support from Cleveland's government. For instance, during a conversation with a senior city official, whose career had been mostly spent in neighborhood work, I argued that the downtown strategy was antagonistic to neighborhood redevelopment. He interrupted:

I don't buy that. . . . I buy the notion that . . . there is a . . . kind of an unspoken covenant, between the people who live in the city and the powers that be in the city. And that part of that covenant is that the downtown is a sector that is regional in terms of who it serves . . . that builds spirit, that builds traffic, that builds an employment base. That is part of that covenant . . . that a city should help a downtown deliver, in this unspoken agreement to the citizens is a healthy downtown economy . . . it's a [collection?] of commercial services, it's an entertainment district. It's the intangibles, the symbolism of "We count" as a community. I mean the stadia, major league, we are major league.

The corporate and foundation sector, though, recognized that regional renewal required a way of staving off the total deterioration in Cleveland's neighborhoods, yet wanted to bring this about without reactivating the annoying protest movement. As a compromise, to both fund renewal but curtail Alinsky-style organizations, money would be awarded only to CBDOs doing housing and working in various public-private-corporate partnerships. This undirected campaign accomplished little.

Next, the corporate and foundation leaders decided to support the neighborhood movement indirectly through local intermediaries set up and funded by themselves, with government playing a passive role. To do so, working through Cleveland Tomorrow, the partnership organization formed to promote regional growth, the corporate-foundation regime set up Neighborhood Progress Inc. (NPI), a public/private/CBDO/foundation/corporate partnership, to act as a local developmental intermediary to guide community renewal. With NPI in place, rather than providing money to individual CBDOs, the foundations, as well as national intermediaries such as LISC, could target funds at projects and development organizations chosen by NPI, that in turn would encourage CBDOs to "produce to scale," focus on housing and larger-scale economic development projects, but eschew both confrontational endeavor or programs of holistic renewal. Concurrently, the city working with NPI encouraged community-based development organizations to move away from programs targeted at the very poorest and to increase efforts to rebuild middle-class housing to lure back middle-income families to inner-city neighborhoods (Yin 1994, pp. 68–69).

These efforts changed the direction of the community development movement with their actions being determined by a foundation-sponsored intermediary, and several CBDOs becoming little more than passive production machines. For instance, I traced out the history of a CBDO that began as a community-based housing advocacy organization that undertook direct actions against slumlords as well as banks who were negligent in their community reinvestment obligations. As a result of the first cutback in foundation money, this CBDO merged with another less aggressive community group, joined a coalition of housing producers, and became one of the leaders in the city in producing affordable housing. It also withdrew from broader advocacy work, and while producing homes for the poor, also began efforts to supply middle-class housing.


### The Political Environment for Community-Based Development In Chicago

Measured by the variety of CBDOs, the number of activist coalitions, and the forceful vibrancy of its community activists, the environment for community-based development is richer in Chicago than in any other city examined. Chicago's community-based development organizations range from those that use physical development as a tool to bring about radical social reform, to other groups that are virtually little more than neighborhood business associations. All of the CBDOs, though, have been affected by Chicago's traditions of neighborhood activism, with many actively participating in protests, especially those to force banks to comply with the Community Reinvestment Act (Squires 1992, p. 18).

In addition, community-based development organizations in Chicago have formed activist coalitions. During the course of the study both CANDO and CWED, two of the economic development coalitions and the Chicago Rehab Network, a housing coalition, carried out advocacy and lobbying campaigns that gained significant concessions from the public sector for neighborhood redevelopment. The tolerance of those in power to such campaigns was made apparent when the developmental activist who spearheaded a campaign to protect manufacturing districts from gentrification was appointed to a ranking city position by a mainstream mayor. Chicago's political culture accepts organized protest as legitimate.

The present-day environment for community development in Chicago was shaped by the events during the progressive mayoralty of Harold Washington (1983–87). During this regime, developmental activists gained access to decision-makers, had an effective say into the allocation of Community Development Block Grant funds, helped open up the budget process, and were successful in retargeting capital expenditures at poor and minority communities ( Rich 1993, pp. 208, 215). Further, many economic development and planning officials in the Washington's regime were closely associated with the Community Workshop on Economic Development, a left-wing organization of developmental activists. Once in positions of political power, these individuals dramatically increased the funding for community organizations, made visible the city's hidden capital budget and used public sector pressure to encourage for-profit organizations to partner with CBDOs. In addition, CWED activists prepared a set of ideological documents, the Washington papers, that strongly supported renewal policies based on premises of economic justice and community control. These documents

> emphasized *job development* over real estate development. They emphasized *neighborhood development* instead of central business district devel-

opment. They emphasized *retention and expansion* over attraction of industry. They emphasized *small business* over large. The articulated a belief in *targeting resources* rather than widespread distribution of all resources. (Wiewel and Alpern 1993, p. 117)

Further, during the Washington administration, neighborhood organizations were appointed as the delegate agencies for the city, responsible for community-based economic, housing, and social service issues. Activists described that rather then being contract service providers for the city, they themselves initiated the idea and gave direction to the programs. Further as delegate agencies, CBDOs received money for operating expenses, yet, as Wiewel and Clavel describe, "since the vast majority of these agencies had multiple sources of funding, they were not wholly dependent on the city and retained significant autonomy" (Wiewel and Clavel 1991, p. 278).

Continuing funding for these programs provided the CBDOs with a political staying power that in many ways made the city, with its more transient set of administrators, somewhat dependent on the community groups for developmental expertise. A director of a CBDO explained:

> [T]here's been so many changes of administration [in Chicago]. . . . And it gets to where if anybody wants to know what the city's policy is on the northwest side, you don't call the mayor's office, you call me because I've lived through it.

Still, the continuing governmental instability after Washington's death, made life difficult for the community groups. The housing director of a CBDO described the fate of a large-scale neighborhood project started under the progressive regime. But with the mayor's death,

> the program never got announced to hit the street. It was being designed. . . . Under the Sawyer Administration the design was finished and RFPs hit the street. [CBDO] applied for the land under the Sawyer Administration pursuant to their RFP, when the Daley Administration came in they rescinded that RFP since nothing had gotten started yet and said, "Let's start all over again" adding some new dimensions to the program, doing some additional work on the program design, so [CBDO] applied again for this same piece of land under the Daley Administration and we got approved.

Still, the Washington administration enabled the CBDOs to strengthen their financial base, to learn how to mesh advocacy with development, and to acquire knowledge on how, by working in coalitions, to influence the public sector. A coalition director claimed that such bottom-up influence continue with the

> interesting thing about Chicago is that all but maybe two of the housing issues that have come up in the last ten years . . . have come from

the community up . . . tax reactivation, the city trust fund, the state trust fund, the Housing Abandonment Prevention Program. All those programs have been designed by community groups.

Of course, after programs are adopted, the mayor, though, always received full credit from the community groups.

Still Chicago is far from a CBDO paradise. Money is in short supply, some banks continue to resist CRA pressures, and downtown still receives the dominant share of money. But Chicago's CBDOs have gained confidence in both their political and developmental abilities. In recent times, under more conservative governing regimes, CBDOs have been able to fight back because of knowledge gained and networks set up during the Washington administration. In chapter 10, I will describe some of these efforts.

*The Impact of the Minneapolis' Neighborhood Revitalization*
*Program upon the Local Community Development Movement*

During 1991, Minneapolis established the Neighborhood Revitalization Program— NRP—a community-focused renewal effort intended to spend $400 million in the neighborhoods, encourage line agencies to coordinate their work in the neighborhoods, and empower community members through establishing a full-fledged, democratic neighborhood planning process. NRP drastically disturbed the funding for the CBDOs, roiled the relationship between development organizations and neighborhood associations, led to the demise of three CBDOs, and increased tensions between homeowners and renters.[3]

**The Initial Setting.** The Neighborhood Revitalization Program was the second stage of a continuing effort to move power back to the neighborhoods from downtown. A generation ago, Minneapolis, not unlike other cities, had been focusing much of its renewal work on downtown. Community members rebelled and a coalition of neighborhood activists and CDC participants united and got behind a winning political slate that supported neighborhood work.

Once in office, this new city council used both federal pass-through money from CDBG, as well as local funds, to support neighborhood and housing renewal efforts. To carry out the work, the council merged several separate governmental agencies into the MCDA (Minneapolis Community Development Agency), and worked with CBDOs to build multifamily homes. Many development organizations became part of the city delivery system, receiving fixed amounts for doing standard projects. Some researchers felt that with these funds available CBDOs were dominating neighborhood associations (Nickel 1995). Two observers noted:

[A] tight trilateral relationship exists between the city (represented by the Council and the MCDA), the neighborhood organizations, and

the CDCs. . . . [C]ity council's control of the agency has led to development determined by political considerations rather than more objec-
tive planning efforts. (Goetz and Sidney 1994b, p. 28)

Political responsibility for development remained split, with a strong city
council controlling the MCDA, with a mayor in charge of the planning department, leading to ongoing political warfare. To make matters more difficult, during this time, the funds available from federal sources for affordable housing were
in sharp decline, leading to MCDA's housing budget decreasing by 25 percent
just during the first year of my study alone.

To expand resources for neighborhood development, the council discovered
that it could use money from the downtown Tax Increment Financing (TIF)
District. In a TIF, taxes that are shared by separate governmental entities are
frozen at a given date, money is then invested within the TIF, often from borrowed resources, and then repaid by capturing any increases in tax revenues
within the district. Generally, TIF districts provide capital loans for businesses
while reducing the funds available for other governmental services. But Minneapolis officials convinced the state legislature to accept a scheme that allowed
the city to use TIF funds in neighborhoods, providing a source of funding for the
Neighborhood Revitalization Program.

**The Neighborhood Revitalization Program: Structure and Philosophy.** NRP
projects were to be chosen from comprehensive plans prepared by elected members of community organizations for each of the eighty-one separate neighborhoods in Minneapolis. Over twenty years, the plan would use the $400 million
from TIF to catalyze neighborhood renewal, while encouraging better coordina-
tion of both services and capital investments from the separate line agencies. The
NRP staff quickly recognized the impossibility of simultaneously incorporating all
eighty-one neighborhoods into NRP, so a lottery, biased to favor neighborhoods
most in need, was set up to determine the order in which neighborhoods would
receive funds.

To carry out the NRP plan, a policy board—consisting of elected city, county,
and special district officials, state legislative representatives, four neighborhood
representatives, and representatives from citywide nonprofits—was set up. To
package the Neighborhood Action Plans into a "multiyear, cohesive, coordinated
service package for each of the participating jurisdictions," an implementation
committee was established. Finally, a small staff under a director would administer
the program.

But problems began immediately. While the CDCs were nervous about NRP,
they were assuaged, in part, because of the persuasive arguments made by its
founding director. Unfortunately, this individual died in an airplane crash and was
replaced by Robert Miller, who moved from a city-county social services/anticrime
program, CARE, that he had directed. Miller had far less contact with the CDCs

than did his predecessor, while he strongly believe in a development philosophy that argued for the dominant role of the neighborhood associations over the CDCs. A spokesperson for a coalition of CBDOs explained the difficulties:

> I mean the reality is that nonprofit development corporations have been the providers . . . but in this whole NRP process we are not recognized. The neighborhood organization is the place where all the planning happens, which theoretically, I don't have any philosophical problem with that, but neighborhood organizations are not development oriented. And all that money is very scary for a neighborhood organization that does not know how to do development, doesn't know how to think about development.

My conversations with supporters of the NRP in public office indicated that these fears of the developmental activists were not misplaced. One advocate for NRP, for instance, pontificated against CDCs, admitting that the purpose of the program was to re-empower neighborhood associations rather than the CDCs. Further, developmental activists resented the need to go through the cumbersome NRP structure, lamented that NRP would end their direct relationship with MCDA, yet felt little choice but to go along. One reflected:

> But maybe through this NRP program, there is going to be additional money. In the end we are going develop a plan, we are going to have a process. We just want the money. That is the ultimate test. . . . I'll suffer through any number of these policy board meetings because there is a brass ring at the end. And, that is why we . . . suffer through this; we're going to have thirty-five different meetings of some sort over the next six months cause we want to get our plan done, so we can put it on the table, so we can get funding for these projects we want to do.

Other developmental activists felt that the NRP was being too picayune in analyzing the community plans. He pointed out NRP's inconsistency in talking about neighborhood control, yet at the same time supporting a strong centralized review structure:

> You've got the city commitment to neighborhood revitalization and everybody has talked about it, touted it, but they don't believe a word of it. . . . Look, they asked us how we can best organize our plan, our neighborhood, and get participation in developing the plan. We told them and if they really believed that neighborhoods should determine their future, they should say fine. . . . And, they don't believe it any more now despite all the rhetoric.

Another developmental activist wondered if the whole reason for the cumbersome procedures was simply to discredit the community development process.

Further, as dramatic as $20 million new dollars per year might seem, it was but a drop in the bucket, in comparison to need. The hope among NRP staff was that this drop would encourage both line and service agencies to increase their coordinated efforts in the neighborhoods. Developmental activists were cynical about such coordination, feeling that the governmental agencies would want to maintain control over their own budgets. Further, they wondered about an approval structure in which social service agencies on the NRP boards would end up with authoritative control over the city's development budget. I observed at meetings the puzzlement of representatives from the social service agencies as they learned how high the costs were of doing physical rehabilitation work within the inner city. The $75,000 to rehab an apartment would pay for a lot of a social worker's time.

Further, the transition to the NRP model slowed and, at times, stopped the flow of development funds, putting many CDCs in a financial bind. In response, NRP set about to approve a list of about $5 million in CDC projects that would be funded in the transition period. However, the very approval of this list required CDCs to gain support of NRP's Priorities Committee, further delaying when the CDCs would receive needed overhead money. Some felt that this delay was an attempt to cull out less favored community-based development organizations. One director whose CDC died the next year fretted:

> they are not approving projects anymore; they are blaming it on this new twenty year plan. It is kind of wait and watch. I think half of that is genuine and half the council is doing it because they know it is going kill of some of the nonprofits. We don't get enough money out of foundations to stay alive without the fees for the projects. . . . So, you know, if they strangle the projects, they strangle the nonprofits and only the ones with the large pockets will survive. . . . But I think about half the council that is exactly what they wanted to do, they wanted kill off about half the nonprofits.

But more was involved than immediate concerns with money or the bureaucratic awkwardness. NRP's core philosophy was for neighborhood empowerment to precede development, with the control of redevelopment planning in the hands of democratically elected neighborhood organizations. Developmental activist questioned these premises and were cynical about who from the neighborhoods would participate in planning efforts. They felt that activist

> groups tend to be made of people who have more of a vested interest in what is going on in the neighborhoods. We find in this city, that neighborhood groups in many cases are made up of homeowners.

Further, they argued that new money brought out the worse in people:

when you start waving around 20+ million dollars in front of neighborhoods around the city, you'd be surprised what would come out of the
woodwork and so we have not been surprised and despite all the protes-
tations people saying NRP not about money and not about what we're
really doing, . . . for the average Joe out there . . . it's about money.

His feelings were echoed by a government official from MCDA. This official
pointed out that

the landlords have come out in force for the NRP organizing. So the
questions is, well, "How much should we reach out to renters? They are
not going to participate anyway." . . . So, you know, that's there is little
fights erupting all over this city and as near as anybody can tell, a lot of
it is related to the NRP. As neighborhoods gain more power through a
process like NRP it creates a lot of power issues and a lot of people who
might have their own personal agenda start to manipulate groups so
that their agenda can carry the day.

Further, development activists felt that time spent in creating active neighborhood organizations where none existed distracted them from the work needed
to accomplish desperately needed physical repairs. To complicate matters, an academic study done by Rutgers and paid for by local foundations agreed with many
of the concerns of the developmental activists, pointing out the cumbersome
organization of the NRP and demonstrating that mandated participation in community planning was likely to favor homeowners over renters. Further, the study
showed CDCs were more likely to represent typical community members than
were the elected neighborhood groups mandated by the NRP (Fainstein 1993).

But motivating community people to control developers seemed to be at the
heart of what NRP was all about. A city official and a close observer of the NRP
process argued:

What NRP does, and I like, is it makes those developers . . . more
accountable again to democratic process. The way [the] system works
now is [a] developer driven model. [A] developer comes in with a project we kind of massage and then we take it out to a neighborhood
group and they say "yes or no."
    The developers decide what happens in the city. NRP switches the
equation, or at least has the potential to switch the equation. [The]
neighborhood defines what has to happen there to match resources to
that and then see if developers want to do it they'll just have to respond
to those neighborhood needs.

At the very least, as a ranking NRP official argued, NRP would bring together different elements within the neighborhoods:

The beauty of NRP is that . . . we bring in a hell of a lot of people into the process and the more people that come into that process the less likely it is that an organization that wants to maintain [itself] as an isolated and kind of controlling body the less likelihood they can do that. If they don't adjust their thinking they'll be gone, and that's one of the real ultimate beauties of the program because of the fact that it tends to bring in people who have never participated before and therefore have some different interests and different ideas.

But for the community-based development organizations, more was needed than rhetorically stated goals; CBDOs want to have the means to carry out those goals, and the ability to adjust when one idea does not pan out. The entire NRP process belied such realities of doing inner-city renewal.

**Turbulence for Community-Based Development Organizations.** NRP created great difficulties for several CDCs. One lost support of its neighborhood association, and failed to receive any transition money, and, as a result, in the gleeful words of an NRP official, was "for all intents and purposes . . . moribund. Deader than a door nail. . . . Nobody wants to work with them." Another CDC had apparently promised more than it could deliver and had disappointed its neighborhood. In this case, NRP officials who had worked with the CDC wanted to keep the organization alive, but apparently because NRP had already committed resources to the group. In general, NRP exacerbated tensions between CDCs and conservative elements within the neighborhoods who opposed affordable housing (Goetz and Sidney 1994b, pp. 59, 60).

The most dramatic conflict caused by the NRP occurred with the Whittier Alliance, a combination CDC and neighborhood association that up to that time had been the city's best-known community developer. The Whittier CDC had made its reputation through converting large numbers of derelict World War II houses into affordable family housing and had been active in promoting cooperatives, started several economic development projects, and had extended its neighborhood outreach efforts to include a community anticrime program. Yet, as a result of the NRP planning process, wealthier community members and landlords who opposed Whittier's socially progressive redevelopment agenda became active in the alliance and forced the executive director and two senior staff members to resign, ultimately ending the organization.

The Whittier CDC had been working with minorities who had fled violence in Milwaukee and Chicago to move to Minneapolis. It tried to house these newcomers in affordable rental properties and cooperatives, worked to encourage private sector landlords to treat new tenants fairly, and set up programs with the police to assure that these social changes did not increase crime. To support these poor newcomers, employees of the alliance led protests against landlords who refused to house the poor and had actually "picketed the suburban home of one landlord." (Goetz and Sidney 1994, p. 330). At a community meeting, an employee of the alliance actually kicked a dissenting landlord out of the room. To further embitter matters, the alliance was administering an anticrime program, but rather than focus on the entire neighborhood, as the homeowners wished, the program was seen as concentrating on the buildings owned or managed by the CBDO.

These tensions were present when the NRP came on line. Even though the staff of the alliance rejected the NRP idea, they understand the need to work with the program and so Whittier's director put together a lengthy proposal, asking for $26 million to guide an integrated redevelopment scheme for the neighborhood. The document proposed building affordable rental buildings and cooperatives and pushed for providing services to the needy in the community, services that would be coordinated by the CDC itself. One of the proposed projects involved repairing a neighborhood park to serve the youngsters. The park, though, was surrounded by private homes of the wealthier members of the community, who took strong exception.

As a technical document, the Comprehensive Plan was well done, and was the first of the neighborhood plans to achieve NRP approval, doing so before NRP's founding director died. After his death, other NRP officials objected to the amount of money requested, aggregately $26 million (including $7.8 million from NRP) and criticized the plan for not taking advantage of the resources that were already in the neighborhood.

Within the Whittier neighborhood, arguments continued on both the content of the plan and the process by which approval had been achieved. Landlords in the neighborhood objected to the parts of the plan that put forth a strong antiracist agenda. They also opposed the community center and an idea to rebuild a school in ways that would facilitate providing community social services to the newer arrivals to the city.

Debate ensued on how thoroughly and publicly the plan had been discussed before its submission to NRP. Opponents claimed that few public meetings were held, though the Action Plan itself documented meetings in the different quadrants of the neighborhood. Whittier officials claimed that

> the planning process was inclusive. . . . [W]e went out and James, our organizer, went and visited people in buildings. So we represent and included the input from the whole range of the neighborhood, but the people that got elected to our board represent business and homeownership interests predominately. . . . [W]e've got the plan that had a broad neighborhood constituencies and then we have the . . . alliance board that represent narrow constituencies. . . . [T]hey're projecting their interest as the neighborhood's.

Homeowners and landlords claimed the neighborhood meetings were fixed to enable those who were housed by the CDC to more readily participate. The meetings mandated by the NRP process, though, took on a totally different tone. The Rutgers Evaluation Team pointed out that homeowners and landlords dominated, even though the neighborhood was close to 90 percent rental. Officials from NRP sided with the homeowners. As one argued:

> what happened in Whittier was an example of what happens when an organization becomes so insulated in terms of its leadership and its staff that it no longer really responds to the community. It sees itself as an advocate for causes as opposed to a provider of services to a community based on that community's needs and priorities.

With continued pressure from NRP, further discussions on the plan took place at subsequent meetings of the alliance. This time, though, an organized faction of homeowners and landlords were present and the meetings became quite raucous. During one, the white executive director of the alliance marched out, accusing the homeowners of racism against the black clientele of the CBDO.

In response, homeowners and landlords organized for the next set of elections for the supervisory board of the alliance. According to the alliance's bylaws, the entire board was elected at one time. The homeowners, including allies of the slumlord who had been targeted for protest, took over the board, leading to the ouster of the executive director, the anticrime chief, and the housing director, and a rethinking of the community redevelopment plan. An observer from a city department described:

> What happened was a lot of white homeowners all said we no longer felt represented by the . . . alliance and they took over the board and they are pushing their own racist agenda. . . . What happened here was that neighborhood, through NRP, really got energized to say "We're not sure that that's the direction we want to be moving anymore." And . . . even though the staff was successful in getting their vision incorporated into the plan, it was obvious that their vision didn't reflect what many of the neighborhood people wanted because they turned out in force to basically say, "We don't want this."

Goetz and Sidney concur, pointing out that after the elections "the organization has come to espouse the ideology of property ownership even though the neighborhood is 89% renter" (Goetz and Sidney 1994a, p. 321).

With the departure of the executive director and housing director, the developmental efforts of the CBDO were dramatically reduced. A temporary director was hired, then replaced by an outsider, who within a short period of time lost his job. By the end of my study, "for a nonprofit organization that had been among the most productive in the Twin Cities, the Whittier Alliance has essentially stopped its development activities" (Goetz and Sidney 1994b, p. 12).

A year later, renters organized and took back the organization but were unable to keep it afloat.


## REFLECTIONS ON DEPENDENCE UPON GOVERNMENT

For developmental activists, the governmental environment is uncertain, changing, and differs from time to time and from locale to locale. National policies change, often radically. In cities, developmental officials and politicians can differ over what redevelopment is about, though relationships vary dramatically as shown in the contrasting mini-studies of Chicago, Cleveland, and Minneapolis. Overall, developmental activists recognize the financial dependence of their organizations upon government, yet fear that those in office do not understand what the community development movement is about.

These observations speak to the broader theoretical questions of interorganizational power, dominance, and agenda setting. They show that public money counts, can shape agendas (and destroy organizations), while mission whip does take place. But the portrait of the government environment hints that in the very complexity of fund raising there is scope for the weak to skillfully play the system. A social service agency with but a narrow task to perform has to comply with the whims of the one funding agency supporting its cause. In contrast, CBDOs take on multiple tasks and work with multiple funders at one and the same time. A potential exists that by selectively piecing together funds from alternative sources, CBDOs can have an impact on the redevelopment agenda.

Further, the very complexity and instability within the funding environment necessitates that the community development movement set up structures to cope with the uncertainty. To interpret the broader environment, developmental activists work together, exchange ideas, and most important, form coalitions and trade associations to speak for the movement as a whole. As later chapters will show, the very support structure required to understand the vagaries of government (and as the next chapter indicates, the vagaries of the intermediaries) provides a means for the CBDOs to influence the overall image of what development should be about.

CHAPTER 5

# Interacting with Intermediaries, Foundations, and Other Support Organizations

I don't like the idea that LISC speaks for me.
— a national leader in the CBDO movement

We've got to teach intermediaries that our circle of control . . . is not necessarily their circle of control.
— a head of a neighborhood association on completion of its first housing project

To carry out their projects, community-based development organizations re-quire investments from the private sector as well as funding from government. As the last chapter described, obtaining these funds entangles CBDOs within a complicated, evolving, and controlling political world. In addition to requiring funds for routine projects, community-based development organizations need access to risk capital, as well as the technical help to carry out complicated projects. Risk capital and technical assistance are obtained from a wide array of support organizations.

As support organizations, financial intermediaries help the CBDOs package money from government and the foundations and put together loans and tax credit deals from the private sector, while making available technical assistance. Foundations fund risky or innovative projects while running on a small scale numerous programs for community renewal. Training institutes teach CBDOs how to carry out projects, while information services keep developmental activists abreast of changes in laws and grant programs, while diffusing the experience of CBDOs to others in the movement.

Those who work for support organizations frequently share common ideologies with the developmental activists, attend the same meetings together, have overlapping career paths, and on occasion are even joined through marriages. Connections between CBDOs and support organizations are

sustained by long-standing relationships based on trust, loyalty, and, reciprocity among the individuals within the support institutions and

the nonprofit housing groups. Key individuals are former colleagues, . . .
or have switched positions from one part of the system to another. (Keyes
1996, p. 211)

Developmental activists are dependent on benevolent support organizations
to provide the funds that catalyze different projects, as well as advice on how to
bring about deals. But tensions arise as the agendas of support organizations can
end up parroting the wishes of the business or political notables that serve on
their boards, rather than reflecting the ideologies that emerge from the community development movement itself.

## THE VARIETY OF SUPPORT ORGANIZATIONS

Community-based development organizations are helped by support organizations that more or less group into four categories—foundations, government-
sponsored enterprises, information providers, and most important, financial
intermediaries. Foundations fund a wide variety of efforts for which they have
established standard programs—micro-enterprise development, for instance—
and are receptive to individual proposals from the CBDOs. The Urban Institute
reports that

> 512 independent, corporate, and community foundations granted $179
> million to support community-based development in 1991. . . . The . . .
> figures show that foundation support for community-based development
> expanded dramatically from 1987 to 1991, increasing from $74 million
> to $179 million. (Center for Public Finance 1994, p. 46)

Foundation support often appears at crucial moments when other institutions
are unwilling to join in on a risky project, while few innovations that emerge from
CBDOs get tested without initial foundation support. For instance, the Aspen
Foundation's program for micro-enterprise development among the poor, grew
out of its initial willingness to risk supporting feminist organizations that were
helping women set up their own businesses.

A second source of funding and technical assistance is obtained from mainstream government sponsored enterprises (GSEs)—such as Fannie Mae, Freddie
Mac, and Federal Home Loan Bank (FHLB), as well as their spinoff foundations—that coordinate and regulate the banking industry. GSEs encourage member banks to establish affordable housing programs and create secondary markets
to repurchase loans made for affordable housing. GSEs sponsor training institutions and help fund meetings at which developmental activists share information
with one another. Of equal import, GSEs have established foundations that support projects and widely diffuse reports of successful community projects that

have won the Maxwell Awards of Excellence Program for community renewal. The Maxwell Award winners become examples whose projects are imitated by others.

A third cluster of support organizations provides information on the changing economic and political background that shapes the world of community-based developments. HANDSNET is a computer service that circulates news relevant to CBDOs, and maintains an ongoing information forum, while the more focused Community Information Exchange shares information on funding opportunities, as well as maintaining a library of successful projects. For those CBDOs affiliated with the Center for Community Change, information is provided through LINK, a computer network.

Most important are the intermediaries that bridge the financial and perceptual gaps between the world of capitalist investment and that of community-based development. The best known of the intermediaries are the national behemoths, the Local Initiatives Support Corporation, LISC, the Enterprise Foundation, and the quasi-public Neighborhood Reinvestment Corporation, the parent of the Neighborhood Housing Service organizations (for LISC's early history, see Vidal 1986).

Intermediaries package funds from the for-profit sector and apportion this money to the CBDOs. Intermediaries obtain money from foundations that is programmed to provide CBDOs with both technical assistance, and for a selective few, their operating expenses. As the largest of the financial intermediaries, with a asset base of $150 million, LISC has profound influence, both as a packager of funds, a sponsor of training programs, and an innovator in moving CBDOs to work on both housing and economic development projects. Still, among progressive developmental activists, LISC's board is seen to represent the corporate and banking sector and, as such, is considered a tool for the mainstream capitalistic sector.

LISC has established a network of citywide, and a few statewide affiliates, though the structure of these thirty or so organizations differs from place to place. In Indianapolis, LISC works through a local partnership, the Indianapolis Neighborhood Housing Partnership (INHP), that encourages an active city role, while in Cleveland much of LISC's efforts were funneled through Neighborhood Progress, Inc., itself a citywide intermediary, that pointedly excludes the city. LISC in Minneapolis and in Cincinnati never really took off, while Chicago's LISC was considered as a success by itself, taking credit for the development of almost four thousand units of housing and three-fourths of a million square feet of commercial space.

Foundations often work through intermediaries in complicated efforts. For instance, in Chicago, the Fund for Community Development (FCD) was started as a grant program by the MacArthur Foundation, but administered by the local LISC office. Initially, the fund was set up to provide operating support to a variety of Chicago's CBDOs who, in turn, would engage in risky, large-scale economic development projects. How such funding would encourage groups to follow FCD's agenda was explained to me by one of the fund's administrators:

> At its core [is] operating support; and it is fifty grand a year for five years. The vehicle to access the operating support is the strategic plan . . . unlike a lot of grants where you just write the proposal and get the money, here you write the proposal, you get into FCD, you do a strategic plan and you get the money. And, the notion is . . . to help groups really move away from operating on just an annual business planning cycle and to think ahead.
>
> In addition . . . there are predevelopment financing of $25,000 per project, you can get up to three of those. It is kind of one of [the] nicer innovations of LISC called a recoverable grant which means the project goes ahead, we'd like to have the money back, but if it doesn't go ahead we are not going to collect it. . . . And, there is technical assistance money in FCD, too. And, that can be up to $5,000 a year, again five years. . . . There [are] consulting contracts, computer systems, there is training for staff, you name it, pretty flexible in that. So that is FCD.

In many ways, the Center for Community Change (CCC), a national advocacy organization, acts as an intermediary linking activist community development groups to needed technical expertise. Unlike other support organizations set up primarily as development entities, the center came about in 1967 as a protest organization, and to this very day, actively continues this tradition. It targets its help on those most in need, as an CCC official explained, "we're particularly focused on very low income organizations mostly lead by people of color" and CCC "really is an organization that believes in [the] grass roots of empowerment and skills transformation."

It helps organizations focus their missions, provides technical assistance on projects and works to help CBDOs navigate the political environment, tasks quite similar to other intermediaries. In doing so, though, it actively pushes groups to buy into CCC's empowerment agenda. A CCC official described the mating dance that occurs:

> Most of the time a group hears about us from some network . . . and they approach us for help very limited basis. Typically it is something like "help us with a specific housing project" or "help us raise money" or "could you come in and run a retreat?" . . .
>
> We go through fairly careful consideration internally about whether we have the resources . . . and whether the group sounds if it fits our criteria for the kinds of groups that we like to work with. . . . And then assuming that they meet our standards which are essentially

that we are looking for a democratically controlled organization, more or less democratically controlled, which is interested in building the power and capacity of low-income people. And that could benefit from some assistance from us.

As part of this study, I examined in more detail three contrasting local models of intermediaries—Neighborhood Progress, Inc. in Cleveland, the Ohio Community Development Finance Fund, and the Indianapolis Neighborhood Housing Partnership. As described in the last chapter, Neighborhood Progress Inc.—NPI— in Cleveland came about when the foundation community and the corporate sector tried to increase the productivity of the CBDOs. As an NPI official described:

> NPI really represents an attempt to sort of rationalize . . . by pooling the grant money within a strategic framework for developing capacity within the neighborhood groups. And giving the board of NPI the control in terms of how the distribution of funds takes place.

NPI is administered by a core corporation, governed by representatives from foundations, businesses, and the community sector. In addition, NPI controls several operating divisions such as "Village Capital Corporation . . . which has a separate board of directors. And, that board is primarily investment banker, real estate development type people. . . . There is no neighborhood representation on that board." Capital funding for projects comes through this subsidiary corporation. LISC and to some extent Enterprise run their Cleveland programs through NPI (Tittle 1992, p. 92). With foundation support, during the two-year funding cycle at the beginning of my study, NPI "dispersed some $7 million for Cleveland's neighborhoods" (Mihaly 1993, p. 72).

The Indianapolis Neighborhood Housing Partnership (INHP) began as a city-wide, affordable housing partnership bringing together public, private, foundation, and CBDO participation. The mission statement of INHP indicated its purpose was to "function primarily as an intermediary" (INHP 1990, p. 1) that coordinates resources for community development within Indianapolis, but by so doing

> mobilize[s] our community's organizations, financial intermediaries, and the City to expand the supply and sustainability of safe, quality, and affordable housing for the benefit of low/moderate-income citizens through coordinating and leveraging the resources of the public and private sectors.

The partnership started after the city's corporate sector admitted to itself that the lack of affordable housing was a blight on an otherwise growing city. An INHP official described the situation:

> Corporate executives . . . were saying, "we've got the domed stadium. We've got the basketball arena, we got the zoo, we got sports this and

sports that. But what about the people who live here?" And, so it was beginning, the executives saying we got to take care of some other fundamental problems. And housing is very fundamental. And it is measurable, quantifiable.

Believing that Indianapolis' community-development movement lacked direction and focus, corporate executive contracted with consultants to examine ways of improving the community groups. The resulting report praised the accomplishment of some CBDOs but pointed out "that financing is arranged on a project by project basis. Consequently, long-term solutions to Indianapolis' housing needs are not being created" (Executive Summary 1990). The report argued that there was a "window of opportunity" now present to increase low-income housing if a leadership role were taken by the Indianapolis Neighborhood Housing Partnership (Indianapolis Neighborhood Housing Partnership, 1990). At the same time, the Indianapolis-based Lily Foundation had been dramatically increasing its support of community development work. The foundation was readily persuaded to provide the local intermediary with operating funds, to set aside a pool of twenty million dollars as capital for community development projects, and to fund the core expenses of several community-based development organizations.

Both INHP and NPI were set up with the strong support of the business sector, in both cases reinforced by major foundations. The provenance of the Ohio Community Development Finance Fund (CDFF) differs sharply. CDFF is a private nonprofit statewide organization set up to encourage partnerships among community-based development organizations, banks and benevolent depositors (brochure, p. 2) in ways that use benevolent bank deposits to reduce the interest costs for affordable housing projects.

CDFF came about as a result of a lobbying effort on the state legislature lead by the Ohio CDC Association along with other affordable housing advocates. Unlike other intermediaries whose boards reflect either corporate or foundation control, CDFF

> has eight community based representative slots on its board and seven others. We did not want a top down kind of intermediary in Ohio. Not like LISC . . . we wanted an intermediary that would really be responsive to the clients. We felt the clients really ought to own this intermediary.

The formative board of CDFF aggressively recruited as the director a person who had been an outspoken advocate for CBDO-controlled development work.

## RECEIVING HELP FROM THE SUPPORT SECTOR

Support organizations provide capital funding for projects, money to pay for the operating expenses of individual CBDOs, as well as indirect support for the movement as a whole that comes about as intermediaries and foundations try to persuade government and the corporate sector that CBDOs are worth helping after all. Financial help, though, is selectively given to those CBDOs that are most likely to carry out the support organization's agenda. For instance, Neighborhood Progress Inc. provides money for only a dozen of the CBDOs in Cleveland, and the INHP distributed core operating funding for eight of the fifteen CBDOs in Indianapolis, while FCD had funded fewer than a quarter of Chicago's development organizations.

Operating support is vital, but a more dramatic role of the support sector is to raise equity capital. For instance, over eleven years (to 1991) Enterprise had worked with local organizations in building 24,500 homes, by raising in aggregate $655 million for grants, loans, and tax credits for affordable housing (Enterprise 1993). In 1993 alone, the Local Initiatives Support Corporation provided CDCs with $12.6 million in grants, $37.4 million in low-interest loans, as well as $158 million in equity investments (LISC 1994, p. 15). At the time my interviewing began, LISC had packaged funds from 850 foundations and corporations and participated in providing 40,000 affordable homes (LISC 1992). Most important, LISC and other intermediaries have helped CBDOs raise money from corporations for tax credit projects, having collectively raised $740 millions in the first eight years of the LIHTC Program (Center for Public Finance 1994, p. 67)

In addition, support organizations leverage the amount of money that banks and for-profits provide to the community development movement. LISC, for example, in 1987 established the National Equity Fund, an investment pool that diffused risk for investors in low-income housing projects, and then through a spinoff organization, Local Initiatives Managed Assets Corporations (LIMAC), LISC created a secondary market to repurchase loans made in support of low-income housing. LISC has worked with Enterprise and major foundations to leverage money on a national scale, through mechanisms such as the National Community Development Initiative that combines foundation money with money from HUD for development programs.

Those in support organizations understand the need to parley investment funds. An official in a support organization remarked, "It is like you are playing a game of financing chicken, . . . where we will give you money if they will give you money. They will give you money if we give you money." For instance, a leader of the Ohio CDFF described how it leverages the benevolent (low or no interest) deposits made by churches:

> What CDFF does is it leverages the benevolent deposit. . . . CDFF will put in half of the money [from a state grant]. So, [church funds are] leveraged one to one right there. . . . [T]here's no risk . . . because in most cases . . . money is placed in FDIC increments of $100,000 or less. . . . [T]he loan which results from the deposits is usually not the entire project, it's usually only a portion of the entire project and we calculate

that usually that is about 50%—40 to 60% of a project—so they're going to then leverage beyond just the deposit.

CDFF then pressures banks to reduce the interest rate charged, to improve their CRA ratings, while CDFF works with CBDOs to help the community groups further package funds. A CDFF official continued:

> We try and be as friendly as possible. . . . I understand that nobody ever says "Yes" until you all get together in a room. . . . So, the idea is that we want to make this as flexible as we can. If our commitment can act as a seed commitment to leverage these grants or will stand out to enable a lender to get involved, or will enable this group to go to a foundation to get a grant, we will do that.

LISC uses both its own profits, as well as pass-through money from foundations, to help CBDOs that are tempting riskier or more innovative community projects, and only demands repayment if the project is carried out. Astute developmental activists have learned how to use such seed money to leverage further funding for their projects. Further, intermediaries can be indulgent in ways the public sector cannot be. One of the nation's better-known developmental activists complained that when borrowing from the public sector

> the city constantly sends you past due, past due, past due. So before you get the thing out on the ground, you look up and you've accumulated outstanding obligations to the tune of thousands and thousands.

In contrast, she explained that LISC was quite willing to postpone loan due dates so long as realistic reasons are given.

Support organizations bail out CBDOs caught in economic binds. In one case, a CBDO had been in default, but then got its financial house in order. As part of showing it was back in the development game, the CBDO worked out a clever scheme to build a laundromat in a storefront of an apartment building it owned. But with its dubious history, the CBDO had not been able to regain the trust of local financial institutions. The CBDO director went to a supportive state-wide intermediary and "got the $12,000 for the predevelopment money from [the intermediary]," a vote of confidence that was then sufficient to encourage banks to invest.

Another developer was trying to package a complicated project to refurbish an old school to house the elderly and to provide shelter for women with children. She contrasted the support her organization received from a state-wide intermediary to the near disdain from governmental agencies:

> [The director] is wonderful. . . . [F]irst of all, he knows what he is doing and he also respects what we're doing. He's probably the only one, he and the religious and the foundations are the only people who give us

any kind of support. At the state level all of the bureaucrats just treat us with total disrespect and disgust that they have to deal with us. They would much rather be dealing with for-profit developers.

With the seed money from the intermediary, she was able to leverage other funds, and carry out the project.

A virtual mythology permeates the field about smaller foundations that enable development organizations with ideas, but little track record, to take a risk. A rural CBDO had some successes in establishing female-owned businesses, but concluded that setting up a flexible manufacturing facility would be far more helpful to the community, yet had no way of getting money for such an innovative project. The developmental activist described it:

I had come across stuff about flexible manufacturing networks. . . . And I had this one place [foundation] that I always every year wrote a grant knowing I won't get it right but just sort of my fantasy. So I wrote one, it was to the———Foundation. . . . It is the most wonderful foundation. They are incredible. . . . Anyway, they were so good, they always liked the stuff 'cause our ideas were always innovative.

To the surprise of the developmental activist, the grant was funded. Other CBDOs described similar successes with this same foundation, one that needed help to set up an incubator, another that needed seed money for an ethnically focused job-training program, and a third that needed help for an innovative welfare-to-work program.

I interviewed the program officer of that foundation and asked about its policy of taking such high risks. The foundation official chuckled and explained why these projects were funded:

We try to be open to ideas and we want people who think they have an idea that will have impact . . . to come to us and to argue with us on our current priorities or strategies are misplaced or we are missing an opportunity. . . . The insight is the people[s] that are operating the project, not ours. We didn't come up with this and say we want to support that sort of project. It is them coming to us and saying "this is worthwhile, this is what we should be doing. We think we have an insight into how to make it work and to demonstrate how to make it work. Or we have an opportunity to change the way the economy functions in some significant way."

And so it is their idea, we are enabling them. It is not our idea, so we don't have ownership of the project the way that some funders feel, we're not contracting with them for a delivery of a service.

Later as the first flexible manufacturing networks idea appeared successful, the foundation sponsored workshops to disseminate the approach.

Developmental activists portrayed some community foundations almost as knights errant. In a smaller city, a CBDO discovered that it had misjudged expenses on a project that tied together housing, social services, and an effort to renew the physical appearance of a skid row, and desperately needed money to continue.

> So I quickly called up the president [of the foundation]. . . . I said "I've got a restaurant; I need your help. I got a $100,000 problem and we'll lose the whole project. It's really not [going to be] a project [if] we don't have 10 percent in by December 31st; that's the tax credit requirements."
>
> And . . . she said, "Well we just had our quarterly meeting. . . . If you're telling that the only way that this project is going to go forward is if I give this $100,000 to you before the end of December . . . I'll see what I can do."
>
> She said, "I'd prefer you wait till our next quarterly meeting." And I said, "I can't" and she said," Ok, get something to me right away and I'll see what I can do to get it. We'll do it go around the corner to the trustees and see if we can get it approved." She said, "I'll support it for $100,000." One phone call that's where the personal asset stuff comes in, you know.

Other help in building CBDO capacity is provided, though not always the help developmental activists want. LISC is involved in setting up CBDOs from scratch in both the southern and southwestern parts of the country, areas that lack an indigenous community development movement. NPI provides technical training to developmental activists, but also insists that the recipient organizations restructure to become administratively more efficient. As I will discuss in chapter 9, developmental activists attend the Development Training Institute to learn how to package economic deals. Doing so can be quite expensive, both to pay the attendee's salary and to come up with a tuition of $18,000. Many of these expenses are picked up either by intermediaries or through local support partnerships. Similarly, local and national intermediaries pay for the consultants needed to undertake specialized projects and to help CBDOs write up grant requests.

In addition, support organizations partner with individual CBDOs on projects. The Fund for Community Development helped bring about several neighborhood renewal efforts, while Neighborhood Progress Inc. partnered in setting up an incubator. LISC partners with CBDOs to develop inner-city supermarkets. In such partnerships, though, the guidance provided can be quite detailed. A development activist described working with the Center for Community Change in a project to convert an old school into a community center:

The Center stays right by our side. . . . . [T]hey flew out . . . came into [city name] to help us negotiate more tax credits. They come here once a month. . . . [The expert from CCC], who is our lead technical assistance person, was here three or four weeks ago to help us complete the general contractor's contract, to go over budgets. . . . We had an environmental problem . . . and [she] got a hold of these people from the EPA and we had conference calls. She called me at home twice because she felt that I was emotionally a wreck over this and she just wanted to call me at home to say, "Don't take this all on your shoulders all by yourself we're all in this together." If it doesn't work, we're all going to have to leave town, you know, but, I mean it, [they are] really sharing that liability and that's the Center, that's how they are. They're just fabulous people.

Support organizations also help developmental activists stay on top of a wide array of information on the technicalities of packaging deals. Enterprise Foundation publishes booklets on step-by-step approaches to refurbishing homes and apartments, while the Center for Community Change produces a constant stream of information on the sociology and economics of distressed communities, helps its partner organizations negotiate Community Reinvestment Act (CRA) agreements, and provides step-by-step consultation on physical projects. An activist described how the CCC staff and other CBDOs in the CCC network helped them in their first major CRA fight:

the Center for Community Change helped us dramatically. . . . People on our [CCC computer] network befriended us. And so we share war stories. . . . And so then we'd put an S-O-S out on [the computer] network and say, "Hey we're thinking about doing this, here's our strategy, what do ya think? " I mean [we] put together our [CRA] contracts that we were signing contracts with banks, reinvestment contracts . . . and five different groups across the country critiqued our contract. . . . And so we're sharing war stories and they're—you know somebody in San Francisco and somebody in Atlanta————that they're just friends of ours through the network. You know and so then of course we send it to the Center for Community Change [and] they critiqued it.

Support organization also sponsor conferences to explicate changes in federal regulations. LISC and the Center for Community Change circulate understandable brochures on changing laws such as those embedded within the obtuse technicalities of the Cranston-Gonzales Housing Bill. The Center for Community Change makes available to its affiliates a computerized data base that keeps updates on tactics in organizing and the development field, and provides documents on CRA tactics that those in the movement can copy from one another.

Foundation officials give voice to the strivings of a movement in ways that those in the establishment must hear and that activists appreciate. With the fanfare only possible to a multibillion dollar foundation, the president of the MacArthur Foundation included a long preface to the Foundations Annual Report (MacArthur 1992, pp. 2–6) entitled "Renewing Democracy from the Bottom Up" that emphasized the holistic views toward community development that those in the movement were promoting. The progress reports prepared by the National Congress for Community Economic Development are funded by the foundations that also produce films shown on public television lauding the successes of the community development movement.

Board members of foundations and intermediaries, usually people of economic note, end up meeting with developmental activists and discussing alternative views of economic change. A ranking officer in a national foundation remarked:

> Three years ago we bought seven community development leaders, including [a radical community activist], in front of the entire [foundation] board, we had a whole day and [radical activist] was one of the people that were talking about their work.
>
> At the end of that, [a nationally known conservative], who's on the board, came up to me, and said, . . . "[We] have just discovered today—rediscovered today—what democracy is all about."

The foundation officer continued to explain the brokering role played by the foundation:

> We took them [the board] on tours. And you take very, very conservative people and sit them down with articulate [community] leaders. . . . [T]hese gentlemen, to their credit, responded to those discussions; they see women who care about their kids, who are worried sick about whether their sons are going to get shot. They were overwhelmed with respect for what these women tried to do and we went from one of these gentlemen saying, "Why are we funding these women in public housing? They're having babies so the government will pay for them" to their saying, "How can we find more of these groups?"

Officials in intermediaries explain to conventional bankers the differences between doing deals and paying attention to social concerns. The head of a city branch of LISC described it thus:

> [T]hat's why I took the job, to inform the bankers of why that [social] cost is necessary and justifying the cost. . . . LISC does not have a problem with the [social] costs. The real banks have a problem with those costs and my job is to bring them to a level of understanding of why the cost is necessary, This is not a brick and mortar project. . . . [T]he purpose was not to create a nice building. . . . [T]his is not a house, this is a

home. . . . It's not the house that makes the payment, it's the person who lives in that home that makes the payment and we need to take care of that in order for that person to continue to provide you with that mortgage payment.

I mean, my whole job is to make sure everybody who's involved in the project turns out win, win, win, win, win, . . . trying to make everybody understand it's not a real estate development project, this is a community development project and, yes, I can build a house for $50,000 in this neighborhood and this one's costing $75,000, but you know what? In ten years we're going to have to go back and redo this house, or tear it down and start all over, this $75,000 that we have now provide[s] a skill and a level of training for this person to remain in it and be able to maintain it, we're taking them through counseling so they know they've got a reserve.

Support organizations also actively work to bring about changes in governmental policies. LISC maintains a full-time office in Washington with professionals who join in the markup sessions for federal legislation, as well as lobby for supportive legislation, for instance, suggesting important modifications made to the Cranston-Gonzales Housing Bill. The Center for Community Change has lobbied government to increase funding for low-income housing, worked to expand antihunger programs, and has been at the forefront of efforts to maintain and expand the Community Reinvestment Act. Recently, CCC has focused much of its advocacy effort to encourage states and localities to set up Housing Trust Funds that provide a dedicated, albeit often small, income stream for filling in the gap in low-income housing development work. As a result, the CCC staff has helped set up eighty such Trust Funds that generate about $300 million a year for affordable housing (Center for Community Change 1994, p. 2).

By law, foundations and GSEs must be circumspect in advocacy work. Still, support is provided. For instance, under its Public Policy Initiative, MacArthur funded community organizations that researched and documented government neglect of the infra-structure needs of poor communities that led to several action campaigns (Teamworks 1991). GSEs have hired community activists who lobby for programs needed by CBDOs, while both foundations and GSEs help fund trade associations that in turn are active lobbyists.

## BUT WHOSE AGENDA PREVAILS?

Community-based development organizations could not succeed without the support of the foundations and intermediaries. Yet this support does not come unencumbered. Whether for better or worse, intermediaries and foundations have their images about what the role of the CBDOs should be in bringing about community change. Developmental activists fear that in accepting help they will end up having to comply with the ideologies put forth by the intermediaries or the foundations. In Baltimore, for instance, Enterprise moved the agenda of the community coalition BUILD from one of empowerment to that of social therapy (McDougall 1993, p. 157), while, as Groenjberg describes it, funding from intermediaries and foundations often distorts community agendas (Groenjberg 1993, p. 309).

Developmental activists appreciate the difference between an intermediary or foundation mandating that the CBDO do it their way, and the constructive interaction that can occur between knowledgeable foundation or intermediary officials and community activists. One activist described how his CBDO become involved in an innovative welfare-to-work program that became a national exemplar:

> We were on our way to doing self-employment four years ago, when we got diverted into doing child care. . . . We went to [foundation name], they often have an appetite for innovation, and we were talking about that we wanted to get into self-employment and trying to go through our transition from doing industrial property. . . . So we made a request to them for like a $50,000 seed loan to get started. And they said, "we don't have any doubt based upon your track record that you can do this project. But we think it might be a wiser move if what we did was to instead of giving you 50 give you 5,000 and give you a chance to be a little more thoughtful about where you are trying to go with self-employment. And start by spending time looking, and talking with people in community and doing some of your own market research."

In response, "[they] took kind of a two-year hiatus away from what [they] were trying" and thought about the broader approach. The idea that resulted was an innovative effort that linked day-care, self-employment training, and housing renewal in ways that ended up reshaping both the neighborhood and the mission of the CBDO.

Such active involvement has helped CBDOs think out their community missions. A senior planner for a support organization described how the low-key pressure was applied, while at the same time helping the CBDO set up a project:

> [The CBDO] did . . . a comprehensive plan for a very small portion of their neighborhood. What came back was after all of the people had been talked to in the neighborhood . . . they said, "Oh, we should rebuild commercial and put housing on this site but mostly commercial."
>
> They sent the plan to me. . . . Well I went over the plan; I had been to [the CBDO] twice; I went out one more time after looking at the plan and I came back to them and I said,

I think the horse is before the cart. Surrounding this neighborhood are destroyed and dying commercial strips. How can you expect that if you invest money and build a new commercial strip in the center that your fate will be any better given what this report says has happened to the economics of people in this community?

Now they . . . wouldn't have sent [the report] to me to ask me what I thought if they hadn't had that baseline discomfort. Then we sat down together and processed through what people felt the neighborhood needed, given that this was untenable and that's how we came up with totally low-income housing on that site. . . .

Now I wouldn't say that the [support organization] drove that. Had they gone on to do commercial development with housing attached we would have still worked with them. But they asked the question . . . and our response was this is not the right use of this property at this point and time.

And the director of the CBDO later indicated to me no complaints about the involvement of the support organization since "they are very involved and very progressive on issues. . . . They promote organizing and developing. . . . And they stay honest."

Still in many other cases, developmental activists expressed intensely negatively feelings that support organizations simply don't understand what community development is about. These activists fear that by pushing for brick-and-mortar projects, LISC distracts attention from the more radical social change needed to repair a capitalist economy. As one developmental activist emoted:

Shoot the fucking intermediaries, especially LISC. . . . [The] MacArthur [Foundation] [that now funds LISC] . . . used to be the most progressive funder in town and actually required you to have low-income people on your board of directors . . . who do they give the program to administer but LISC, who'd rather you don't mess up your development work with involving low-income people.

The woman who had labeled herself as a social banker described the personal nature of the tensions by indicating changes in relationships with others in the movement when she left a CBDO to work for LISC:

[The city's leading developmental activist] has been a mentor of mine and a very good friend for several years. He was not happy when he heard I was going over to THEM. . . . WE and THEY. . . . WE being the community developers, implementors, THEY being the funders. I've been in this field for twelve years, have always been a "we," been very proud to be a "we," . . . [leading development activist] and I went through a year of a, a strained relationship. He was trying to figure out, "Why did you go over to be a they?"

The image of a 'they' comes about because many developmental activists feel that LISC chooses its tasks to accomplish its own bureaucratic agenda and is

> not really interested in local initiative. They're interested in the pro-duction that is necessary to raise more money to support the [LISC] bureaucracy from the large corporations and large foundations that fund them and I think that's awful.

Worse yet, developmental activists feel that intermediaries absorb money from the community foundations that would have funded the CBDOs in their inde-pendent efforts at social change.

Developmental activists feel pressured by the intermediaries to produce jobs, homes, and businesses irrespective of other goals:

> they only base the end of production. They're not interested in capacity buildings, or helping a group make a strong administration to run the program. They're basing it on production. If you do not have the num-bers we're pissed and we're going to reprimand you for it.

Social agendas can fall by the wayside. A developmental activist described that his African-American neighborhood was seen as dangerous by outsiders, had a deteriorated housing infrastructure, and desperately needed visible signs that it could be resurrected. Yet he felt that LISC, who had helped fund housing in his neighborhood, was unwilling to cooperate in his group's effort to symbolize the possibilities for community renewal. He detailed the difficulties in convincing LISC to sell a house at a loss, framing his narrative in terms of a conversation he had with a LISC official:

> You come out the first time and said "that's a beautiful place . . . to develop that house." It was fine then, but economics have hit the com-munity. You've got gangs on that corner, you've got drug dealers on the next corner, you allow four more building to become vacant. How the hell we gonna rehab that building and sell that building and put that building back on the market?
> . . . Who the hell's gonna buy that house? You said, "production." You're not dealing with the times. Times have changed. That neigh-borhood is not the best neighborhood right now, because four or five people got killed there lately.

He continued by described his argument with LISC to

> drop the [price of the] house, give it to some poor person for $5[,000] or 10,000. "Oh, no, [name], it's not that type a program."

Well, hell, we'll be sitting on the house, so taxes got to be paid, water bill's got to be paid, gas got to be paid, lights still got to be paid. . . . We sit on that house for a year and a half. We could not sell the house at all . . . a police [officer] got killed across the street, couple of guys got shot gang related right down the block and all. . . .

So we get this guy from the north side, a black couple, "Well, you got any houses for sale? "We said, "Well, we got some to sell." He said, "Well, I've been living in a bourgeois neighborhood all my life, I just want to experiment being in the heart of the black community. I'm black." . . .

And I said, "Well, you know I've got a house . . . it's in the heart of the rough areas, I'm going to be honest with you." He said, "Let me look at it." He looked at the house, he called me back he said, "I want the house." . . . . He said, "Well, now the whole catch to this; I've got a limited amount of money that I'm going to spend and I'm not going over." He said, "I will spend $50,000 for the house." I said, "Hell, we can't sell the house for fifty, we've got $60,000 in the house and the house is appraised at $65,000. We gonna take a beating." So the guy says, "Well, maybe it's no deal."

So I calls LISC up and says, "Hey, we've got a house over here we've been sitting on it for a fucking year and a half and you guys are saying you want your money. You know we can't give you our money out of our pocket. We don't have it. We've got to sell that house to give you your money back that you loaned to us for the program, and he's only wanting to pay $50,000. . . . Now can you guys take a beating?"

"Oh, no, we can't take a beating."

Other developmental activists summarized their understanding of the intermediaries as follows:

[T]he reality is that they [intermediaries] are driven by a business side mentality that says, "I give you; you produce; and you report back." . . . They did not come here to be a people thing, they came to be a production-based thing.

They described that the pressure to produce is part of the intermediaries' efforts to please their corporate funders:

[G]o to the annual meeting [of LISC]. . . . [T]hey have a stream of corporate people from Amoco Corporation, from IBM, and from . . . all these people come up and talk and get awards. Somebody from Rockefeller Foundation, somebody from Ford Foundation talks and then they show a little video of seven or eight community projects. They don't want to let the community folks up there to talk because they might say something that's not controllable and so you know we're all on video; we're all edited out. . . . It's backwards.

Structural changes in some of the intermediaries gives credence to the developmental activists' concerns. In Indianapolis, the original director of the housing partnership, along with the community organizer the intermediary had funded, were replaced, an action interpreted as against taking on a broader social mission. In Cleveland, though CBDOs successfully lobbied for representation on the NPI board, corporate and foundation representatives pushed the intermediary to concentrate on physical production. One influential foundation official noted that

> NPI's initial philosophy was around physical revitalization. That was heavily pushed by the funders and I think we continue to feel that the primary criterion for evaluating NPI is production and hopefully production to scale. In practice, the community groups that were producing large-scale, visible projects demanded by NPI were the only ones receiving help. (Mihaly 1993 )

Other evidence points to the desire of the intermediary to dominate the redevelopment agenda. A major report put out by NPI, *Policy Recommendations 1993–1994* (NPI 1992), described how resources would be allocated by a "centralized production engines but decentralized operating units." In case the point was missed, the report included a diagram that placed NPI at the center of the developmental efforts, surrounded by its affiliates, with the CDCs themselves pictorially relegated to the outer edge of the paper.

The multiple roles played by intermediaries complicate their relationship with the CBDOs, making it hard for the community groups to stick up for their own agendas. For instance, the same intermediaries that supply capital funds for projects and operating support, can also be the organizations to which CBDOs turn for technical assistance. At one and the same time, a CBDO requests the funds indicating its competence to do a project, yet it is also asking the funding source to teach-me-how-to-do-so, thereby deferring to the funder's agenda. When LISC provides technical assistance, a CBDO wants to be open about any difficulties so that the problems can be solved, yet with LISC as a funder, the CBDO wants to present an image of success to keep the stream of money coming in. An economic development director explained:

> LISC tries to wear to many hats in the development process. On the one hand [it] . . . is a grant maker and funder just like a foundation. They also try to play the role of being your partner in development [and] technical assistance adviser in development.
>
> Sometimes those two operate at cross purposes . . . at least, they don't support each other. I mean you tell certain things to your partner that you will not tell to a foundation. Or you will create an image of

comprehensiveness with a foundation about community benefits that a real estate development partner doesn't want to hear about.

So LISC on the one hand says you've got to legitimize yourself on the community benefit front in order for us to fund you . . . and yet all through the rest of that year we are being evaluated on the basis of real estate and only real estate.

She continued by emoting:

You talk about the confusing roles . . . LISC on the one hand they're a lender, they're a funder, not a lender, they're a funder. On the other hand, then, they're an adviser and so here I am learning the process of development with my funder as my adviser on the process. It can get very sticky.

The head of a local intermediary explained the obverse side of this quandary:

We're backing you; your problem is my problem. I'm putting equity into you because you are going to produce the . . . houses. . . . And so if that partner has an accounting problem, it is my self-interest to help get it done, because my equity is in there and I want a product out the back door. . . . And so we are an equity partner, we are not a funder that is going to cut you off because you do not hit your goals. Now if you really screw it up and you didn't hit your goals, that is one thing. But if you are doing your best and all these kinds of things take place, that's understandable.

But this desire to help can evolve into pressures for the CBDO to accommodate the intermediary by changing its organizational form or reformulating its mission. In Cleveland, developmental activists complained when, as a condition of funding, intermediaries demanded that smaller CBDOs merge into a larger, multifunctioned organization. Elsewhere an old-time director employed by a fiscally quite solvent organization claimed that an intermediary refused to fund the CBDO's operating costs unless he, as executive director, signed a two-year contract. Another described an exchange with the intermediary over a provision in a loan agreement that gave the intermediary a say in personnel selections made by the CBDO:

We ended up taking it, but we just objected to this provision. It is this provision in this loan we just got that further disbursements are dependent on their being no changes in significance in personnel. . . .

And if I decide to fire our project manager, what are they doing? [Pretending to quote the intermediary:] "Well, of course, we don't want to select your new manager." Yah, but if you don't like the one I replace him with, you might hold up that payment. . . . And they impose this unilaterally across the country. It came out of New York.

With quasi-governmental organizations, tensions can be worse. For example, many housing trust funders are run by organizations who along with the developmental activists worry whether this money should be allocated for a few deep subsidies on projects for the very poorest or spent on a larger number of projects that benefit a greater number. Still, directors of the trust funds tend to encourage spreading the money around, in part, because it pleases the politicians to whom they report. A ranking official working for a housing trust fund remarked:

> The politicians . . . want production. When I go to [the capital] nobody says to me, "Tell me the incomes of the people you serve." What they say is "How many units has the trust fund created? And, how much money have you leveraged? . . . They don't say, "Did you get at those people who earn 30% of [median income?]" . . . They don't care about that. They want to know how many units you do. . . . But I'm sensitive to the fact that the more subsidy we put, the lower we can do the rents and so we have to do some of those . . . where your rents are $175. But you can't do all of them. Or you'll end up instead of doing 4,000 units in the first two years, you'll do 1,500.

Similarly, developmental activists resented it when they felt that intermediaries were encouraging CBDOs to become equity owners of income-producing properties rather than simply catalysts for their development. Helping a CBDO build its own financial base is far from an unreasonable goal and certainly has support within the community development movement. But activists worried that by immediately pushing for ownership, intermediaries encouraged ill-prepared community groups to work on "hero projects" that exceed the CBDO's capacity.

These tensions were apparent in the programs sponsored by Chicago's Fund for Community Development (FCD). Developmental activists were sanguine about the FCD since it dramatically increased the money available for projects while providing operating support for thirty CBDOs. Yet the FCD was resented for pressuring CBDOs to bring off large-scale, visually dramatic real estate developments. The threat for not doing so, was the withdrawal of the $50,000 subsidy for operating support. One developmental activist described how LISC responded when his successful CBDO refused to become an equity owner:

> they tried to defund us and remove us from the . . . program. We raised hell because if you look at the . . . program guidelines, renewal of support is suppose to be predicated on the extent to which you follow your own strategic plan. Well, they had accepted our strategic plan for that

year and they had accepted every interim report we had given them and yet out of the blue they said you will be defunded within thirty days unless you have this [physical development] deal consummated. . . . I mean it was made such eminent good sense from our perspective to play the catalyst role in that deal. The outcomes were exactly the same. I mean we stabilized the real estate, we rehabbed it, we organized the block club around that building, built the networks. . . .

[The funder] didn't like it and on that basis they were going to defund us. Forget all of their own guidelines about adhering to your own strategic plan.

Many FCD projects were successful, especially those done by the older, established community-based development organizations, one of which managed to construct and manage an affordable housing project for the elderly on the south side of the city, while another successfully turned an old industrial building into profitable incubator space. But developmental activists thought such pressure was quite harmful especially for the newer, less experienced groups that would either fail at the effort or simply become extensions of the intermediary. One argued that LISC officials (through the FCD)

are strongly urging, dangling lots of money in front of groups, into the field of owning and managing real estate. That's the wrong thing to do. . . . [T]here are groups all over town that are starting up and looking first at doing real estate development. And that's the last thing you should do because that's where the money is, that's where the glamour is, that's what LISC is talking about. There are groups all over town that are getting money from LISC that are doing the wrong thing and in two years they're not going to have a project or three years they're going to have a project that goes under. . . . The neighborhood's going to be worse and then the funders and LISC are going to look around and say groups weren't very good or their going to say, "Ah, this economic development stuff doesn't really work."

He continued by arguing that physical development is a means for community renewal, not an end in and of itself.

The FCD was seen as being too aggressive in pushing smaller CBDOs into megaprojects that, in the words of a coalition leader, "looked good in their annual report." The iconic example was the pressure on a small CBDO to work out a $60 million plan for the entire redevelopment plan of a commercial area surrounding the final stop on a transit line. The project caused nothing but headaches. Neighborhood housing organizations opposed the project fearing it would lead to gentrification. With LISC's help a federal grant was obtained, but insufficient progress was made to even use the money. A consultant for the project, who himself was a successful community commercial developer, reflected on the consequences, claiming the CBDO

> will be the first ones to tell you they did it wrong because they shouldn't have started with the big, what they call a sizzle, project because six years later they have nothing to show for their efforts because it takes seven or eight years to put together a 60 million dollar project. And, in the meantime people in the neighborhood think that they are no good, think that they are incompetent.

Officials rebutted claims that they were imposing an agenda simply to produce. One explained that "LISC is changing. LISC is creating a community-building program" and pointed out in an annual report that LISC spent $23 million to support "social community development such as child care, health care, crime prevention and education" (LISC 1993, p. 6). Others said that the CBDOs who resisted these pressures were just making excuses for their own incompetence or inexperience.

To complicate matters, both intermediaries and CBDOs end up having to respond to the changing funding fashions of the larger foundations. Just during the years of this study, the MacArthur Foundation, a major supporter of community work, moved full circle in what types of community actions it encouraged. Initially, the Foundation was heavily supporting advocacy efforts, then it moved to funding physical development work, and by the time this study ended had circled back to supporting holistic programs of community renewal, often lead by religious leaders rather than developmental activists. Further, foundations and intermediaries are heavily networked to each other, and, as a result ideas that succeed in one part of the country are rapidly tried in another, irrespective of the differences in setting, leading to complaints about "cookie-cutter" development models that are being imposed.

LISC officials deny this is the case, as explained to me by a director of a city-wide LISC affiliate:

> I don't think there was ever an attempt that LISC should be a cookie-cutter. . . . There are a lot of good reasons to criticize LISC, but one of them is not that it is New York–directed and has like this sort of national agenda that crushes local initiative. Just the opposite: it really attempts to foster as much innovation locally as it can and just to illustrate that . . . in California . . . we now have three cities there, San Francisco, Los Angeles, and San Diego have programs. . . . Because the notion of neighborhoods is rather different than in the East Coast, the initial push for organizing CDCs came from ethnic constituencies and from social service agencies. And so LISC rather than sort of being

purist about it, . . . said we'll work with what is there. And what was there, you know, Japanese-American service leagues, and homeless advocates with single room occupancy building (SROs).

Still, models that the intermediaries adopt rapidly spread. For instance, what is now known as consensus organizing came about as follows: LISC had been funding activists in the Mon Valley where a dozen CDCs worked together in response to the closing of the steel mills to implement Michael Eichler's [the proponent of consensus organizing] plan to create new community organizations that would combat de-industrialization, but avoid the confrontations associated with direct action groups. The MacArthur Foundation learned of these activities and funded Eichler to experiment with this new approach in Florida. LISC became involved since

> one of the long-term strategic objectives of LISC is to help foment community development activity in the regions of the country that completely lack traditions of local organization. . . . Mike Eichler . . . sets up what he calls a development team that goes out and works in different neighborhoods. . . . The development team is actually insulated from LISC, it is not LISC directly but it is kind of this vehicle for organizing CDCs and then at the same time a LISC program is organized to marshal the resources needed for development.

Senior foundation officials were pleased, for

> Eichler I think has moved the idea of community development and organizing into the next paradigm. And what Mike Eichler is doing is he's figured out how to organize around consensus as opposed I would suggest to Alinsky's adversarial organizing.

But many community activists view the Eichler model of consensus organizing as a sophisticated form of co-optation, while recent studies question its overall effectiveness (Gittell and Vidal 1998).

## TWO CASES OF CONTENTIONS OVER THE AGENDA

Intermediaries are crucial actors in helping CBDOs bring about renewal. But the needs of the intermediaries, especially to show successful production, and those of the community-based development organizations, to assert local control, do not always coincide. Quite vicious contests sometimes occur, mostly carried out behind the scenes. Below I detail two battles, using pseudonyms to protect the informants.

*An Entangled Interorganizational Web*

In this first incident, the anger of intermediary at a less efficient CBDO almost lead to the demise of this development organization. Enterprise had been working in this city and to assure production had established a network of community-based housing providers. Both the network as a collective, and the individual CBDOs within the network were eligible recipients of Enterprise money. The network was particularly active within the city's poorest neighborhood, a crescent-shaped neighborhood that contained numerous not-for-profit organizations, several of whom were rivals with one another.

Within the crescent, Empowering the Poor (ETP), a CBDO governed by a neighborhood-based board from an African-American community, developed, owned, and managed large numbers of affordable apartments. ETP served the poorest population, was probably inefficiently managed, and survived primarily with the help of city hall. Helping the Alcoholic—HA—was the best known organization in the community. While nominally it was a social service agency set up for the rehabilitation of alcoholics, it was lead by a well-known social activist who advocated on many different issues, including an approach to affordable housing that differed from that taken by ETP.

At the time of the controversy, ETP had just partnered with Enterprise in a major housing project that failed. Accusations were made by Enterprise that the ETP was both corrupt and uncooperative with the intermediary and as a result Enterprise withdrew from supporting ETP. Concurrent with the ETP-Enterprise imbroglio, the head of HA, a Caucasian who had support from some on ETP's board, pressured the director of ETP, an African-American, to undertake administrative changes to the housing organization. The director of ETP described the situation:

> I had two staff positions here that needed to be filled and [HA director] pressured me, and pressured me, and pressured me till I filled . . . the business manager position with one of his people. . . . Well that business person . . . started gathering information to lodge allegations against my mismanagement and misconduct. So he brought forth these twenty-two allegations of mismanagement and misconduct against me. It was real public. . . . So that business manager conspired with the five white members of our board and the Enterprise Foundation and they all met separately in these little secret meetings. . . . [T]hey went over this list of allegations and finally they brought them forth to the board. . . . And that hit the papers for about six months.
>
> Then, the city did their own investigation. . . . Ultimately, the city came out and said I was all clear of all twenty-two allegations. They said, "Well, there's some unorthodox business practices. . . . there's what we wouldn't call mismanagement, it's unorthodox."

From what I could ascertain, the CBDO had been inefficient in collecting rents, preferring not to evict those who did not pay, and had worked out arrangements for tenants to provide janitorial services in lieu of rent. In addition, a board member had misused the CBDO's credit card on a personal trip.

ETP's executive director was angered at the head of the social service agency who had spied on his CBDO, but his fury and disappointment were focused on the intermediary whom he felt made the negative case because he refused to carry out projects its way. As he explained,

> Enterprise Foundation was to come in and help us build our organization internally, . . . be our limited partner in this deal. Well, because we were so closely connected with Enterprise Foundation, the people that formed the allegations went to Enterprise Foundation . . . and said, "Look, these are all things that [his name] is doing wrong and you need to look into 'em." So Enterprise Foundation gets scared right away. . . . And where they made their mistake is when they started meeting separately with members of the board—all the white members. That's where they messed up and further made that split between black and white.
>
> So, what happened, the Enterprise Foundation gave us an ultimatum, the board, and said, "You either do this, this, this and this, or we're not going to work with you." And one of them was for me to leave the organization and the board supported me. Remember, I had six blacks there. They said, "Oh, no. You're not going to get rid of [director's name]."
>
> Enterprise told me, they said, "One, we will work out a orderly process for you to leave the organization over a six-month period. Two, we will find you a job in another city. . . . Or, three, if you choose to stay with the organization, we won't help you. We won't support you. Matter of fact, we'll fight you." I picked number three. And the board was behind me.
>
> The community rose up behind me. We marched 250 people to city hall and told them that Enterprise wasn't going to tell us what to do. And, I chose to stay. . . . [Enterprise] started writing letters to the city council, lobbying against giving us any funding, lobbying and asking the city to take the buildings from us and give them to another group in the city that they wanted to work with. All of that failed. It was at that point I had to get real seriously and heavily involved in organizing, community organizing.

Though the director had been able to make his case with the city council that no corruption was involved, Enterprise still ended its relationship with the CBDO. The CBDO was ordered by the city to hire a property management firm.

Unfortunately, this firm was less responsive to the tenants than was the CBDO. It refused to send anyone into the neighborhood to collect rents and insisted that no cash be used for rent payment, two conveniences that the CBDO had offered its tenants. Several years later, the neighborhood CBDO is still afloat and run by the same executive director, while Enterprise has withdrawn from the neighborhood.

### Contestation over the Developmental Agenda in Flat City

This second case study describes a battle between a citywide intermediary—Helping Communities Progress (HCP)—that tried to impose its own vision for community change and the CBDOs that rebelled. The dispute came about as local foundations that had previously supported the CBDOs and their broader mission now felt, as a foundation official described, that

> the breadth of groups in Flat City was so great that we could not support all of them. Not all of them merited support. We felt the need to begin to focus our resources on those groups where there did appear to be some capacity demonstrated already and some potential for these groups to make a significant difference in the physical environment in the neighborhood.

To carry out their ideas, the foundation community contracted with consultants who concluded (after privately clearing their report with foundation and corporate leaders) that hundreds of millions of new money should be invested in physical repair of the neighborhoods, but that the effort must be coordinated by a local intermediary, HCP, that would assure the money would be spent to achieve "production of scale." HCP was set up, the foundations agreed to increase the money made available for redevelopment, though doing so only through HCP, while LISC's local affiliate agreed to follow HCP's lead in distributing project funds.

Both public officials and many in the community development movement supported HCP's board structure. A city official, who had come from the community-development movement, indicated that HCP's board is

> composed of half a dozen or more neighborhood activists in various constituencies and half a dozen or so corporate leaders, the foundation distribution committee people, the CEO and the board that is chaired by [major company head] and you have [head of a CBDO housing alliance] they are calling each other by their first names and they are working on subcommittees and they are working through problems.

Still, observers from the community movement worried that the board would be dominated by directors from the foundations and larger businesses. Developmental activist were also aware, as a foundation official later confirmed to me in an interview, that the foundations questioned whether CBDOs should have any representation on the board at all.

The increase in funding was appreciated, though its allocation to selected community-based development organizations caused some concern. Developmental activists were pleased that there is now "more foundation money . . . more corporate money, direct grant loan than before. That money has increased the pot significantly." A citywide housing alliance received an additional $125,000 in operating money from HCP, plus had easier access to the equity funds made available through the intermediary. A CBDO that had tried to set up a commercial incubator, now partnered with HCP, and as a result received well over a million dollars in loans and grants, while thirty other projects with start-up funding ranging from $34,000 up to $150,000 were begun throughout the city's neighborhoods. In addition, HCP distributed funds to train CBDO employees while HCP itself provided both technical assistance and hired consultants to work with the community groups.

Still, each of these actions were viewed with suspicion by some of those in the CBDO movement. For instance, a survey funded by HCP to determine what skills and resources developmental activists required was interpreted as a backdoor way of replacing oldtimers, many who started out as organizers, with hired technocrats. Others felt that technical assistance was only provided to those CBDOs most compliant with the wishes of HCP, leading to dissension among the developers. At one coalition meeting, two activists, one from a CBDO that was the major development partner of HCP, the other from an excluded organization, stood up in front of over sixty people and hurled epithets at each other, more or less to the effect that the partnered organization had "sold out," while the excluded organization was simply incompetent.

Further, several developmental activists disparaged the quality of the technical advice received from HCP instead interpreting it as a form of ineffective, yet condescending control. A developmental activist whose group had begun a project recommended by HCP but then had difficulties in completing the task complained that an HCP employee

> was supposed to be our coach on this project . . . he came here and actually sat in my office and told me all the things I had done wrong and the things I should have done different. . . . And I lost it, I said, "Like who do you think you are? Sit here and tell what I should have done. You were the damn coach. Where were you? You know, if things weren't done right, you should have been telling us that."

Both developmental activists and those in the intermediary built up negative images of each other, a dynamic that was accelerated after John Ball, a strong, assertive, successful developer hired from an adjacent city, became head of

HCP. In describing John Ball, a leading CBDO activist and recipient of HCP funds commented,

> John is a very talented person. . . . But I think his weakness is that when he doesn't want to think about something he absolutely will not, no matter what you say, he totally rejects it.

She then described how Ball ignored her ideas about community participation in redevelopment while indicating her sense of resentment at Ball's public criticism of prior work done by the CBDOs.

In reaction to these criticisms, Ball claimed that the CBDOs were angered by the demands placed on them to produce more. His supporters agreed, as indicated by a housing activist whose organization produced numerous homes but did so following the HCP model:

> I think there are some nonprofits that don't want to be held account-able to strict production standards. And so instead of looking at them-selves and saying, "How can we do better, how can we do more housing and more commercial development or whatever?". . . they're killing the messengers, or beating up the messengers, which is HCP, who's basi-cally reflecting the thinking of the folks with money, the foundations, who are saying, "We've been funding this stuff for such a long time and we don't see a lot of improvement." In fact, there's a group of us who call them the whiners, because all they do is whine about, "Oh, poor us, you know, funders don't understand how hard it is."

Funded organizations received extensive technical assistance paid for by HCP, making other activists jealous and accusing the recipient CBDOs as simply being fronts for whatever HCP wanted to accomplish. Funded groups disagreed. The developmental activist whose CBDO had received the largest share of HCP money claimed:

> I don't feel subordinate. I feel like we are real up and up partners. We are both learning. We are growing together and I feel comfortable with the partnership. . . . Some people would say, "If HCP wasn't there you wouldn't do it." Possibly, but I would have done it anyway—it would just have been slower.

Ball recognized that HCP could support but a handful of organizations, but felt doing so was both right and efficient:

> We made some decisions. One, where is the highest quality . . . person-nel, by which I mean not just staff, but board, assemblies of neighbor-hood stakeholders, where is that done well? Where is their high-quality staff? 2nd. . . .Where are the opportunities to leverage private invest-

ment? Where can we make the most difference? I can tell you underlying all this is my perception, . . . that this city doesn't have a lot of time left, that given the rate of disinvestment and the plight of the middle class.

Leaders of the community movement were more cynical, feeling Ball was responding to foundation pressures to sculpt the community movement according to the agenda of the foundations and the corporations:

I mean when [Ball] was hired there was discussion [with the foundations] as to: Here was what our agenda is, we're tired of putting money in the neighborhoods and not seeing a lot of turn around. We want to see focused concentration. . . . So it goes back and forth, but he always uses the excuse the foundations . . . like they're holding it over his head. I mean, if he doesn't come up with a good model he's not going to get the money. So it gives him total control of how to pick and choose the groups.

Ball bragged to me, and I assume to others, how through targeted financing he was slowly able to change the missions of selected CBDOs. I traced out several such cases and watched how HCP convinced one organization, Southeast Development, to switch its focus to working on a larger and quite visible commercial building, rather than continuing its older agenda of aiding the small merchants in the community. I wondered about the borderline between persuasion, seduction, and ideological rape.

To the woman directing the CBDO, HCP initially appeared as a knight on the white horse since "the money looked wonderful, they had a press conference at the City Club, champagne, we were like the, you know, got our pictures in the paper." And Southeast Development was quickly placed on the HCP dole.

When HCP first came and they picked their first victims we were thrilled to death that we were one of the groups. Well, we're going to be on the gravy train, we're going to get this money and then slowly, you know, at first it's like we write our proposal and they write their proposal and jibe with what we're doing.

Certain compromises were made, as John Ball wanted a large building to be refurbished, rather than the smaller projects usually done by Southeast Development. Repeating to me what she claimed Ball said, the director explained,

He loves this building that we took over, this old vacant building, and we renovated it and we brought in, well sure, that's part of it, I mean, when there's an empty building we will serve as developer as a last resort.

But then as the CBDO shortly discovered, all its efforts were being refocused on this one project, and the executive director started to question the wisdom of HCP's goal "to do large-scale glitzy developments." She wondered,

> Is that serving the needs of the people in my neighborhood? No. They need jobs, they need job training. My little merchants need these store-front [projects] that will do most good. John could care less about store-front renovations—came right out and told me that he won't fund for it. . . . He does not see where building by building, slowly that's making a difference in my neighborhood.

She began to disagree with HCP's demands, but was feeling more like a captive of the intermediary. Ball was telling her:

> Production, production do this, we don't care about your other agendas, its not important. . . .
>
> And, yeah, big production. Not, like they say my little storefronts, but what were some of my other benchmarks, . . . for one merchant to finally be able to acquire a grimy used car lot to create parking so that he can stay in business. That is very important to our neighborhood. I mean, it's like because it's one little project, it's only going to me an acquisition of a parking lot that might total $100,000, it just doesn't matter. It's very important for us to do that. John says, "I don't care about that." . . . I mean all these things that my board and my staff and my neighborhood I believe think are so important, John doesn't care about. . . . The only ones with physical development with big-scale projects are all he cares about.

But by this time, however, her group's financial dependence on HCP had increased:

> My budget's only $176,000. They're giving me $57–60,000 of my budget. Do I just say, "No, right here, I'm not doing this stuff, I don't want your money, or do I go for it?"

To increase the pressure on her, so she thought, the issuance of her operating budget from HCP was delayed. In desperation she called Ball:

> I said John, "I need money."
>
> "Well, let me see what I can do, I'm leaving in two weeks on vacation."
>
> I said, "John I've got to have the money before you leave on vacation. I'm not going to make payroll."
>
> That was kind of a lie—I could have borrowed money from another account, but the fact is that the day before he leaves on vacation he comes by the office saying something like you'll get your check if you're willing to sign this letter.

Bottom line is, what the letter said was, "we're going to give you your money through December . . . providing this is what you do by January, and if that's not done by January, you're not going to get your next amount." Basically, tight control of both properties and preliminary financing in place. . . . I mean, I feel like I am being held hostage. Literally, I had my choices were to not sign it and try to fight with 'em and go to my board and say I can't repay 'em.

Later in a sort of reconciliation she claimed that Ball offered her a year's sabbatical to get more training. She refused, thinking it was simply a way of allowing HCP to replace her in her absence.

The seduction of Southeast Development was symbolic of the broader conflicts HCP created in Flat City. Some developmental activists felt that the production models imposed by the intermediary would alienate their organizations from their neighborhoods and require the CBDOs to "totally [sell] out and just ignore . . . what we think important and what we think our communities think are important in order to stay alive in order to get the dollars."

When presented with this argument, Ball retorted,

I understand the rhetoric, the language, I've been there. My challenge to that is, "Show me what's the outcome of your activity?" . . . [Y]ou can show me you had so many community meetings around public safety, you did this with the police, you did that, and has it changed the crime statistics? Has it slowed the out-migration? Has it increased investment? What's the outcome? What's the change? We'll fund projects or institutions that do those things, but give us more than anecdotes. We gotta see something that's definable. And people by and large engaged in that kind of discussions can't show you the outcome.

A case in point was the refurbishment of an old community school that a CBDO had transformed into an office building. The developmental activist admitted having real difficulty with the project and appreciated the help provided by HCP, but felt that she had to fight to get support. The community group wanted to save the building since it "is esthetically pleasing, it has historical significance to people outside the community." But when asked for help,

John wanted that building torn down and he came back to us repeatedly and said, "You need to tear that building down and put up a matching one-story cinder block like the other one and that's what needs to go there. And you will see, because you will not be able to do the project. You will see that that's right."

Still the CBDO director admitted

once our intention was clear and once it became known that we could do this project, then HCP got on board and did provide some assistance.

Yet the pressure remained:

> [W]hat we're told repeatedly is that it comes down to production. That the foundations are going to invest in neighborhoods, but they don't want to invest without being able to measure and evaluate what their money bought and the only way they can do that easily or more easily is to be able to count units.

Ball's narrative provided a different cast to the same story. He admitted that he preferred tearing down the building, but continued,

> [T]hat project was defined by them, not by us. . . . When I came to Flat City that project was already two or three years old and the neighborhood that defined———School as a priority. . . . If you genuinely committed to building a decentralized infrastructure to some degree you have to allow people to set their own priorities.
>
> The issue for me was let's find out why it wasn't working and get it done. . . . But———School is not what I would have picked. . . . But they did select it, so we did it, mobilized a lot to get it done for them. I even had to bring a consultant . . . to help shape the deal for them.

An observer from the development community implied that Ball agreed to help on the school project only to claim the credit:

> John's great at hedging around it. . . . [HCP] reluctantly participated in it. And I think John was a real naysayer about if it could come together. [W]ell, it came together and then all of sudden you know, he'd like to be considered part of it, or associated with the success.

The battle over who would set the renewal agenda in Flat City continued. The foundation community prepared a set of Policy Recommendations for the Future of HCP, proposed the development community focus upon housing production, downplayed efforts to bring about economic development, and suggested all community programs follow the HCP model. As such, CBDOs' "primary obligation [are] to be a production engine" while HCP would provide overall direction to the movement. Further, the recommendations suggested eliminating the CBDOs' role in the governance of HCP by arguing that those from the CBDOs who were on the board faced a conflict of interest, since their organizations received money from HCP. A ranking foundation official remarked:

> I was not an advocate of having the neighborhood groups on the board myself. That was somewhat of a compromise. I was more of the opinion that HCP should be a vehicle for coordinating the private sector's response to the neighborhood development and that it was important it be sensitive and responsive to the neighborhood development.

To roil the waters further, foundation support for HCP itself was not all that firm, nor was their support for John Ball, whom the foundation people felt was too accommodating to the CBDOs.

The battle continued in numerous small incidents and behind-the-scene events. Though the foundations claimed they were not talking to the developmental activists in private, several activists described such meetings at which they made direct complaints about both HCP and John Ball's heavy-handed style. As a result of such nonconversations, HCP decided to hold a retreat to discuss the overall direction of the community development movement. Rather than calm the waters, the retreat exacerbated tensions. Developmental activists claimed that they had reached compromises with HCP on the new direction and governance of the intermediary, but the compromises were simply ignored in a revised draft of HCP's developmental agenda.

I discussed this meeting with Ball and mentioned that the developmental activists had not fought back because they feared losing funding. With animation he responded:

> Well, fuck em. If they haven't got the guts to deal with that, I can't help it. . . . I'm sorry. . . . [I]f you want to then go off and bitch under a rock somewhere, nobody will pay any attention to you.
>
> My grantees are the ones we fight the most with. . . . If you can't cope with that kind of environment . . . how the fuck are you going to save your neighborhood? . . . So I don't buy it.

Another forum through which the CBDOs battled HCP was at the meetings of their coalitions. For instance, the Housing Alliance, a consortium of the leading producers of affordable housing in Flat City, held several sessions primarily to argue about HCP's suggestion to eliminate some of the old-line street activists from the Housing Alliance's board. Still, the alliance was following HCP's mandate and pushing its members to produce more homes.

Other attempts to curtail HCP were spearheaded by the citywide commercial and industrial development coalition, the Association for Business Development (ABD), that included most of the CBDOs doing economic development work. ABD prepared and forwarded to HCP a strongly written letter that argued that the focus on production distracted from holistic community building, blasted the proposed changes in HCP's board structure, and argued that HCP "should not operate as a top-down gatekeeper of development resources needed by that community." Further, ABD pointed out how by ignoring the industrial retention work done by CBDOs, HCP was going against the "specifically tailored community development and capacity-building agendas" of established CBDOs.

Ball argued with me against the thrust of the ABD letter. He pointed out, quite vociferously, that pressure to produce had become a necessity, even if it ruffled feathers in the community-development movement:

We had to make some difference. We had to really drive a tough hard aggressive agenda. . . . [T]he City's dying, it is literally dying. . . . Go look at East St. Louis, there is a pattern we can look at if we're not careful.

So, there is a sense of desperation around here. . . . [I]n order to drive the kind of agenda I believe these neighborhoods need . . . you have to have institutions of sufficient weight that they can truly manage a sophisticated, long-term hard agenda. . . . We're going to select certain places and opportunities. So I've done it and there's no way around it. And that occasions a lot of hard feelings.

The dispute continued. As my study drew to a close, the relationships between funders, intermediaries, and the community development movement (as well as within the latter) remained unsettled. Ball later left the city.

## REFLECTIONS ON DEPENDENCE UPON THE INTERMEDIARIES AND THE FOUNDATIONS

In spite of such conflicts, most often both intermediaries and foundations worked with the developmental activists in constructive efforts to help renew poor neighborhoods and joined together to lobby government to support the community development movement. The squabbles portrayed are akin to family arguments. The participants recognize that they share a common goal, must work together against a world that can be hostile, and participants understand one another's perspectives. At conferences or in the anterooms of foundations, developmental activists, foundation officials, and those from the intermediaries engage in serious conversations about what community renewal should entail.

These narratives point out that the community development world is entangled in terms of interpersonal relationships and complicated interorganizational networks. Within this world, the battles over direction are rarely one sided, with the victor determined only by brute force. At the extreme, some CBDOs are defunded by intermediaries and other community-based development organizations stand little chance of receiving money from foundations.

But more often, there is frank discussion about ideas, about the direction of the movement, in which money speaks loudly, but does not drown out other conversations. Foundation personnel are willing to take a chance, and while intermediaries need to respond to their corporate funders, intermediaries also need to find ideas that will work. As the next chapter argues, the ideas come about from the discoveries made by the developmental activists as they ponder their experiences of neighborhood work and recast these reflections as an organic theory of community renewal.

CHAPTER 6

# Being a Conscience and a Carpenter

## An Organic Theory of Community-based Development

> You are not real estate developers, you are community developers, and
> there's a difference.
> —a newcomer to the field repeating the words of her mentor
>
> The mission of [CBDO name] is to create assets for our community, its
> residents, neighborhoods and institutions.
> —part of the mission statement of a CBDO

Up to this point, the book has described the accomplishments of the community-based development organizations, the tensions that developmental activists face as they try to balance off contending missions, and the pressures to comply with agendas put forth by the funders of community development work. The image communicated is that of small organizations buffeted both by contradictory local circumstances and a powerful exogenous environment.

In this chapter, I begin to discuss how, in spite of these internal tensions and external pressures, developmental activists collectively are able to frame, both for themselves and for their financial supporters, what community-based development can be about. In subsequent chapters I describe the institutional techniques—of leveraging external funding so that CBDOs can accomplish their own agendas; of setting up coalitions and trade associations that advocate for the movement and propagandize its ideology—through which this framing is communicated to others.

In this chapter, I focus on the ideology itself, what I have labeled as the organic theory of development. An *organic theory* is a coherent set of political, economic, and social ideas that provides both a vision of what ought to be and how that vision can be obtained. An organic theory guides developmental activists to enable them to reconcile the tensions CBDOs face as the development organizations seek to bring about what at first appear to be contradictory goals. The emerging organic theory then is diffused to intermediaries, foundations, and to a lesser extent government, as the ideological image of what community development ought to be about.

## THE GUIDING THEORIES OF ORGANIC INTELLECTUALS

Organic theories emerge as activists, reflecting on their experiences, induce what works, why, and what are the broader goals. A home builder explained how his understanding of what development should be about emerged experientially:

> I didn't get it out of no book, I got it out of the streets. I got—[what] was a real problem, I listened to the people I was there holding their hands. I know what the problems are.

Organic theories are tested in the cauldron of practice and respond to the problems at hand.

Such reflective practitioners, Gramsci's *organic intellectuals*, share experiences with one another and by doing so create a shared ideological shape for a movement, one that emerges, not through appeal to abstract principles or an imposed tradition, but rather by deliberating about which efforts at social change have failed and which succeeded. As such,

> organic intellectuals . . . conduct their intellectual inquiries through the practical activities of social contestation. . . . They create symbols and slogans that disclose the commonalities among seemingly atomized experiences, and they establish principles that unite disparate groups into effective coalitions. (Lipsitz 1995, pp. 9–10)

In creating an organic theory, a multipart conversation takes place, in which organic intellectuals communicate both with others in their social movement and reflexively with themselves. Through contemplation about praxis they bring forth an ideology on what needs to be accomplished and why. These self-reflections are then shared at meetings, through professional associations, writings, and training sessions. Within the community development movement, an organic theory provides reasons why a narrow concern with physical production devoid of attention to community empowerment will fail. It communicates that building homes or businesses are a means to achieve broader values, not an end in and of themselves. An organic theory communicates to the staff of the CBDO, to funders, and to the developmental activists themselves that "doing the deal" involves more than a technical solution to a narrowly defined problem.

A developmental activist, now working for a coalition, described the process of thinking about what constitutes the guiding theories as "almost like the historical dialectic." Another illustrated the dialect as he explained to me how his organization reflected on what it had accomplished in light of its overall goals. At a retreat for the staff and board of his CBDO, the participants were evaluating whether or not an economically successfully industrial park had accomplished what the CBDO wanted to achieve. The park was profitable for the CBDO as an organization, but did not seem to help the neighborhood poor:

> We had an agreement that [businesses in the industrial park] would try to work toward hiring neighborhood residences and yet every time [the staff] would come to the board with an industrial park project [a board member] would say "the guy next door to me doesn't have a job yet."

"Getting the guy next door a job" became an iconic statement of the core of the organic theory of what this CBDO was about: not simply increasing income within the community, or for the CBDO, but ensuring that individuals in the community benefit.

From numerous conversations with developmental activists and by listening to their speeches at meetings and reading their publications, I have tried to piece together the components of the organic theory. First, the theory speaks to the moral necessity of not abandoning communities that are facing overwhelming difficulties. Next, it argues that the projects undertaken should be part of broader scheme of holistic renewal intended to create and maintain wealth within the communities in ways that empower both individuals and the community as a whole. The completed project—a school refurbished as a community center, attractive single-family homes that replace burnt-out shells, a shopping center where none existed before—manifest to the world that there are opportunities, and not just needs, within neighborhoods in which CBDOs work. Finally, the theory suggests that though small and fiscally dependent, CBDOs can bring about the goals of holistic renewal by mastering tactics of niche organizations that can strategically leverage resources from a wide variety of funders so that the agenda of the CBDO itself is achieved.

## THE MORAL MISSION OF COMMUNITY-BASED DEVELOPMENT ORGANIZATIONS

An organic theory begins with statements of the ought, why community-based development organizations must attempt to bring hope to neighborhoods of deprivation. Such ideas are illustrated in the mission statements of the CBDOs that emerge only after development activists, board and staff argue at retreats over the purpose of the organization. Such sessions are treated quite seriously, as a developmental activist described them:

> [Our organization is] going through a whole about year long strategy-planning activity where we are rewriting our whole mission statement. . . . That process has been tedious, hopefully it has been sensitizing. At times, it has been angry.

The emerging mission statements articulate what the CBDO is now about. An Hispanic economic development organization stated its overall purpose as

bring[ing] low-income residents of [city's] Hispanic community into the
economic mainstream. . . . While questions of poverty and racism will
and should continue to be debated, it is our belief that we can "do"
something about these problems right now. The slogan of [CBDO] is
"meter mano," which means "put our hand in."

And it then articulated an overall model of how this can come about through
commitment "to the development of a sustainable regional economy, based upon
economic justice, self-determination, and respect for diversity."

Mission statements evolve as developers learn more what has to be accomplished and why. An established housing and business development organization
added the phrase "and for comprehensive social service development" to the
older mission statement of helping low-income people in the neighborhood. The
executive director explained:

[W]e've gone from a strategic plan that emphasized that we are the
developers of quality housing and the creator of jobs . . . to redefine
ourselves in terms of a totally different mission statement. A mission
statement that talks about that the purpose of [the CBDO] is to *"build
assets toward community for its residents and for its institutions and to do it
by investing land, buildings, people and industry."*

I hope that begins to signify a maturity of the organization. That
it's going to begin to look at itself differently in terms of preserving
institutions and value, creating wealth. And that part of that charge
includes . . . to get people into higher performing possibilities so that
education has to be fully integrated into our economic development
strategies; that mutual accountability and responsibility [is included] in
trying to help focus not simply people's understanding of their role in
the economy but also their role in the community. . . . [P]eople who are
part of our system need to begin to value themselves in relationship to
their community. That they need to be take responsibility for the Boy
Scout troops, the Little Leagues, the Girl Scout troops, the church cho-
rus, the things that help make community work and function as well as
the boards and the committees and all of those issues.

Such mission statements articulate a vision of how empowerment for the
community comes about through a process of holistic development. In a statement
prepared both for the CBDO's board and staff, a developmental activist argued,

We are a community-controlled developer, not simply a not-for-profit
developer building in a low-income community. Our projects are a
means for people to take control of their lives, to be empowered in a
number of ways.

Another developmental activist reflected that even though the organization mainly worked with the business community, "we are not an industrial group, we're a community development organization. Our constituency is much broader than just the manufacturers."

Within these statements of underlying purpose, the uniform tone is one of hope and possibility along with a rejection of the structural inevitability of community decline. The director of a community-based industrial development organization shared these thoughts:

> People said it couldn't be done because there are international forces were at work that were going to devastate [the region]. And we said that there are some things that we can do. And that we have to do or it disables you if you don't.
>
> We can't do anything about the yen or the dollar or the deutschmark. But we can do something about the brick going through the window of the CEO's car. . . . So we set about doing things that we had some control over. And we found out real fast that we control a hell of a lot more than we really thought.

A developmental activists communicated this fundamental motivating belief that success can occur by thanking the organization's supporters for keeping those in the CBDO "profoundly ignorant of the impossible" while this guiding ideal appears in the motto of the national trade association, the National Congress for Community Economic Development:

WORKING
WONDERS
in America's Communities

Central to the moral mission is an obligation to act as the developer of last resort to fight back against problems of systemic economic injustice. A speaker at a national conference noted,

> The idea then is to create institutions within the community that will off set those two things that our system of economics [creates], which is the rich get rich and the poor get poorer.

And this is done, as explained by a Republican lawyer turned developmental activist, by attempting what others fear to try:

> It is a tough row to hoe these days, especially since financing has just dried up, but, and it is tough because that is why we are doing it. **That is why not-for-profits do it, because it is tough, because the for-profits won't do it.**

This moral obligation requires looking beyond the mere bottom line since

economic development must include putting money into the community, **which will not make money for the investor**. This investment will create an institutional structure within the community which will move people into the economic mainstream.

Further, as an executive director of a small CBDO that had just completed its first housing project reflected, the physical redevelopment is a means to a broader end:

Our mission is to empower and educate and advocate. . . . It's not to produce anybody's anything or deliver anybody's anything. It's to empower and educate and advocate for the kind of changes that will make the neighborhood a neat place to live. And it's going to keep it a neat place to live. And they [funders] don't understand that.

And this work must be accomplished no matter what. On a tour for visiting activists, the executive director of a commercial and industrial redevelopment group remarked, "This is the heart of the central business district. It is the most difficult place to work." I asked him then why do they work there:

Because that is where the CDC should be, where the private sector, where the private market doesn't operate, doesn't function.

Still, developmental activists recognize the overwhelming difficulties they face, working in the worst of the country's neighborhoods. Soon after one of the homes his organization had built was torched, the head of the group reflected:

I thought to myself, "Well, you're really not engaged in affordable housing if you don't have an arson every now and then." I mean that's like the reality of what's going on in urban neighborhoods . . . and it increasingly is out of your control.

Yet continuing even in the face of failure is part of the moral mission:

It makes us more authentic to have "failures" because I don't think you can work in this kind of a ministry without [failure], I mean you're dealing with people who are living right on the edge and if everything was wonderful you probably weren't selecting the right folks for your families.

These beliefs enable developmental activists to accept setbacks, and then continue on with their tasks. As one shared, "I am very optimistic in the morning, I am less optimistic in the afternoon," while another, working in one neighborhoods still unrepaired from the sixties, admitted "I know there are times when I come the street and have my rose-colored glasses on and I see things developing and evolving and I that keeps [me] going and I also see the reality of what is there."

This sense of fighting back in spite of the difficulties is especially important for nascent community-based development organizations. A director of a new organization reflected:

> I have a mentor who expects very big things of us, of me. And when things get discouraging and none of the board members know and I don't know, I can get on the phone and say, "Oh fuck. This thing is falling apart. You know it's just never gonna happen." And this person can pump me back up and say "Oh yeah but it's going to. Talk to so and so. They know such and such." These people are major lovers that way. They are really into sharing.

But developmental activists recognize that what they are doing constitutes but a drop in the bucket; their mission is not to solve the problem but rather to become an exemplar to encourage others to become involved. In spite of his group being one of the larger housing developers in his city, the head of the CBDO explained:

> We think of ourselves as catalysts. . . . Over the years we've done over six hundred units of housing. And there is I am sure there are at least fifty families in this community that could use it for everyone we've served. . . . But the fact of the matter is, it is a drop in a bucket. So if that drop doesn't . . . ignite activism and ignite a sense among people about what can be done when people work collectively and struggle for what is needed, then we've done little.

Being a catalyst is made possible because a CBDO can take risks and need not profit from each and every endeavor:

> When there's an empty building we will serve as developer as a last resort. That's how we view ourselves. If there's a party that can't get off the ground, can't get private investment, then we'll do it, but my goal is to bring the private sector in and do that on my own and keep these merchants and their little stores going. . . . We are losing money on the deal but it makes it all work.

For-profit developers cannot take chances on deals that appear to be risky. But a

> nonprofit development corporation or neighborhood development community based organization can do the deals that might be marginal. Can do the deals that can the save the neighborhood. That can do the deals to lead the way and provide the window of opportunity for private development to take place.

CBDOs can take political risks and try innovative types of projects that others might fear to attempt. Doing so bridges the gap between what for-profits feel is financially possible and what the neighborhood needs:

> We know there is a gap in every project. We know there is a bad image in every neighborhood. . . . So our job is, how you turn these liabilities into assets how do you get over these hurdles?

Bridging such gaps though requires experimentation, but that is the job of the CBDO.

> Every project involves a certain amount of risk. That's why CBO's [sic] are there in the first place. Because we absorb that risk and impact in order to improve the community. You know, we'll go out on a limb and try something. If it fails, it fails. You know, but our jobs are to be out there making changes, and taking those risks that the business community won't do.

Further what the CBDO accomplishes remains as a physical symbol that change is possible, especially when change can "bring back ownership and control to those who have been deprived".

## TOWARD A THEORY OF HOLISTIC DEVELOPMENT

The core of the organic theory describes the symbiotic connection between the physical changes made to the geographic community and the social and personal consequences that affect the individuals within the community. The goal is to do work that empowers both the community as a whole and those already living there by enabling them to control assets.

Empowerment for the individual comes about by gaining the resources—the assets—both in an economic sense and in terms of individual character development—that builds toward independence. Assets are financial, but are also measured by the increased capabilities of individuals to grow. Homes are provided, but also the knowledge on how to maintain them. Job opportunities are created, but in ways that enable those in the neighborhood, not outsiders, to have an opportunity to work.

Community-based development organizations create housing, job training, and employment programs that recycle money inside the community, not simply distribute wealth that can be spent elsewhere. Doing so both empowers the collective community as well as the individuals. An innovative developmental activist shared with me the chart in table 6.1, which presents his theory of how a CBDO links investment in human development skills to the physical changes made in the neighborhood:

## Table 6.1. Human Investment Strategy

*Education*

| | |
|---|---|
| Focus and Specialization | High School Diploma |
| Job Improvement Assistance | Home Ownership Training |
| Job Apprenticeship | Self Training |

*Assets*

| | |
|---|---|
| Sweat Equity | Individual Development Accounts |
| Equity | Joint Savings |
| Institutional Affiliation | Avocation |

*Community*

| | |
|---|---|
| Mutual Accountability | Committee Boards |
| Mutual Support | Work Groups Classes |
| Shared Housing | |

*Character*

| | |
|---|---|
| Lease | Loan Repayments |
| Leadership | Voluntarism |
| Conflict Resolution | Attendance |
| | Parenting |

This portrait was not of some abstract theory, but rather synthesized a series of projects already underway to bring about holistic redevelopment of the neighborhood. Separately, each project either built a visible product or provided a member of the community with measurable skills so as to please a funder, but taken together the separate activities created an overall program of holistic community renewal.

The CBDO worked to teach people in the neighborhood how to repair homes, and by doing so both improve the physical appearance of the community, while providing job skills to those involved in the construction. Some homes were sold or rented at affordable rates to community members, but only after these individuals attended education and training programs that taught about the responsibilities of home ownership or of apartment living. Individuals literally gained a stake and commitment in their community. The physical environment of the neighborhood was improved, while those housed learned the importance of mutual accountability through sharing committee work in tenants' and owners' associations.

Holistic development requires concurrently focusing on creating physical improvements within the community, while working on the social needs that enable the physical projects to succeed. Material improvements cycle back into social betterment. Individuals who feel empowered after gaining skills or owner-ship of property, contribute to the neighborhood through volunteer work, or by being role models for the young. Home ownership joins together the ecology of community change and individual betterment, as it physically improves the appearance of the community, as well as sheltering individuals. It creates both material and social assets for the poor that in turn build toward a sense of collec-tive social responsibility.

Core to the organic theory is the understanding that CBDOs cannot fix one social problem without responding to others—poor education leads to poor jobs, hurting parenting, and so forth. The goal is to work with the individuals to solve their problems in ways that the community as a whole is improved. Let us step back and examine the separate components of the theory of holistic change.

*Building toward Community Autarchy*

Core to the organic theory is the premise that neighborhoods are worth preserv-ing and should not simply be tossed on the dustheaps of social change. Organic theorists oppose social programs that end up encouraging beneficiaries to flee from neighborhoods of the poor (Lemann 1994), a process that extracts (social and economic) wealth from neighborhoods of need. CBDO directors argue that, for some, flight is impossible, while preserving communities is vital since people missed by inadequately funded social welfare programs have no choice but to stay. Instead development should be about creating locally controlled assets to bring about "the vision of a neighborhood-based economy where assets would be con-trolled by the people who lived here . . . the vision of the neighborhood being neighborhood owned." A community gains power **over** rather than dependence **on** outsiders. As a CBDO argued in its newsletter "the philosophy . . . is that peo-ple in our communities can do something about our economic conditions, instead of waiting for and depending on government assistance."

The model builds upon experiential insights that parallel those presented in import substitution theory (Persky et al. 1993). One theorist, the developer of the auto-repair place previously described, explained:

What we have is a community that exports more money than it imports. Part of what we are trying to do is to change that balance of payments. . . . Over 53% of the community is rental despite being mostly single family. On Friday people export rent checks. The utility bills are higher than they ought to be because of the age of the housing stock and lack of energy conservation measures so we export more wealth than we ought to in the form of utilities. And, when people have to go outside of the community to buy goods and services that are no longer here that's gone in terms of exporting. What we really are trying to do over

time is to change the balance of payments, to try to create wealth here
in this community by importing dollars not exporting them.

Another CBDO leader, who ran a CBDO half-time, and then acted as a consultant to other development groups, interpreted the L.A. disturbances of 1992 in
terms of the model of community ownership:

> I didn't see houses burning, I didn't see factories burning . . . I saw retail
> chains burning and being looted. . . . In a retail store you take products
> that are made somewhere else and put them on display for distribution
> in a community and in that exchange take income or cash of which
> there's precious little to begin with and send it somewhere else.

Organic theorists justify projects in terms of how well they enable a community to become more self-sufficient. In an Hispanic neighborhood, a CBDO
planned to refurbish an old building and rent space to local entrepreneurs who
would employ community members. The executive director explained the reasons for the project:

> There are eight bars. . . . They don't hire anybody from the community
> to tend bar. They are all owned by people from outside. . . . I mean all
> the cash those eight bars generate, none of it even changes hands in
> the community even once. It leaves at 2 [in the morning] and it is
> gone. So our idea is to have some development in the restaurant and
> nightclub bar kind of thing and store and shops and maintain owner-
> ship either [by the CBDO] or [by the] community people.

Waste recycling can become a means to control wealth, while at the same
time making the community a better place in which to live:

> the role of that [recycling] center was . . . to put cash in the hands of
> local residents, kind of trash for cash philosophy and then secondly, to
> make an impact on the environment. . . . [T]here would be spinoff
> opportunities in terms of remanufacture of materials and whether it was
> park benches or fire logs or pencils that could be made.
>     . . . At some point once we stabilized the employment piece that
> we would offer some kind of ownership to the folks working there, to
> really empower them and make them real stakeholders in the project,
> so that was really important in terms of the development of our guiding
> principles in developing this project.

Keeping wealth in a community also becomes an assertion of neighborhood
and ethnic pride:

> First we're trying to recreate a neighborhood that is a vital part of . . . the
> African-American culture in [city]. . . . We're gonna rehab some of the
> stock there and we're going to build new housing stock when necessary

and . . . we're going to create a scattered site limited equity cooperative. Why a cooperative? Because . . . [it] maintain[s] an African-American presence in an ownership position. We're not going to create a rental neighborhood. We're not trying to create a low-income neighborhood; we're trying to create a balanced neighborhood of owners rather than renters.

A project to build a Mercado, a facility with individual stalls for community entrepreneurs within a larger, commonly maintained facility, became an expression of community pride and ownership. As the organic theorist described:

> Small business entrepreneurship is not our vision of the answer to economic problems and unemployment problems. But [the Mercado] really fits our criteria. . . . It focuses on local ownership versus the outside tell[ing] us what to do, in a collective way, as opposed to just individual entrepreneurs helping start individual businesses. It focuses culturally on the typical foods that different ethnic groups now travel to get. Blacks travel . . . to get the cut of ribs they want. Hispanics travel all over town to get what they want. Focus here, "Hey, my ethnic group is important, I'm going to stay."

The project was designed to keep wealth within the community and to create new wealth for community members. Similarly, by intent, community-based development organizations create local employment through their own enterprises. A CBDO that housed its own social service programs in buildings that it rebuilt found that "we are ourselves are now a significant employer on the west side. We have 450 employees. . . . And we hire from within and we promote from within."

Arguing for community autarchy, though, does not mean excusing the rest of society from providing the capital needed for redevelopment. But having an locally controlled economic base, allows requests for capital to be made from a position of strength, not from dependence. As the activists in New Community's Corporation argue,

> [The CBDO] has already borrowed over 90 million dollars to construct housing. Self-reliance is not building a tent city. It is using all the available resources without losing control. (Linder and Shattuck 1991, p. 16)

Or, as described in a handout describing the auto repair center, "Don't give us a piece of the pie . . . just help us gather the ingredients and we'll make our own."

**Complementary Housing and Commercial Development Activities.** Building toward an economically autarchic community, requires focusing on work that recycles money within the community. To build such a community, both affordable housing and commercial opportunities are needed. In a minority area of a smaller city, an African-American activist reflected:

> We suddenly realized that we had developed a lot of housing, but . . . there was absolutely nothing here in terms of economic activity. So as a result of that you had housing that either would die over the long run from lack of infra-structure support or would begin to attract the very worse element.

With this understanding in mind, this developer of numerous apartment units, refocused the CBDO's efforts to construct a small, inner-city shopping mall with a full-service supermarket, drug store, hairdresser, video store, and dry cleaner.

Another organic theorist described the importance of linking housing and commercial development in ways that create an economically self-reliant and integrated community:

> In order for our neighborhood to be a good place to live . . . we have to build economic balance. . . [T]here aren't going to be any bakeries here if there is no middle class people with enough money to afford jelly-rolls. . . . The commercial work we did was not only to provide economic development and jobs and bring investment in, but, . . . if you are looking to buy a house . . . the . . . commercial corridors are the display windows of our neighborhood. . . . A residential block can be beautiful, can have lovely lawns and beautiful homes and well-dressed kids playing . . . but you will never see it. . . . So the commercial work is really key towards this overall logic and strategy which says we want to build a community of balance here.

Housing is simply not enough. The vision of integrating housing with commercial redevelopment is carried out, at times, even at a financial risk to the CBDO. A community-based development organization that had successfully completed several apartment complexes recognized that more was needed to bring about the renewal of the neighborhood. It attempted to set up a small strip of stores, including a needed supermarket, across from the apartments it owned. When commercial investors refused to join in, the CBDO started to fund the project itself. I commented about the costs to the CBDO and heard the following reply that argued for the need for a holistic approach:

> [I]t's a risky thing but from our perspective for the neighborhood to change and to support other economic development there has to be some things happening. You know it's a question of the chicken and the egg. [Do] you have residential first or do you have . . . retail first? Which comes first? . . .

If you get the rents low enough, people will move anywhere. . . . But if you expect to integrate the neighborhood in terms of incomes you've got to provide the retail services. Which means the same effort that's been put into housing in terms of subsidizing the rents down to the point that they can be affordable to people, you have to do the same thing with retail.

The CBDO though was handling the risk with caution.

It's probably the scariest thing we've gotten into since I've been here. . . . We're not going to let the agency go down the tubes. . . . We're trying to do be careful about it . . . the grocery store. . . . We use volunteers that are supportive of what we're trying to do. . . . It's scary.

The CBDO was being cautious to protect itself, yet recognized that the risky project was core to its broader mission of neighborhood renewal.

### Creating Material and Psychic Assets for the Poor

Development enables both communities and individuals to obtain material and psychological assets. Material assets empower by creating a stronger self-worth, for as a developmental activist argued, "If you own your own house, you are empowered." Assets enable the community as a whole to gain sufficient confidence to continue to reinvest in itself:

[B]uildings are real. . . . You can see them. And it does something to the community. It transforms a community in a way when you take something that wasn't there and put it there. And it builds power for the people on a whole new level.

Developmental activists learn that what they are about is not simply building structures, but creating community assets. An increase in material assets builds a psychic sense of empowerment, both to individuals, the community as a whole, and the organization itself. For instance, lease-purchase programs are meant to empower through providing ownership in ways that make those housed feel more responsible for their neighborhood. In general, quality housing empowers the poor, as a former street activist turned builder put it:

When people have a decent please to live, to go home every day, their ability to deal with every other issue that's out there is greatly increased. I don't have to worry about where I am going to live, what I am going to pay for rent. I can move onto that next step and worry about a whole lot of other things. . . . It is a self-actualization thing. You take care of your most basic needs and then you can move onto to the secondary level, up the ladder.

In general,

We have become more interested in entrepreneurship by poor people themselves as [the] preferred way of helping them. Just as we would prefer home ownership strategy over developing rental housing for the same reason. **Poor people need to own things**.

These models of enabling people to own assets paralleled ideas in Michael Sherradan's (1991) book *Assets and the Poor*, which argues that people can be helped out of poverty by establishing individual developmental accounts (IDAs). An IDA combines money that people earn with money given to them (as a social transfer) when they pass a life stage—completing school or training, or turning a certain age. These earned funds become a stake that is then used to acquire a valuable asset—equipment for a job, part of a down payment on a house, or college tuition. A leading organic theorist carried out the IDA model as an empowerment strategy.

Part of what we have experimented with this year in our teen-parents program is that we pay the kids $4 and then we take the fifth dollar and put it into a savings account in the credit union here. So that at the end of their year of working with us, they are going to have $1,500 . . . because you're making an investment in yourself now, we are going to help cause an asset to be created that you can invest in your future.

But organic theories evolve, based on experience. I interviewed this theorist a year and a half later and he explained how the assets-building approach had been modified based upon what had been learned:

The reality is that when you take it to young people in the youth investment program, they weren't happy about it. Because what they want is car, clothes, jewelry. . . . And, what you offer them is education, home ownership, employment opportunities, self-employment, or pension.

He restructured the program to teach the young about the value of longer-term investments by setting up mentorship programs between them and tradespeople in the community who had already invested in their own futures and could show the young people how and why to do so.

Confidence expands as people acquire material assets that show them the value of having a stake in society. In turn, this stake creates an ambition and a desire to own even more. A program to help train women as day-care providers had succeeded, at least in helping the participants set up such services in their homes. But these women wanted a cooperative that they would run. . . . Now before they were just individual women out there powerless in their houses locked in on welfare. And now they're starting what amounts to a business. They're going to have a loan fund and their going to have a fund that will take care of insurance, health insurance. . . . [T]hey've gone through [a training program] they've seen what they can do and they've got confidence from it.

CBDOs help set up tenants' councils that provide people with the psychic ownership of their residential environment. In such developments,

the tenants will be involved in making key decisions. . . . They will decide who will be renting the unit next door, they will be deciding what are the rules about storing broken-down cars on the property, they will decide various policies about maintenance. . . . We are giving . . . the renter a whole lot of things. Number 1, we're giving a sense of ownership; we're giving them a stake. We're letting them see how their actions or failure to act in certain cases . . . has impact upon the housing.

Empowerment, though, requires more than simply the ownership of assets. It comes about when the poor are responsible for maintaining these assets that root them to the social community. When, at first, I did not understand this concept of empowering responsibility, an organic theorist illustrated what it would mean for me:

Activist:    You own things. . . . You own stuff. What do you own?

HJR:        Me, now personally? Home, couple cars, hefty retirement funds. . . . Large bank accounts. Computers, . . .

Activist:    You have mothers and fathers and brothers. **But you own the problem. But it keeps you linked somehow to all this stuff.** History, memory, all kinds of things that you own, through the psychic as well as material. You own all kinds of stuff. You own education, you own things, how many books have you written? . . . They can't take that away from you. It's got your name on the cover, right? . . .

What does the "beneath the underclass" own? . . . [T]hey own nothing. How do you begin to develop ownership? In a successful family? Well, you give 'em the same thing that everybody's got.

Material ownership creates the responsibilities that enable people to respect themselves and take care of others.

Further, providing the poor with assets puts them on an even keel with those who grow up in wealthier circumstances:

if you want community people to get in business, you're going to have give them an edge because right now the playing field is dominated by capital and by people who have experience.

A level playing field involves protecting people from the inevitable failures that occur as they learn how to run a business. For the middle and upper class, parents provide such protection. By providing an economic shelter for start-up businesses, CBDOs give the poor similar protection so that new businesses have a better chance of succeeding and then perhaps bootstrapping to other efforts. In one of the programs to help welfare women return to work,

> each of the women who heads a household is expected to pursue a career development initiative for at least twenty hours a week, whether it is further education, service work, job training work. . . . One of them says she wants to be a lawyer. I mean, that's probably a longer-term venture than maybe she is going to be committed to pursue. But there are a lot of steps along the way that help show what it is going to take to try to get there. . . . [W]e are giving people a chance to begin that to think about it. Think about what could be possible.

Helping individuals gain the social skills they need is as vital as providing them with material assets. A developmental activist who ran a micro-enterprise fund remarked, "You pay as much attention to developing the business owner as you are paying to the developing the business," for example, by teaching people how to maintain checking accounts. As such, "our biggest measure of success is how have we empowered people so they can take control."

Empowerment involves teaching skills, but in a way that recognizes where those in need begin. The micro-enterprise director continued:

> I need to take a look at what at has been limiting her and help her to see what her capacity is and actually help her to see that her capacity can be limitless. . . . The process again is building her self-esteem skills, her success skills, so that she believes that. Then she begins to see what happens when she has small successes and her children begin to be affected by what she is doing. . . . As her successes increase and her business starts to move forward, more people take notice. The suppliers that she works with, the community in which she operates. So that building capacity for us means starting very small going at a step by step process and building on that process as you go so that developing the business owner goes hand in hand with developing her business.

However, balance is needed between working to empower by providing material assets and working to ensure that people learn to be responsible for what they now own. So, for instance, CBDOs that set up tenant-owned cooperatives still maintain management responsibility, though working to empower the tenants by slowly turning over these responsibilities to them. This

> step-by-step conversion will enable the cooperative to gain the necessary skills for managing their own homes while under the supervision of [the CBDO]. . . . Control over one's environment is the most important step toward controlling one's life. Therefore the CO-OP [housing cooperative] project is an empowerment program, bolstering independence and self-confidence and fulfilling the American dream of home ownership for our participants.

The border line, though, between enabling somebody to succeed and doing it for them can be fine. The promoter of the Mercado explained that there is a

> big difference between technical assistance and doing things. We are not going to do anybody's books. That's important. We'd love to lease a space to a bookkeeper and have them offer their services at decent rates. We think that would be a great marriage but we are not going to make that happen. . . . **There is a difference between hand holding and enabling.**

Organic theories of empowerment are tempered by hard-nosed realism, as developmental activists learn from experience that people can be disempowered because of their ignorance of social norms, as much as by lacking opportunities. Enabling people to get good jobs, in part, requires teaching people what jobs are all about. An activist in an inner-city community explained, "We're not talking to people who got laid off. We're talking to people who never worked and have no idea what they want to do and they get on the job for a week and they say, 'Oh, I hate this' and they walk away." Another theorist, an oldline community organizer, whose CBDO was working in a program that linked job training to affordable housing, fretted that when we

> take a person and move them from unemployment to employment, than we've got to look at why has this person not been employed? . . . What are the things that we have to overcome? . . . We have a young man say who grew up in a household, he's seventeen years old. Well, all of his life, he's never seen anyone . . . get up on a daily basis and [go] to work. And he's saw people coming to his household that may have a had a personal strange purse, he may have seen them selling little funny packages. So he thinks that is how you earn money. You know, he's never seen people who got up and go to a job.
> So all of a sudden we are going to this seventeen-year-old and say, "Okay, this is how you earn money." That is not going to happen over-

night. Because his values don't say that. His values go say and I am going out and snatch a purse, or I'll sell drugs to earn money.

In the effort to empower people, organic theorists realize they must understand how the broader problems in the community end up handicapping those in need.

As such, to the organic theorist, empowerment implies almost a communitarian spirit to teach people to take responsibilities for their actions. There is the need for "tough love," of imposing rules and regulations that build toward a collective responsibility. For instance,

> when we give someone a house [on a lease-purchase agreement], that's probably the best house that they ever lived in, . . . then they have something to protect. We set down the rules and the rules are that anybody who stays with you more than forty-eight hours has to go on the lease. Then they've got a definable set of parameters to share with people who would otherwise want to come in and be part of their good fortune.

The organization is helping people protect themselves from negative aspects of community life, but doing so requires modifying social behavior. People who are empowered through gaining new assets have a responsibility to work to protect their gains.

## Linking Community and Individual Empowerment

Programs that encourage people who gain skills to leave the community simply belie the essence of community-based and community-preserving development. The assets that people gain must also redound to the benefit of targeted communities. Getting someone a job is good, but it is better if people work near where they live and so can recycle money within the neighborhood's commercial areas.

The logic of helping individuals while helping the broader community can be seen in the development of an innovative day-care program. Initially, the CBDO had planned to build a day-care center within an industrial park adjacent to the neighborhood on a commuter route to downtown. In that location the center would serve the children of suburban parents commuting to downtown, and perhaps might provide jobs for a few community members. Yet this approach bothered the developmental activist, who saw little from the effort in the way of neighborhood uplift. Instead of immediately building the day-care center, the CBDO surveyed the community and learned that there were day-care needs within the neighborhood itself, that, at best, were being met through an informal, uncertified home day-care industry.

The CBDO then began a multistaged project. First, it taught individual women now on welfare how to manage a home day-care center. At the same time, the CBDO worked through another of its programs to construct up-to-code day-care facilities in the homes that these women would own. When certified as day-care providers, these women would then have the facilities in which to work and to serve other families within the community. The educational and monetary assets made available to needy individuals within the neighborhood would then redound to the benefit of the poor community as whole.

Other approaches can ensure that the broader community benefits, or at least is not harmed, by programs that initially can help only a few individuals. For instance, when a CBDO provides affordable cooperative housing to individuals, the new owners might want to sell out at a profit, especially if an area is gentrifying. Such an outcome flies in the face of the ideology that the benefit should be for the community. A developmental activist explained how he got around this problem in a cooperative built for the working poor in a neighborhood adjacent to a gentrifying community. He asked:

> [W]here does the community fit in, including the unemployed community? . . . Why should those [co-op owners], many of whom live in the community, and are about to be low income if they are laid off, be the only ones to control what may be a huge amount of capital that's put in [the housing]? Is there no broader [community] accountability? . . . We believe that the fifty people who live in that house are not the only ones who have the right to have some say over [neighborhood housing].

To handle the problem,

> we wrote into the partnership agreement [that] . . . [the CBDO has] a veto over any decisions to sell it for profit. If the tenants go condo, we could veto. And they have the right to transfer that right to any other nonprofit group . . . such as a tenant group. . . . That's putting the control over capital, the control over resources in the hands of people who wouldn't ordinarily have it.

And, as he summarized, "the whole approach is community-controlled development and empowerment through development." Further, the legal structure ends up empowering the poor against the rich:

> The yuppie realtors hate it. They are always trying to solicit the low-income tenants to sell their shares. They have no notion what a co-op, a true limited-equity co-op is. Why there is no financial incentive for them to do that.

Physical development projects sponsored by the CBDOs provide jobs or better homes, but of equal import they become signifiers of future hope. A project to improve the facades of commercial buildings, or provide a parking lot next to a neighborhood restaurant, brings traffic to the community, and assures owners of companies that they need not flee. A shopping strip was built as an open structure because of the "psychological implications of putting a lot of glass back in the neighborhood would have on people's appreciation [of the neighborhood]." Further, the shopping strip becomes a source of community pride:

> It's a very prestigious piece in the eyes of a lot of admirers. A lot of people in our community feel proud about it. . . . [It] is a showplace; people who come to town they bring people and they show it to them.

Successful projects show the young that there is still hope for people like themselves. The auto-repair shop provided jobs for adults, but also employment for the young. Work there

> gave the [youth] an exposure that is not the summer job where you push a broom, pick up paper, cut grass. We put them in the computers and work in the departments. You put them with a role model, a person [who] looks like them, eats like them, lives where they live, didn't have a lot of education. . . . You take a kid and have him go to a lawyer downtown [a program the city sponsored], he is an alien to them. They don't think they can be ever like that guy. They don't ever want to be like that guy. But if we assign a student to José, who has a fourth-grade education and who is now the general manager here, they know, they say, "Hey, I could be a general manager of a place because José did it." . . . That makes a whole different world. Those are people you need to put those kids with, people they can identify with who have made it.

Further, as workers gain a financial stake in the community, the community gains politically. For instance, those newly empowered with a job and property now want a political voice. The developmental activist who set up the auto-repair shop explained:

> [Voting] didn't come by getting them at meetings and telling how important voting is. It came by them starting to have some economic independence. José, our general manager, never voted before in his life. . . . He just bought a house and he had a job. He said, "I want to vote for that Hispanic guy." Something I couldn't get him to do for fifteen years. He says, "I got a house now, I got a car, I got a job. And my kids, you know, are in the school."
>
> Hey, that's social change, you know. It didn't happen by having voter registration drives. It happened by giving people a stake economically and then they turn on.

*The Strategy Implied by the Organic Theory Is One of Holistic Development*

The organic theory implies the need to link social, economic, and physical development, an approach that not all funders understand:

> Physical development is very easily seen, very sexy, everybody wants
> to get into physical development, a shopping mall, or rehab some houses,
> things that people could see. . . . It is not that easy on human develop-
> ment and some of the results are not always immediately seen because
> you are talking about changing attitudes, values, and behavior. . . .
> [W]hen [other developers] are talking about rehabbing housing and
> bringing low and moderate families into those new rehabbed facilities,
> . . . if they don't do something on the human develop side those build-
> ings are going to need rehabbing in ten years from now. They are
> going to be torn up again.

Activists understand that unless the social fabric is repaired, physical redevelopment will not last. An activist argued strongly, "We just can't fix houses,
that we got to fix neighborhoods" and further:

> when you deal with economic development, community development,
> you end up taking into consideration people, you know. . . . It is an
> education process and it is giving kids opportunities.

A national leader in the field, a successful home builder, asked rhetorically, if
CBDOs were only meant to build properties, "Why would I do condominiums in
a neighborhood where people don't have jobs?"

I asked a major housing developer to illustrate what holistic development
entailed. She answered by describing a welfare-to-work program her group set up:

> That would be our welfare mothers. . . . Our problem was twofold. One
> [in order] is to help women get off of welfare, you need day care. And,
> so we negotiated with the state . . . to pay for day care in our commu-
> nity. . . . And obviously if you just gotten a job, you're working at five,
> six dollars an hour, you still need day-care assistance. . . .
>
> Then you come to find out that there . . . isn't enough day care
> here. . . . Let's train welfare mothers to become day-care home
> providers, be self-employ[ed]. . . . [W]e then brought in the two local
> groups . . . to train women in our community. And come to find out
> that they cannot get licensed unless they are doing day care in the
> licensable space. And most of them were living in apartments that
> would not pass muster.
>
> So we said well why don't we combine that with our self-help hous-
> ing and let them move into brand-new houses. Well, here you have a

welfare women who is going to be self-employed, well how do you get a
mortgage for her. Okay? It is just about impossible. To get a mortgage
you have to been employed two years in the same place and . . . self-
employment is just a horror of all horrors to any mortgage company.

So we had to figure out, how could we do this . . . we got the right
to draw down on about $1,800 per person [from a federal program to
get people off of welfare] . . . as a work incentive thing. . . . We then
plunked that in a bank account which we put into that bank account
as they earn it on the sweat [equity].

That money, along with the sweat equity, became the down payment for a home
that both housed the former welfare client and provided her with an appropriate
place for day-care services. Social services and physical redevelopment flow one
from the other.

A theory of holistic development is about enabling people to build social
relationships, in part, by embedding the CBDO within the broader structure of
the neighborhood, through its staff living and volunteering within the community. And social capital is acquired through mentoring relationships in which
small startup businesses are put in touch with experienced business people, or
when, perhaps paternalistically, a CBDO encourages the families they house to
join "a family support program, using volunteer families from the many churches.
. . . It might mean helping finding a job. . . . It might mean helping getting the
kids enrolled in the nearby school."

In Appalachia, an activist argued how important it was to build social networks between those being helped whose lives are often in turmoil and others
whose lives are far more stable. This CBDO originally thought it best to use its
limited resources to help only those whose needs were the greatest, but rapidly
discovered that businesses run by just the very poor quickly ended up in trouble:

[H]aving all low income people in a business [means] you don't have
any stability. Everybody's life in crisis, . . . the car is still breaking down,
unless you can give people enough money that they can get a car that
is not breaking down. Somehow they have to learn to deal with all the
addictions in their family. Like this one is extorting money, gambler,
this one does drugs.

The solution found by the CBDO was to set up businesses that linked the individuals they were trying to help with more stable members of the community.

Social empowerment is as about developing relationships, a process CBDOs
try to encourage. A developmental activist described how his organization helped
small businesses:

The place I go to [for] lunch quite often . . . he's got a Mexican restaurant, he is starting to catch on. And, you know, maybe what we would

do is loan him a $1,000 to buy a new refrigeration system. And [he] begins to pay us back and . . . we expand it to $5,000 so he can do some remodeling. . . . All the while what we are doing is help him build a credit history. And then we are working with a bank that . . . has agreed to buy any loan that is performing out of our portfolio. . .

The idea here is not to make [the community entrepreneur] a permanent client of [the CBDO] but to serve as the bridge to get into banking relationship[s].

Another approach to help the community as a whole while working with individuals might be to set up crime watch patrols. For instance, Bethel New Life, in Chicago, has run aggressive campaigns attacking the drug trade, both by holding prayer vigils outside of drug distribution centers in the CBDO's neighborhood and marching to the suburbs from which the purchasers of the drugs come. Or to help reduce the image of crime in a neighborhood, a CBDO might undertake physical development work that might not make full sense economically. In one illustrative case, a CBDO acquired an expensive, yet derelict, building that had been the center of drug trade for the south side of a major city. The CBDO recognized that "nobody in the world was going to want to buy a house knowing that they are next to a crime-infested [building]." The project was justified in terms of its broader community impact.

The organic theory recognizes that physical development programs have a collective social impact far beyond the goods offered or the shelter provided. For instance,

you [can] . . . focus on housing as an issue related to character development. . . . Housing here isn't an end, it is a means. Housing as an end is this idealized two-car garage, air conditioning, privacy, in the suburbs. . . . It is a means in that a couple of grade schools have a 100 percent turnover in their student body. Housing as a means is a place where people can live for an extended period of time having stability so the kids can now attend the school system, have a relationship with the teacher. So an outcome of our work is to reduce the turnover in the grade schools.

More generally,

we are concerned about how the quality of housing affects the quality of life. We understand very strongly about the relationship of quality of housing with educational achievement. We understand very strongly the relationship of quality of housing and cost of housing to marital stability. We understand very strongly the connection, albeit sort of an amorphous connection, but the connection between quality of housing and the establishment of positive self-concept, which in turn informs things like educational achievement, the avoidance of juvenile delinquency, etc.

Similar linkages between the social and the economic occur in job creation programs. The director of the auto-repair shop argued that having a stable community employment for adults ended up socializing the young to be both better family and community members. He explained that one worker,

Ernie, . . . used to go across the street to the bar and get a couple of beers. And there were two young kids [working in the shop] who would go with him. . . . And, it was the best role model we could have. I mean Ernie would have two beers and then he would get up and say, "It is time for dinner, let's go." And they go. So what do you teach them? You didn't tell them they can't drink, 'cause they are going to drink. They taught them after you work you go out two beers and then you go home and eat dinner. You don't sit there until ten o'clock at night getting messed up. . . . It is not guaranteeing anything, but that is the role model you want for kids, because they can relate to it.

But funders fail to recognize the necessity for joining social programs to physical redevelopment ones and have difficulty understanding why buildings cost so much.

## EMPOWERMENT WITHIN THE NICHE

But how does a small, community-based organization that lacks its own resources bring about programs of holistic renewal? To answer this question, organic theorists have worked on how CBDOs can act as niche organizations. A niche organizations catalyzes other organizations to act, then builds upon the successes to encourage further groups to participate. A niche organization can succeed by bridging the gap between sectors. For instance, a CBDO can simultaneously speak the language of capitalism, that of community concern, and when necessary, advocacy.

Part of the responsibility of a niche organization is to catalyze others into action:

What we've been doing here is more of encouraging development to take place rather than doing it all. . . . We start off with the commercial side [and show] that we can build a commercial area that can survive, there is a market there for businesses. . . . On the housing side what we did was begin to show people . . . that the neighborhood is beginning to turn around.

Such catalytic activity ramifies. A rural developer who introduced the idea of flexible manufacturing to her area of the country described how "when you do something and it just starts. You know rip. . . **like a stone in a pond, it sends out**

**ripples.**" Setting up ripples is what a CBDO should be about. A housing developer explained the strategy for selective purchasing of buildings that hopefully would stimulate further change:

> there are twenty buildings in all that were considered to be the anchor buildings that were strategically located and they are like . . . the ends of the block . . . and the whole thought process, that is, somebody really put together development that would anchor the block, then the private market could do the infill in the middle of the block. . . . Those twenty buildings . . . were designed to serve as a catalyst. To stop the whole cycle of deterioration. . . . To make it possible for other people to reinvest in the community and to prevent further abandonment . . . and that would serve as a catalyst to energize that little section of the neighborhood.
>
> . . . So at best what [this CBDO] can sort of do is act as a catalyst and as sort of a leader and as a mobilizer . . . of resources in the community to bring attention to the area and do something about the area.

When acting as a catalytic niche, each and every activity need not show a profit, so long as the actions lead to further improvements. An activist explained:

> We look at [projects] them in terms of how many jobs get created and what's the potential for the business to grow. . . . Our waste metal container business and metal fabrication shop it may be profitable two years from now but we're not all that concerned about whether it makes money. . . . We're concerned with its developing a training program, developing or creating jobs within it.

A niche organization works to interrupt cycles of decay through strategic interventions. In neighborhoods with housing abandonment, a CBDO might work to stop the housing foreclosures that accelerate abandonment. A developmental activist explained the logic of this approach:

> We had to do a little bit of homework. . . to see what . . . kind of loses banks, for instance, were suffering from foreclosures. We found that an average of . . . $27,000 per home. . . .
>
> So, what we did was we said, "How much would it really cost to help these people . . . to get them up current, to put them in some kind of program with credit counseling, . . . enhance their employment and job income producing capabilities?" . . . Get the homes back in shape again. . . . [G]et the family back together again . . . deal with issues of abuse and things like that would more than likely happen when money is tight.
>
> We figured that it would cost us . . . $500–$600 month. We figured for a few months it would cost $2,500 per family for just the house

payments, and then we got other parts of the credit counseling and things like that . . . we're saving, you know, $25,000 or more by preventing the default.

By handling overhead social costs, the CBDO acting in the niche enables others to contribute to the renewal process. Many inner-city locations are ideal for small start-up businesses, but refurbishing a shell of an abandoned building to house these businesses is simply too expensive for a commercial developer. The CBDO obtains the grant to cover this renovation, a renovation that helps keep a neighborhood alive by providing spaces for needed businesses. Or a community-based development organization can take the time and effort to do background work that is not profitable for commercial firms to do. Why should a commercial developer check complicated titles or do land clearance work when green fields are available in the suburbs? A neighborhood developer, the former lawyer, explained that

> the titles of these properties are the most screwed-up titles you've ever seen in your life. And it discourages other people from developing this. Well, I got nothing else to do but develop the homes in this area. So, of course, I am going to keep on it until I finally get it. It took me two years and I cleared up the title and we will start construction.

But to succeed within the niche, the CBDO itself must become a recognized and respected organization or its suggestions will be simply tossed aside by the capitalistic businesses that often treat non-profits with disdain. Image counts and, as such, CBDOs must show they can become owners and players in the economic game. An organic theorist, a director of the only organization in a small city, explained:

> Just as I think that poor people need to own things, . . . community-based economic development organizations also have to own things. . . . [T]here is pride in that ownership [that] did something to cause the overall development of the organization.

And, with this image of success, the CBDO had become an important enough in the community to be consulted by both government and businesses before plans were made for renewal programs.

Further, having some semblance of economic independence empowers the CBDO itself:

> Part of it's a financial base, but I think much more it's an attitudinal base, an attitudinal approach. Everybody talks about self-sufficiency with poor people, and I think that's the way we think institutionally is that we [CBDOs] want to have a certain level of self sufficiency so that we're not in a dependent relationship to funders.

Success and ownership of property facilitates gaining even more funds since "once you are known and something comes up and they say, 'This is the group in this city or in the Midwest whatever that we think can do it'."

But capitalistic firms, as well as many government agencies, seem reluctant to grant even a successful CBDO respect. Hear the anger of a leading housing developer, who at the end of an interview shouted at me:

> the most common experience that I have in the external environment is absolute either disregard or disrespect for CDCs. . . . [T]here is palpable disrespect and animosity you know toward CDCs. . . . [It] is my most common experience in working externally with funders, predominately in the finance arena, bankers and city and government types. It is incredible, like feeling that CDCs are not worth all the time and effort.

A national leader described that banks might want the CBDOs as community groups to pay for social costs, but then at the same time treat CBDOs disrespectfully since they are not profit making entities:

> Banks . . . treat you like a nonprofit until you get to the table about development then they treat you like a for-profit deal. And then you try to tell them how you replace a for-profit and . . . then they get very leery again. . . . And then they want to take the development responsibility away from you.

Yet when CBDOs succeed, "then you're treated differently too. Then they say you're ripping off the poor people to get rich," but if you don't have a record of success banks and funders "put regimentation on the nonprofit that they won't put on the for-profit."

The depth of feeling on the topic of respect and dignity was made clear to me when during an interview a developmental activist momentarily excused himself to take a call from a banker. In about ten minutes, he reentered the room and started banging on the table, while shouting out that the banker said:

> "I'll be glad to listen your story." [Gets quiet] "Okay, I don't know what you mean by story? It is a real project, with $5,000,000 in [tax] credits." And, I said, "we have some real hard numbers and we're experienced at this and we want to review those numbers with you in detail. And we want a yes or no." He said, "Oh, that is what I meant." Okay, fine. But, you know, "I'll hear your story'" [said with sarcastic tone].

But as a niche organization seeking to gain the money to leverage a project, some capitulation is necessary:

> Now I go to see this banker next Monday. . . . That he said, "Yes, I will listen to your story" that pissed me off. Quite frankly, I think it is con-

descending. I don't like it. It implies that I don't know how to do business. So I'll be very prepared when I'm going in there to have my salesmanship thing on, you know, . . . have the brakes on to, so I make sure we go over the numbers that we showed them, that I got a good debt coverage ratio. I'll show him what his internal rate of return is, that all those things that are important to a businessman [are] right there, fully disclosed in our pro forma and it is an attractive project.

[Lowers voice] It pisses me off.

Even the titles given to those that head CBDOs imply a concern with the respect that those in the niche require. In common parlance, an "executive director" connotes the head of a social service agency, while the title "president" refers to the CEO of a business. The choice of which terminology to use for the head of a CBDO can take on import:

I sit as the president and CEO of a company and many times people they want to call me the director. They love to call me the director of [CBDO] . . . that's a social program identification, which I don't mind, but from a conceptual point of view, it is the failure to acknowledge the business position of that entity. That's what I struggle for.

And that has a certain connotation of competency and discipline and management, all of those kind[s] of stuff, whereas when you [are called] director, it gives less of a connotation of that level of responsibility. And you don't really perceive that organization as running itself, as much as you see it as being dictated by federal rules and regulations or city rules and regulations, and that kind of stuff, as opposed to the competent skills of the individuals that's making that thing go forward.

Ownership and success can be empowering, but to gain respect requires constantly fighting for the dignity of the CBDO. To be treated as a subordinate agency, a provider of social services, and not a competent developer, albeit one with a community-building agenda, is to enter into a downward cycle of denial and disempowerment.

## GUIDING DEVELOPMENT THROUGH AN ORGANIC THEORY

The organic theory of community development begins by premising the moral obligation to bring back the communities that government and the private sector have abandoned. Doing so is seen as normatively right, repairing what is hurt. But what activities should be attempted?

What choices are made do reflect funding and market realities. When most grants are for housing, to attempt to build a shopping center might prove a futile effort.

But organic theorists have learned that it matters less what is built than that projects introduce assets, both material and social, for those in neighborhoods of deprivation. These assets create an economic stake in society, for both recipients and the CBDO, as well as a set of obligations—paying rent, maintaining property, concern with the quality of the neighborhood—that is socially empowering. The assets benefit individuals in need and the neighborhood as a whole; replacing a drug house with affordable apartments reduces community fear about crime while providing housing for a few. Organic theorists build upon these assets by pyramiding a small success into a larger project, a topic that is covered in the next chapter.

An organic theory is an emerging set of understandings, closely based on first-hand experiences, that are shared and argued over by activists. Organic theories are communicated through stories of success and of failure, parables, if you will, sometimes with lessons explicitly drawn, but more often with the lessons left unstated. The theory represents what the community development movement can achieve and provides the answers to the funders when they ask what community-based development ought to be about.

CHAPTER 7

# The Art of Leveraging

With only five loaves and two fishes, managers must use creative
recipes.
                                        —part of a conference speech

I think money is the killer of vision. I mean you can't get paralyzed by
the fact that you can't see how to get there. So if anything I've learned
in the last seven years is you don't quit and you hang in there.
                          —established development activist known for his theories

It was seat of the pants . . . constant state of emergency, constant learning. . . . It is an adrenaline rush. . . . I mean, it is just mind and mental
exposure. . . . I mean that is as naked as they are ever going to get.
There [is] every possible opportunity to get nailed for something . . .
when you work for a community development corporation.
                                —developer's description of first project of a CBDO

We had eight sources of funding, fourteen attorneys to put together
this crazy package.
                                —small city community developer describing an
                                                        inner-city housing project

Developmental activists learn that obtaining funding for a project from one
source is a near impossibility. Instead, they must package funding from multiple sources. Doing so is administratively inconvenient and time consuming.
Yet, by skillfully leveraging funds from many separate organizations to pay for a
single project, developmental activists can turn an administrative hassle into a
way of providing ideological direction for the projects they attempt. In doing so,
CBDOs obtain financial support, but without totally subordinating their agendas
to those of the funders.

Following the logic of leveraging, a CBDO builds on an initial, usually
small, resource—a grant, a donation, or the like—that can be obtained, consistent with the ideas that emerge from the organic theory. A foundation, or even
an intermediary, can be persuaded to expend $10,000 on an idea that comes from
the CBDO, while a mortgage company is unlikely to initially commit the needed
millions. Based on the initial funding, the CBDO then skillfully leverages the

163

rest of the needed money, but does so in ways that the funds are obtained to support the project chosen by the CBDO itself. The logic parallels that used in social leveraging, in which a CBDO completes one project that catalyzes other efforts to bring about plans of holistic renewal.

## SOCIAL LEVERAGING

Community-based development organizations bring about social leveraging by themselves undertaking projects that "ignite others" to take action. Pressure on banks, for instance, to drop "junk fees" in mortgage applications, enables more of the poor to own a house. Tearing down a derelict building, replacing it with a small store, encourages other businesses to reinvest in the community.

Social leveraging can involve coordinating other organizations, none of whom oppose an idea, but individually find it too complex to put together. To bring about the day-care project described above, the CBDO had to negotiate an agreement between a local high school that provided training, the "county welfare department, whose people handled the licensing for both child-care homes [and] day-care homes," and "sixteen different funding sources." A community-based development organization provided the home for discussion between numerous funders, social action groups, and governmental entities, to save the 640 housing units in the "expiring use" project detailed in chapter 4.

Community-based development organizations can bring together organizations that otherwise would not cooperate with one another. In one city, the power company and the city government were at loggerheads, with the power company owning land needed for a neighborhood renewal project, but refusing to donate it to the city because of a history of previous fights. Neither side would budge and both had powers of eminent domain leading to a legal standoff. A developmental activist persuaded the power company to donate the land to the CBDO (reserving space for a transformer if and when needed). With the title so secured, the CBDO entered into an agreement with the city, enabling the renewal project to come about.

The CBDO can provide a place, sometimes quite literally a physical table and conference room, at which advocacy, social service, and governmental agencies can communicate about shared problems. In a troubled neighborhood, several community social service agencies were quarreling over their images for change, while an advocacy organization was pushing for all to take aggressive actions against those in power. As such, little was being accomplished in bringing about larger plans for holistic renewal. In that community, the CBDO acted as a progressive landlord, had helped tenants organize, and was run in a democratic way. The CBDO spoke the language of development, protest, and community empowerment and, as such, was able to more and more function as a table where people come and sit around . . . because it's a safe table, with a stable group who's not trying to threaten people or take things on. We just want things to happen. And we're willing to put some money and staff to make it happen, . . . and that's enabled a lot of conversations to begin happening.

The CBDO provided a physical place to meet and provided a forum for discussing issues of community change. And, according to the CBDO director, by doing so is

creat[ing] an environment for the light bulbs to go off for other people in terms of the connections. . . . Housing is connected to jobs. Youth is connected to education.

For the contribution of coffee and donuts the CBDO triggered actions on broader efforts at holistic renewal. In this instance, the bottom floors of a building being renewed for housing, became a community facility for local social and artistic events, as well as a home for a program for teens.

In social leveraging, CBDOs join physical development processes to social improvement efforts by working closely with social service agencies. Sometimes, CBDOs are formally part of networks, often religiously based, to which social service agencies belong, and as such, act as referral groups. On other occasions, the CBDO encourages social service agencies to locate in the properties it repairs, directly bringing needed social service skills to the community the CBDO serves. A CBDO director whose group was trying to repair a skidrow block of apartments leased ground-floor space to social service agencies in two buildings, one set up to house the homeless and another built to shelter substance-dependent women, many of whom had been prostitutes:

[We] . . . lease to nonprofit organizations that are providing services. . . . [T]he Salvation Army leases a space from us for homeless assistance reception center. There's a drop-in center . . . it's kind of the living room for the SRO. . . . [H]ere's a . . . clinic which is free health care for the homeless or people in the area. . . . We have the AIDS Resource Center located in our building too.

Through renting out such space, the CBDO became the node of an emerging network of community social service providers, and later was instrumental in forming a neighborhood social services coalition.

Doing social leveraging also means knowing when to cut a deal wearing a gray flannel suit and when to join with allies from the housing advocacy movement in more forceful actions. A CBDO can bridge the gap between advocates and the bankers by turning the results of a protest into a tangible project. Banks are pressured by the advocates to make money available, while CBDOs reassure the financial institutions that concrete projects will result.

## BACKGROUND ON AVAILABLE FUNDING

Successful leveraging requires developmental activists to be aware of what funding sources are available and how each can be approached. Doing so is necessary since for the high-risk projects done within neighborhoods of deprivation, no one source, either charitable or for-profit, wants to place a large proportion of its funds in a single endeavor. The downside is that the financing of deals ends up with complicated agglomerations of money from multiple sources. For instance, when the developer of the successful auto-repair shop previously described sought out funds to renew an office building, he still had to piece together money from eleven different private sources, as well as two large federal grants. The upside is that projects that satisfy both social and economic missions can be done.

The Urban Institute (Center for Public Finance 1994 ) indicates that to fund affordable housing, CBDOs routinely work with seven major federal programs, as well as solicit numerous state, local, and private-sector contributions. A study of Chicago's better known CBDOs showed "that the [researched CBDOs] [aggregately] had no less than eighty different sources of finance for their projects" (Giloth 1992), while an Abt Inc. study that focused on selective apartment housing projects run by CBDOs highlights that the nonprofits "used multiple funding sources, averaged 7.8 sources per development" (Hebert 1993, pp. ES–15).

Packaging money is also needed for the CBDO to stay afloat between projects. Avis Vidal estimates that for routine operating expenses CDCs have a median of six types of funding sources each (Vidal 1992, p. 55). In a detailed study of the CBDOs that received money from the Fund for Community Development in Chicago, the Woodstock Institute discovered a pastiche of separate funding sources (Pogge 1991, p. 12):

| | |
|---|---|
| Sales and Income | 32.5% |
| Local Support | 15.5% |
| United Way | 0.7% |
| Government | 20.8% |
| Foundations | 13.3% |
| Corporations | 9.7% |
| FCD | 7.5% |

What weighs upon the developmental activists is the sheer effort of piecing together money dollar by dollar, grant by grant. A sweat equity program in Indianapolis received money from HUD, the Indianapolis Housing Finance Authority, the City of Indianapolis, a major bank as well as from the local intermediary, the Indianapolis Neighborhood Housing partnership, that, in turn, had packaged its money from a major foundation, as well as national intermediaries. A small CBDO that already owned a building wanted to convert it into fourteen apartments at a cost of $1,096,600. In doing this project the CBDO obtained 2.2% of the funds from the Community Development Block Grant, a state subsidy another 2%, a grant program from the Federal Home Loan Bank 12.7%, local foundations 13.6%, a bank mortgage of 18.2%, with the remaining equity of $550,000 (50.2%) received by selling low-income housing tax credits and historic tax credits.

To convert the convent described on page xii to affordable housing for the elderly cost $680,000, even with the building being tossed in free. Tax credits accounted for about 27 percent of the investment, with state and federal grants and loans another 44 percent. The rest was raised through local solicitations, including money from the original donators of the building. Still, that money proved insufficient, as small gaps appeared, and the project had to be bailed out through a virtual *deus ex machina* when a person donated the last $10,000 in memory of her husband who had grown up in the neighborhood.

To package funding for commercial and industrial projects, CBDOs partner with commercial developers who, in turn, require the CBDO to provide some equity capital. A few CBDOs have their own money, raised from mortgages or as "profits" from housing properties. However, most of the CBDOs' share of the equity comes about from public and foundation programs that only nonprofits can access such as those sponsored by the Office of Community Service. For instance, an established CBDO invested $167,000 of its own money toward the $2.2 million cost to convert a school to a community office center. Of the capital investment $1.1 million came from conventional loans, another $250,000 from syndication proceeds, $47,000 from local intermediaries. In addition, costs were paid through twenty-three grants including $300,000 from OCS, $50,000 from HUD, $37,500 from National Trust for Historic Preservation, as well as numerous small foundation and business contributions ranging from $50,000 down to $150. A $5.7 million dollar conversion of the school to the Medicaid facility involved eleven separate city grants, six grants from intermediaries, $435,000 from OCS, two state grants, two significant grants from the Lily Foundation, as well as a HUD mortgage insurance guarantees that allowed a conventional mortgage to be placed on the building, plus, of course, the proceeds from a tax-credit syndication.

Capital budgets can be quite difficult to piece together with different types of funds needed for each stage of project development, as seen in this complicated effort to build apartments for the elderly:

> We took some money from our [special] taxing district to put options
> on all the properties and then went to a local bank . . . and worked out

a linked deposit program with the state treasurer, for $210,000 in three-year state CDs at eight percent market. . . . And, then we got five savings and loans to lend us $133,000 at market rate but in a totally subordinated position. . . . It took $403,000 to acquire the property.

These efforts resulted in the CBDO's owning the property.

[Then] based on having control of the properties, we were able to go to the State . . . and get a $1,000,000 Build————Grant to support elderly housing. . . . Next we applied for . . . half a million dollars in low-income housing tax credits . . . half from the city, half from the state, . . . [I]t is almost $5,000,000 in low-income housing tax credits. Based on having the tax credits, we have attracted equity investment. . . . The take-out of the construction financing is a bridge loan that capitalizes tax credits and is retired by the pledge payments over the next six years, so the tax credit equity pay-in. . . . And a first mortgage of $1.2 million from————Savings and Loan. There is a little grant from the Affordable Housing Fund of the Federal Home Loan Bank that writes the interest rate of that grant down from 10% to 8%. Okay? And that is the permanent financing that will retire the construction financing. The construction financing is a $4.1 CDFLOAT construction loan which is one of the first four to be made in the city.

The project financing was further complicated as the CBDO wanted to assure that after the tax credit period expired that the development organization would own the property so

we did not put our million dollars in as equity. We put it in as a subordinated mortgage. . . . We will take no principal or interest payment during the tax credit holding period. So will build a considerable lien against the project. . . . The reason for that is that at the end of the fifteen-year tax credit holding period, we want to take title to the building. . . . That way, we can guarantee that this building stays in the service of low income elderly people forever.

Packaging Low Income Housing Tax Credit deals requires attention to numerous details. For example, for corporate investors to receive the tax credits, the apartments must stay leased to individuals with incomes that remain below different measures of the poverty level, lest IRS retroactively demand that the private investor return the credits received.

Just handling legal costs for such deals can be prohibitive. The developmental activist who built a small apartment complex to house abandoned women explained:

> Our hard costs are reasonable, they're about $59 thousand a unit, our soft costs are outrageous, they're almost $37 thousand a unit. . . . [B]ecause when you use tax credits, first of all you have to hire some very expensive professionals . . . [and] none of the investor's money comes into the project until it is done so you have got six years of carrying a loan, so you have minimally 300 thousand in loan fees that you are financing.

She then showed me two bookshelves of binders of financial documents required to obtain money from the different sources. I asked this person, who had a previous career as a private developer, how much the project would have cost if done with just bank loans. She answered that "[with conventional financing] we probably could have done it easily for $3.2 million. And now we are going to do it for $4.2."

LIHTC provides capital that can only be used for housing very low-income people, yet at the same time the funds are not sufficient to reduce rents enough so that what the poor can afford will cover the bank mortgage. When undertaking LIHTC projects a developer almost has to find a secondary subsidy, for instance, housing individuals who have obtained Section 8 vouchers. But during the course of the project, Section 8 subsidies were hard to obtain and "as a result, there are few certificate holders out there and we [the CBDOs] are all running and jumping and grabbing at the same people to fill up our developments."

The very effort of piecing together project funding from numerous sources takes up an inordinate amount of time:

> You have a lot of transaction costs and it takes time. . . . I mean one thing is always different, sources of funds they don't have the same application forms so the city has to apply on behalf of the nonprofits . . . to the state, well their application . . . is different than their application for some other programs so we are always constantly rewriting the same proposal instead of having one.
>
> . . . But it's like there are different forms for different windows and different requirements, they require a certain debt ratio, they require a different debt ratio, the banks have different standards . . . so just coordinating this stuff is a pain in the ass.

To further complicate matters, different types of funds are needed for each stage of the project, money that takes on distinct meanings to the funders. Predevelopment money pays for testing the economic feasibility of a project, or its environmental soundness, but is in essence pure risk investment, obtainable only from those that ideologically support the movement. Money for the bricks and mortar, the "hard costs," that pay for the visible tangible project is easier to obtain than the "soft funds" for preliminary planning, the time spent in investigating a project idea, or the preliminary fees for architectural, land use, or legal advice before embarking on physical development.

As a result, soft costs often have to be absorbed within the operating overhead and the developer's fees, putting increased pressure on these already limited pots. Worse yet, CBDOs find their developers' fees eaten up in unanticipated development costs—the removal of asbestos, or to fund efforts to teach the poor how to maintain property. Further, public agencies rarely allow a nonprofit a fee that comes anywhere close to what a for-profit normally receives.

A wide variety of sources of money are available, but obtaining such funds requires both knowledge about their existence and persistence in seeking the money. Table 7.1 summarizes examples of these funding sources:

Funding sources vary from standard mortgage loans, subsidies from numerous governmental programs, interest rate buy-downs by banks trying to satisfy the requirements of the Community Reinvestment Act, charitable money from churches, direct grants from foundations and pass-through grants from intermediaries, brokered loans through intermediaries, or even program-related investments (PRI) in which foundations invest their endowment capital in projects done by nonprofits.

Government-sponsored enterprises such as the Federal Home Loan Bank, sponsor subsidy programs to help build affordable homes. The federal Office of Community Services provides money for handful of innovative economic development projects, while major foundations such as MacArthur, Ford, and Aspen, as well as community foundations help fund the community development movement. State and city housing partnerships provide subsidies for affordable housing projects, while the costs of homes can be reduced through sweat equity investments of future home owners. The public sector can be persuaded to provide free or repossessed homes, as well as reducing the numerous fees that are associated with construction.

Community-based development organizations are allowed to apply for the standard array of federal programs that support housing, as well as receive money from the community-development block grant. CBDOs that own and manage apartments collect rents and management fees, but this income is often insufficient for ongoing costs. Some commercial investors partner in projects for the chance to earn a market profit, such as has occurred with inner-city supermarkets. Other capitalist firms join in because of the substantial tax write offs allowed through the LIHTC.

In addition, clients of the CBDO can bring money from social service programs to help pay expenses. In housing, Section 8 subsidies offer one such income stream, as do the grants made available for housing for the elderly or the homeless. In commercial and industrial projects, funds for job training provide part of the overall support of a project, as do pass-through fees for supplying community health services, day care, and the such.

## Table 7.1. The Complicated Arena of Funding Sources

| Source | Illustrative Forms of Money or Funding Programs | Description |
|---|---|---|
| The community-based development organization itself | Equity contributions | Capital investments that can come from grants received by the CBDO from foundations or government |
| | In-kind development costs | Expenses paid for out of the general overhead of the CBDO for site exploration, preliminary plans and other administrative costs |
| | Recycled project revenues or developer's fees | "Profits" from projects that CBDOs recycle to handle the uncovered or unanticipated expenses |
| Immediate beneficiaries of the project | Rents, fees | Money tenants pay |
| | Sweat equity | Labor put into projects by future beneficiaries |
| | Pass-through subsidies | Money the government or foundations pay on a capitation basis for individuals who benefit from a project. |
| | Service fees | CBDOs receive administrative fees usually from government for running programs. |
| Private sector investors other than the banking sector | Conventional investment contributions from for-profit partners | For-profit partners provide cash equity toward the construction of the project and receive an ownership share. In commercial projects, for-profit partners often are active in managing the project. In housing projects the for-profit investor is often a passive partner. |
| | Syndication investments | Through sales of syndicated packages, corporations invest in nonprofit projects to gain tax credits. |
| Commercial banking sector and insurance industry as investors | Conventional mortgages | Long term interest bearing liens on the property |

Table 7.1. (continued)

| Source | Illustrative Forms of Money or Funding Programs | Description |
|---|---|---|
| | Buy-downs on mortgages | Mortgages with interest rates pegged considerably below market rates often because banks want to satisfy CRA or charities contribute money to reduce interest rates. |
| | Low Income Housing Tax Credit Investments; Historic Preservation Tax Credits | Investments from corporations and financial firms on properties that house very low-income individuals or are designated as historic restorations. The return to the investor comes from income tax deductions that reduce other taxes owed. |
| | Bridge and construction loans | Temporary, usually higher interest loans made until a project has been completed and permanent financing is in place |
| | Pass-through from intermediaries | Intermediaries package investment funds for tax credit projects from for-profits that are then placed in individual projects |
| Government-sponsored banking enterprises | Housing Program Grants | FHLB, FNMA etc. have set up grant programs that help reduce costs of low-income housing projects |
| | Subsidized mortgages | FHLB, FNMA etc. encourage member banks to provide subsidized mortgages |
| Community-oriented financial institutions | Conventional mortgages with minimal soft costs | Conventional mortgages but with the elimination of many of the fees that occur on closing |
| | Socially responsible mortgages | Mortgages targeted to properties in distressed areas |
| Community loan funds | Revolving loans | Loan funds that recycle as repayments occur |
| Foundations | Negotiated grants | Grants obtained for projects suggested by the community groups |

Table 7.1. (continued)

| Source | Illustrative Forms of Money or Funding Programs | Description |
|---|---|---|
| | Program grants | Foundation funds obtained through competitive applications for programs whose purposes have been established by the foundations |
| ∫ | Pass-through grants managed by intermediaries | Large lump sum grants from foundations to intermediaries that in turn pay both the overhead of intermediaries and provide the capital for projects done by CBDOs |
| | Operating expenses for high risk projects | Foundations might cover the overhead social costs associated with development projects, for instance, providing grants for an on-site business consultant within an incubator set up for low-income entrepreneurs |
| | Program-related investments (PRI) | A foundation invests part of its endowment in projects done by nonprofits, usually as a mortgage loan though one issued at a low-interest rate. |
| | Rescue and bail out funds | Community foundations with established relationships with nonprofits can be persuaded to rescue projects that have developed a small financial gap. |
| Churches | Unrestricted contributions | Unrestricted donations to the CBDO, often intended to pay core expenses as well as handle nonfunded development costs |
| | Benevolent deposits | Money deposited into insured bank accounts, but at very low interest costs to the bank. The money is then relent to the CBDOs at highly subsidized rates |
| Financial intermediaries | Operating expenses | Grants for the core overhead expenses of the CBDO including salaries for developmental activists |

## Table 7.1. (continued)

| Source | Illustrative Forms of Money or Funding Programs | Description |
|---|---|---|
| | Risk money for project development; predevelopment grants | Grants/loans for the costs of testing out project feasibility, preliminary design and architectural fees |
| | Pass through funds from tax credit syndications | Intermediaries package tax credit money from commercial investors that is invested in particular projects done by the CBDOs. Packaging spreads the risk, encouraging banks and commercial investors to participate |
| | Equity contributions | Direct grants for project equity either as a donation or as a partnership between the CBDO and the intermediary |
| | Subordinated mortgages | Loans often at subsidized interest rates or as secondary mortgages |
| Housing partnerships | Predevelopment grants | Money to test out the feasibility of a project, do preliminary market, architectural or environmental studies |
| | Subsidized mortgages | Equity investments from the partnerships |
| | Bridge loans | Money to pay for construction until mortgage are obtained or tax credit money is paid in |
| Government | Community development block grant | The least restrictive source of federal funding for developmental purposes that cities can pass through to CBDOs for virtually any type of expense for community renewal |
| | HOME money and CBDO set-asides | Housing development funds with a set-aside for projects done by CBDOs |

Table 7.1. (continued)

| Source | Illustrative Forms of Money or Funding Programs | Description |
|---|---|---|
| | Client-targeted funding programs—Section 8 as example | Numerous social programs—McKinney Act for the Homeless, Section 8 voucher programs for low-income housing, 202 money for elderly housing, that subsidize rents for individuals in need |
| | Community-focused grant programs such as Nehemiah, NDDP | A variety of smaller competitive grant programs that fund physical development projects with high symbolic value. The iconic example are the Nehemiah single-family home building projects to restore inner-city areas destroyed in the destructive burnings in the late 1960s. |
| | Office of Community Services | Provides the capital and equity funding up to $500,000 a project on a competitive basis for economic development efforts of nonprofits |
| | Housing trust funds | Special programs that dedicate an income stream (a transfer fee on real estate, for instance) to subsidize low-income housing |
| | Special districts assessments, TIF district set-asides | Cities allow taxes collected from merchants in special districts to fund expenses of CBDOs involved in commercial renewal efforts |
| | In-kind property contributions | As an result of urban renewal programs as well as tax foreclosures, government has ended up as owner of real property that can deeded to the nonprofits for rehabilitation work |
| | Fee waivers | Government waives normal fees for building inspections, water tap, etc. for projects done by nonprofits |

Overall, to successfully package financing requires great skill and organizational flexibility as CBDOs must blend different types of money and at times work out the incompatibilities between separate funding programs. Developmental activists regret the need to spend the time to package the funds, but rapidly learn how by leveraging money they can guide the direction that projects take.

## FINANCIAL LEVERAGING

Packaging the funding for community projects involves bootstrapping an idea, a dream, into the initial financing that pays for the capital costs, yet keeps debt service and operating expenses low enough to be covered by the project's income stream. Leveraging starts by the CBDO's soliciting a modest charitable contribution from community members to support the initial idea of the development organization. With this seed money in hand, the CBDO then approaches foundations, government, intermediaries or even the private sector for more substantial sums of money.

For instance, the shopping malls set up by the Kansas City CDC, the nation's best known developer of inner-city shopping, were primarily funded with equity from the Office of Community Services as well as very large secured mortgage loans. But the initial impetus that enabled the CDC to convince others that building the mall, an innovative effort to carry out the CBDO's scheme to create economic autarchy in communities of the poor, came about as the CBDO obtained cash from local churches that literally passed the hat to solicit $10 investments that were supplemented by more sizable investments from black professionals.

A successful first-time developer described how he built upon a small grant to leverage his idea for a Medicaid facility into multimillion dollar housing project:

> You gotta go to all of these entities and sell your project. . . . [T]he first problem with any of this . . . is to find someone to buy into the project. Usually LISC is the first group because they're the ones who give you the predevelopment money. So once you got a LISC money, then you can go out and say, "LISC believes in this project. We want you in on this project."
>
> . . . So you sell that to the city, you sell it to HUD, you sell it to whomever. And as people begin to buy in, then you got more clout when you go to the next person so when you get a list, then you got a nationally competitive grant, then people begin to listen again. You see 'em saying, "Well, jeez these guys got . . . that's nationally competitive, it must be a good project."

And then you go to the next group and say, "Ok, I've got LISC, I've got OCS, I need the city," and the city kicked in $200,000. Then you say, "I got LISC, OCS, the city, I go to the banks and say, hey I got tax credits."

A full bootstrapping logic is followed:

When we got one of those HHS grants, we got $435,000 and then from there it just steamrolled. They gave us $435,000, Lilly said, "We'll kick in . . ." and they gave us $150,000. Then we went to city, the city said, "Well the other guys in," so they gave us $200,000. So that's how we built up the 5 and half million. Just kept on, syndicated it through low income tax credits. . . . We got $2.1 million mortgage insurance through HUD backed by the AFL-CIO.

The entire idea for the multimillion facility originated only after the developmental activist talked with others in the state movement about the types of projects that best symbolized community renewal, yet could be accomplished in ways that remained economically viable. The size and scope of the project was adjusted to keep funders comfortable, but the idea originated from discussions between organic theorists.

Packaging deals requires patience to combine funds needed for physical construction with those to pay for a social subsidy. For instance, to make lease-purchase programs viable, the monthly charges must be affordable by the working poor, while grant money must be found for down payments since the poor rarely have such capital put aside. In such a case, a CBDO might go

after some banks who had CRA problems. . . . And then we went after the State Housing Trust Fund and got a $5,000 a house subsidy to write down the cost. . . . [As intended owners] these women . . . are part of our self-sufficiency program . . . and [as] the down payment . . . we use . . . this wage supplemental program. . . . We are also having them put in ten dollars additional a month in their mortgage payments.

Through the leveraging, the CBDO was able to carry a holistic program of renewal that empowered the women who participated in a jobs training program, improved housing, and increased services available in the community. It successfully carried out these goals that had emerged as part of the organic theory.

In trying to leverage a deal, face-to-face discussions occur between bankers, developmental activists, and intermediaries. At times, such sessions are convened by charitable funders or intermediaries whose presence communicates to the private funders that there is a source of money for gaps in the project funding. Negotiations occur in a round-robin fashion with multiple bargaining games being played simultaneously. When negotiating with LISC and other intermediaries the discussions focus on how much money is in the form of grants, or in the form of loans, and how generous and patient are the terms of repayment for these loans.

With many projects, especially those that assume that the CBDO will receive a federal grant, or in routine apartment construction projects that are tailor-made for tax credits, participants assume that the deal will be consummated. In such cases, the goal of the developmental activist is to ensure that at least one source of investment capital is locked into the deal early on and that this source buys into the CBDO's agenda. After that, the remaining investors end up negotiating with each other and the CBDO on who contributes how much and when and who gets first position and who gets last, that is, who takes the highest risk if the project goes belly-up.

A consensus exists that it is the role of the public sector to take the subordinate position on any loan package, but when to do so involves a strategic decision. Further, officials even after they accept the idea of a project wrestle with how much public money to invest in one effort. An administrator of a Housing Trust Fund explained the tradeoffs involved:

> if we [the trust fund has] so much money in [the deal] so the bank's in at 10% . . . then what good is it? You're not really leveraging—you're leveraging nothing. . . . On the other hand,—we have this argument all the time in loan committee—"Why don't we just take out the first lender? Why don't we put another five hundred thousand into this and forget about [a bank] ?

The seed contributions for the projects the CBDOs want to do can be obtained through gentle pressure tactics. For instance, one CBDO organized local churches to pressure the city to start the process needed to obtain a federal grant required for an innovative community-initiated project:

> We had to sit down with the city and say we want you to become a partner . . . these twenty churches want you to become a partner and this is what we need from you. One we need free land. You are biggest holder, you are the biggest slumlord in our community. . . . What better way of getting land back upon the tax role, increase your revenue in the community than to see to it that a redeveloped plan is in a way that meets your desires. . . . You charge for building permit. We want that fee waived. . . . Two, we want water and sewer tap fee and inspection waived because again that is about [a] $3,500 to $8,000 cost that is going to be passed onto the borrower in terms of savings.

Deal making can require intermediation. Tensions need be overcome, as gray-flannel-suited bankers meet with former street activists, now acting as community developers. A former street activist described how the Federal Home

Loan Bank brokered a meeting between conventional bankers and the staff of an ACORN affiliate:

> When we did this deal with [commercial] Bank and the [State] Housing Trust Fund, we actually got the executive vice-president of the Federal Home Loan Bank here . . . to bring people to the table to have discussions about stuff. . . . And they kind of acted as a neutral third party.
>
> [FHLB Official] was the person who put this all together [FHLB Official] said "look I know these ACORN people. And I know that they are kind of wild. I know they do activism; I know they march in the streets. But I also know, they should be able to do what they say they are going to do, which is build some houses."
>
> And he called up [commercial bank] . . . and we had a very bad relationship with [commercial bank]. We've gone after them a couple of times. And, he said, "Look, let's put some personal feelings aside here, let's sit down and let's see if we can do a deal." And he called up the State Housing Trust Fund; . . . and he said, "You know I'll meet with these ACORN guys who are trying to put together a deal for some low and moderate income housing, can you come over and meet [them]." And he called up some people he knew at the city and said the same thing.
>
> So, he put together really a very interesting meeting. . . . Put some coffee on and shut the door and said let's talk. And what came out of it was this program that we've got.

The resulting program followed the ACORN model of providing low-income people with homes they owned, but assuring that the property remained affordable by establishing an underlying land trust. The CBDO was able to implement part of an organically induced development model.

Initial funding can be obtained by pressuring banks using the threats of the Community Reinvestment Act. Some CRA games seem almost amusing to the developmental activist, at least in retrospect, as the CBDOs pressure banks to make better and better deals, and the banks, afraid of CRA and already locked into the initial deal, capitulate. In the following case, a bank had been partnering with the CBDO that ran short of construction funds when another investor was tardy. The developmental activist approached the banker and argued (successfully):

> "Look, you guys are have been partners in this thing all the way along and right now what your partnership requires is that you get us a 0% loan."
>
> "Helen, bank's don't do 0% loans."
>
> "Well, nonprofits don't pull manna from heaven either, and I have nothing in the construction budget to allow for interest, so we need a

very low construction loan or bridge loan or something, but [the other funder] is not going to come through in time and I'm not going to make payments." So he said, "OK, let me see what I can do."

The intent of this project was to recycle a convent as affordable housing that would allow the elderly to stay in the neighborhood, while symbolizing to others by repairing the old convent that the community was still viable. Initially the banks had opposed the project, suggesting that demolishing the building and starting anew would be more economical, but the preferences of the CBDO prevailed.

Other bargaining tactics involve, more or less, inducing local government into providing that last piece needed to close the deal, that originated from ideas proposed by the community organization:

> We kind of get the city in a piece at a time. We've learned a lot from private developers on that. . . . Private developers . . . ask the city for a loan, then they come back and ask for a little more, then they come back and ask for a little more.
>
> Well, you see the mistakes of neighborhoods sometimes is they come and ask for everything on the front end. And the city goes, "Oh my God, we can't do that, no way."
>
> Well, if you bring the city in a little bit at time, at some point . . . the city kind of figures we are in this deep already, you know. If they get in incrementally, they get in all the way.

Once a city is involved, it can be pressured to do even more, in this case supporting large scale housing and commercial development that carried out a progressive model of cooperative ownership that reflected the CBDO's model for empowering community members.

### Combining Different Development Programs

Deals are leveraged by combining funds meant for quite different purposes in ways that bring about programs of holistic renewal. For instance, the income from a social service effort might finance a physical redevelopment project or a commercial development on the street floor of an apartment building might help subsidize those being housed. The projects simutaneously help solve problems, empower individuals, and improve the community by following models consistant with the organic theory.

In one case, a CBDO was trying to reuse a building that had been a hospital owned by a religious order by converting it to a multi-use facility that included affordable housing. However, the financing was not going to work if the complex were to be used only for low-income housing. So the CBDO repackaged the project to include a series of other activities, including day care for the elderly. The funding finally worked

> by layering. So by having all of these things on the same campus we reduce costs, 'cause you got one set of security guards for the whole campus and one set of standing maintenance and all that kind of stuff. And you reduce administrative costs.

Practical concerns of keeping the project affordable were met, but in solving these problems the CBDO was able to bring together housing, economic development, and social service activities, as part of a holistic approach toward community renewal.

In another case, a CBDO was refurbishing a derelict school building. The CBDO had a federal grant and thought it could get conventional loans, but to make the project work it also required a direct loan from the city that the city was unwilling to provide unless a guaranteed income stream for repayment was in place. The CBDO talked to a neighborhood social service agency and convinced the agency to move into the refurbished building, as a rent-paying tenant. These actions received community support since they made access to the social agency more convenient, and at the same time satisfied the city's concern about repayment.

Elsewhere a CBDO refurbished the interior of a small apartment building to make available sixteen units of Section 8 housing, but could not find the money to repair the exterior of the building, an idea that was part of its overall program to create a better image for the neighborhood. However, in an adjacent building,

> we had another nonprofit organization [that ran a] soup kitchen. They were having major problems with the numbers [of clients] increasing, going up, in terms of people coming through the kitchen . . . serving four hundred in a seating capacity of seventy. They came to us and said we really need more space.

The CBDO director came up with the idea of moving the soup kitchen into the empty commercial space below the Section 8 housing. The combined project then was sold to funders, not simply as a charitable soup kitchen, but as a quality restoration. The CBDO encouraged a architectural firm to do the design work by appealing to their professional pride since the CBDO (to show others that the community still was viable) was attempting a historic restoration of the building with "the brass chandeliers, hanging chandeliers." With this redefinition of the project, foundation funding was easy to obtain, since "everybody wants to fund a soup kitchen."

By combining the funding for restoring both the soup kitchen and the building front, the CBDO was able to reduce the overall mortgage payment for the entire building, and the soup kitchen provided additional rent that allowed the

CBDO to "shorten the amortization period on the loan." Further, the image of the CBDO was enhanced:

> We have an historic building . . . the nicest soup kitchen in the nation.
> . . . Volunteers love it. People in the community look at that and they
> say: [CBDO] really is able to pull some things off that seemed like an
> impossibility. People come in there and say, "This is a soup-kitchen?"

Further, the CBDO had accomplished one more step toward its overall goal of doing physical renewal in ways that also helped community members overcome social problems.

In another case, a CBDO was financially "strung out too far" because it had refurbished a building as a dentist office and built in special piping and a customized layout. Unfortunately,

> the dentist bombed out. . . . This place was supposed to generate
> $2,400 a month. . . . And so as a result of that it strains our cash flow
> from everything else since we still got to pay the note.

To get out of the problem, the CBDO joined together several projects:

> We had this space here. . . . My office was in the building down the
> way. . . . Upstairs there [was a] two bedroom apartment; downstairs on
> one side we had a print shop. On the other side, we had our office, four
> flat I guess you could call it. Had this vacant space over here.
>
> I got to thinking, now how could I make this space work. It is too
> big for any small entrepreneur to want. It is too costly to come in and
> split it up, put a wall down the middle, and try to get two entrepreneurs
> in here; we got that big gate out there, we had to redo that whole
> thing. Too costly, don't have the money to invest in that. Can't find
> another dentist that want it. What do I do?
>
> First decision was I can move my office over here. . . . What do I
> do with this space over here [old building]? I convert that space into
> housing. Why? If I can go to the state and get a————Grant, go to the
> city and get a 50 percent reimbursement on any construction costs that
> I put into the building. I will come out with enough money to convert
> that into housing so I don't have no loan and I got debt-service-free
> revenue coming out of that building, that pays my $2,400 over here.

In this case, the CBDO was backing and filling to handle a financial emergency, rather than directly carrying out an ideological agenda. But that agenda was accomplished none the less and both housing and businesses were added to the community. In addition, the developmental activist persuaded city officials to open a library branch in the new building, a branch that ended up being the most heavily used in the city. As a result of leveraging, a minicommunity center was created, the CBDO showed the neighborhood that the development organization could succeed, and holistic programs integrating housing and commercial development came about.

Community-based development organizations partner with social service agencies in ways that benefit both. As part of a broader experiment to provide the families of children in day care with needed services, a social service agency had received a multiyear grant, thanks to which half of the families of the children would receive a special bundle of social services. The agency, though, required a day-care certified facility within its neighborhood and needed one within a short period of time. The director of the social service agency called the development organization to ask for help. This social service agency could supply a steady income stream, at least for the five years of the grant, enough to enable the CBDO to convince funders to loan the money needed to refurbish an empty building that it owned. Again the CBDO was primarily engaged in real estate work, but work that helped add social wealth to the community.

With clever packaging (and perhaps strategically discrete reporting to funders), an economic synergy occurs between real estate, economic development, and social service projects:

> [W]ith our restaurant we are also doing a meals-on-wheels. . . . The print shop we do a tremendous amount of in-house printing. . . . Like in the food service . . . if you can center it all into the restaurant operation where you're already cooking and . . . you can take advantages of chefs to do various programs. . . . [L]ike the meals-on-wheels programs, you can put into each one of these budgets . . . a chef. . . . You start to do that in two or three different programs and you find that you're funding a chef and a half but you only have a chef. [since the single chef can do all the work]

For financial reasons the CBDO is packaging together several activities, but each is a step toward broader programs of community empowerment.

### Coming to the Table

Leveraging begins with an idea that emerges from the organic theory. A developmental activist described how her organization comes "to the table with the idea and without the skills. We do bring information, we do bring the concept, and we bring the vision." Further, the CBDO has a

> dream. We share the dream with people, "Sound good?"
> "Yah."

Then we bring more people into the dream.
[It sounds] good to more people. "Yah, fine."

Initial ideas might be received with disdain by the hard money folk, who have little faith or understanding of the nonprofit world and immediately "discount all
that when we come to the table. They see you coming begging." Still, the developmental activist who enthusiastically presents an idea, especially one emerging
from the organic theory, can be persuasive:

> because we are not in it, solely for, the tangible numbers or money
> profit. We are looking at it for the bigger picture. . . . That we are a part
> of the community. That we are sensitive to that whole economic devel-
> opment process.

In addition, as a nonprofit, the CBDO brings in the soft money—the grant
money, and the charitable contributions—that no bank, or private investor can
access. The most important of these sums is money obtained from the Office of
Community Services (OCS) that for grant winners virtually guarantees $500,000
of equity in the project. This money is important since it is obtained only after
the CBDO is able to sell an innovative idea, one that is suggested by the organic
theory of development, that in turn is stimulated by the innovative projects
other CBDOs have brought to fruition.
    A grant winner reflected that with soft money from government or foundations

> I can walk into those banks and say, "I got something for you. I got a
> project that is completely funded except for these tax credits. I got a
> project that is practically guaranteed because it has no debt. I got a pro-
> ject that is practically guaranteed from the standpoint of compliance
> because it is destined for low-income housing and the corporation
> which has developed it; restricted it to renting only to low-income peo-
> ple. And further more I've got your CRA. . . . I got lots of PR value
> here for you folks. And I've got the reservations to the tax credits
> because we're nonprofit."

Money from foundations and government provides the comfort level that buffers
the equity loans of the banks and allows the for-profits to earn on their investments. And, of equal import, it is obtained based on the ideas suggested by the
CBDOs themselves.
    Interestingly, some for-profit partners also join in because they sincerely
believe in the mission of the CBDO, though, of course, they also want to make a
profit. In LIHTC projects, for-profits join simply because of the money involved,
but in more intimate partnerships, it is the ideological affinity that also draws
them in. A developmental activist described one such situation, in which the

CBDO located in an African-American part of the city partnered with a successful black developer:

> We were co-developers of this building with . . . one of the city's most respected office developers. The [CBDO] got a OCS grant for $400,000. We got land from the city that we acquired for the parking. . . . What [the CBDO] then did is we went out and found a private developer and asked the private developer to assist us and do it on the basis of a community service. . . . We wanted to build an office building. What we needed was a cash injection on the part of the private investor, but more than that we needed their experience in assisting us in getting this project done and their relationship with the banks to help us get the financing.
>
> . . . We came to [the private developer] with a pro forma, with a building design, with a product what we wanted to do, with our equity. . . . We told him we don't want you to develop this building for us and you walk away and it is a good deed and we don't benefit from the experience of having learned. . . .
>
> And this is what this guy said, "The reason we'll do it is I don't feel that there is enough African-American participation in this city's development. And we are not going to do it for you. We're going to do it with you and to the extent that you learn from us, then hopefully you will be in a position to do this your own self one day and help some other folk."

The CBDO succeeded and afterwards started on another building, this time on its own. Both the CBDO and the partner were working to carrying out an ethnically focused empowerment agenda.


## BOOTSTRAPPING THE DEVELOPMENT MISSION

A completed project becomes both a morale booster for the organization and public proof that the CBDO can succeed (and should be continued to be funded). As such a leading developmental activist argued:

> You gotta celebrate every little victory. It's mandatory. Every little . . . I don't care if you rehabbed one house. You need to take everybody in there. . . . [Y]ou need to open that house up, you need to let the neighbors come in, you need to make your board come in. You need to have punch and cookies there for your staff to say, "We have completed this task. And don't we feel good about ourselves?"

For startup organizations, the initial success is crucial in forming a positive image with the funders, an image that allows the CBDO to better sell its next project. Accordingly, any project that is successful, you sell it. . . . [T]he more successful you are, the easier it is to go to the people next time and say, "Hey, we did this." Then it's a little easier to sell yourself 'cause you have a success.

Promoting an image of success becomes a tactic to be used by the CBDO, both to help its own finances and to promote its ideas for renewal. A wily developer explained how he publicized his first incubator:

> We looked at the largest building in this neighborhood. . . . It was a massive building so it was what would capture the imagination of people. . . . I spent 500 bucks for a sign. What people didn't know was that we were paying rent ourselves to the building owner, it was only $75 a month for a small office but we got in and the newspaper wrote that [points to wall with framed newspaper story on the ownership of the incubator by the CBDO] and that was all I needed to get started. . . . We got twenty-five phone calls just off that newspaper article.

His strategy was successful in an instrumental sense, but it also communicated to the wider city the possibility of catalyzing renewal.

Skillful developmental activists bank the earnings from a successful project and then leverage their reputation, rather than their cash, on the next activity. For instance, the developer of the successful Medicaid facility put away the fees that were earned and persuaded funders to support the next set of projects without putting any of the CBDO's own money at risk. The developer's fee became "the money that I'm showing other people that we have a balance sheet. That you're putting money into an organization that's not in the hole." Because of this initial success, the CBDO received grant money from a local intermediary that paid for its operating expenses, allowing the CBDO not to touch the money in the bank and to have the economic space to experiment with its own ideas.

*Successes bandwagon.* There is an pleasant irony as banks and funders who had avoided the CBDO before, now rush to join in, having found a safe way of satisfying their CRA requirements, though this time carrying out projects designed by the CBDO itself. The women whose organization initially had difficulties in getting funding for a school-to-office conversion, discovered that now that project was a success:

> [T]hose same banks that could just not understand this [previous] deal, just the year before, understand this deal, very, very clearly the next go around. So we actually chose the banks we wanted. No questions asked.

One victory can start a chain of interlinked projects. The New Communities Corporation (NCC) leveraged its successful home building project for the elderly into a building a contiguous community-based nursing home. To support its employment training program, NCC was able to justify setting up a day-care facility and with that facility underway the CBDO learned of babies with AIDS in the community, justifying further efforts to build specialized centers for this tragic population. Success at one effort justifies gaining support for other projects that complement the initial work. Financial bootstrapping does occur, but equally importantly the initial idea itself, in the words of the organic theorist quoted in the last chapter, ripples—"when you do something and it just starts. You know rip . . . **like a stone in a pond, it sends out ripples.**"

The automobile repair shop initially was set up to teach job skills in doing body work on vehicles. This training, though, required learning metal bending and welding, which in turn created a spinoff business to make metallic waste containers for the commercial market. The asbestos business came about as the CBDO started housing renewal work, at the behest of some employees who were becoming bored with the auto work, only to discover the environmental contaminant. Then rather than hire others to remove the carcinogen, the CBDO obtained a grant, trained its employees to do so and spun off another community business. Through group discussions, those in the CBDO, as organic theorists, reflected about what their work had become and discovered it was about setting up ways of keeping money in the community. In response to this self-realization, the CBDO chose, as its next effort, to refurbish a commercial building that would house locally owned businesses that would attract cash to the community from the nearby central business district.

These leveraged images of success are publicized through a series of award ceremonies that propagandize what the movement has accomplished, both to other CBDOs and to the banks and the foundations. Many of these ceremonies are carried out at the conferences discussed in later chapters. The novice developer who converted the convent to the apartments for the elderly explained the importance of such image management:

> I'm learning how to toot our own horn, we're understanding more now that marketing us as an organization is equally as important as marketing us as a neighborhood. . . . We didn't do it just simply because there wasn't the time, and now we've integrated it into everything that we do, [so] that we do take the time to say, "We're doing this. Here's why. Here's the success."

Established CBDOs long ago discovered the importance of "tooting their own horns" and as such produce a steady stream of press releases and reports that show their successes. In these publications and blurbs, the ideologies, the core of the organic theory, that justify the community-based development organizations approaches to renewal work are put forth and shown to be viable ways of renewing hope in poor communities.

## LEVERAGING AS IDEOLOGICAL AND
## STRUCTURAL EMPOWERMENT

The material in this chapter can be interpreted in several complementary ways. Seen as a way of getting funds, leveraging is a clever expedient used to patch together needed money. But in many cases, the patching itself become the technique through which the CBDO shapes the redevelopment agenda that the funders then end up accepting.

The very process of leveraging allows the CBDO to steer redevelopment efforts in ways that carry out the organic theory. Small amounts of seed money are obtained from religious groups, a few risk-acceptant foundations, by using the limited resources owned by the CBDO itself, and, for a selected few each year, the sizable awards from the Office of Community Services. Most of this initial risk capital comes about by convincing funders about the wisdom of the ideas initiated by the CBDOs themselves, ideas that have emerged as the developmental activists work out the organic theories. These small grants allow an idea to be tested and give legitimacy to the perspectives advocated by the CBDOs. As further funds are then leveraged for the project, even though some modifications might be made, the direction, the focus, is the one initiated by the CBDO itself.

The individual projects do not immediately bring about a sea change in the agendas of the larger funders; instead they slowly modify the definition of what can and should be done. Such influence is more of a gentle shove than a dramatic turn, still the shove moves the funders slowly to accept ideas that have come about as part of the organic theory.

To make this incremental influence more effective, developmental activists need ways of diffusing both to others in the movement and the funders alike, information on successful projects and, of equal import, the reasons why such successes occur. Much of this is accomplished through the coalitions and trade associations that support the developmental activists, allow them to share ideas with one another, and communicate to the broader world what community-based development can be about.

CHAPTER 8

# Building a Movement by Creating an Industry

We organize ourselves the way we do . . . to match up with large institutions.
—director of an activist coalition

You get to know each other. Those informal networks [build] relationships so we can call each other on the phone and say how do you do this or who did you use for that or ever heard of this guy.
—nationally known CDC director on why she participates in the NCCED

Through skillful leveraging of funds, developmental activists guide projects in the directions suggested by the organic theories. But to be effective, an organic theory must be shared and refined by the developmental activists, and not the funders. Further, ideas are not enough without resources; institutional means are required to pressure funders to make money available for purposes designated by the CBDOs.

Developmental activists have established a wide array of coalitions, trade associations, and technical assistance providers, an endogenous support sector. These support organizations are controlled by the activists, provide a means for them to frame an image of what community development ought to be about, and have become the institutional tool for vigorously advocating for the resources needed to obtain these goals.

In this chapter, I describe the variety of support organizations, their provenance, and the services they provide. The next chapter examines how the support organizations help bring about an ideological consensus by providing the mechanisms—the publications, training programs, and conferences—that allow practitioners to discuss with one another their ideas. At conferences, organic theorists share with each other narratives about exemplary projects, as well as the philosophies that motivated these projects. In doing so, they vividly communicate the values and ideologies of the movement, both to other developmental activists and indirectly to their funders. Chapter 10 explores how trade associations and coalitions pressure government to adopt programs that financially and politically support the CBDOs.

## THE VARIETY OF SUPPORT ORGANIZATIONS

Community-based development organizations work with a wide variety of support organizations, varying from small technical assistance providers to national trade associations and coalitions. The mere existence of these organizations that represent many CBDOs, communicates to public officials that a movement exists rather than there simply being a handful of suppliant CBDOs.

Developmental activists are well aware of the importance of communicating that they belong to a movement. I had asked a leading developmental activist why he spent so much time on coalition work and he explained the importance of communicating to public officials that his organization was not alone but rather represented many others:

> It is helpful for [my CBDO] to be part of a larger movement because the state won't create programs to fund [my CBDO], but the state will create a program to fund community economic development of which [my CBDO] is likely to become a beneficiary because we have a lot of capacity. . . . So you know trying to help [to] support the movement is . . . selfish, but it is helping to offer contributions to others in the field to help them in their capacity development.
>
> I mean it doesn't do any good for [CBDO] to be terrific and on its own. You know if it is not part of a larger movement there aren't going to be resources to support it.

A single organization is perceived as only after its own survival and, as such, is treated by government as a suppliant; a coalition speaks for a movement and can be funded as part of a cause.

Support organizations form networks that help one another in activist campaigns. For instance, in Chicago, both the Center for Urban Economic Development (CUED), a activist research center at the University of Illinois, and the Woodstock Institute, an activist research shop that gathers data on CRA, have worked with citywide housing and economic development coalitions in campaigns to pressure banks to reinvest in communities of need. Support organizations help maintain unity within the community development movement, in part to overcome the rivalries that exist for limited resources. The Chicago Housing Rehab Network, for instance, a coalition of CBDOs that provide affordable housing, acts to smooth over the competition between CBDOs that wish to carry out direct actions against the city and those whose executive directors are active partners with the established political machine.

Most support organizations are of necessity small, local, and focused on a narrow task. This comes about since technical and political assistance can only be provided on a case-by-case, project-by-project basis: mastering the byzantine, segmented, somewhat closed government of Chicago, but one quite open to deal making, is a far different experience than dealing with the less segmented, more open, yet highly opinionated professionalized bureaucracies in Minneapolis. Research centers such as CUED at the University of Illinois at Chicago or the Center for Neighborhood Development at Cleveland State University provide technical assistance for specific projects carried out in their separate locales.

But being small means that the support organizations operate on a shoe-string budget. The core budget of the Chicago Rehab Network, money with which the coalition provides regular services and guides advocacy campaigns, has ranged between $300,000 and $500,000. The Cleveland Neighborhood Development Corporation had revenues of $174,000 (and actually spent less), while Chicago Workshop on Economic Development runs on about a quarter of a million dollars. Both the Ohio CDC Association and the Massachusetts CDC Association have revenues of between $100,000 and $150,000. The Ohio CDC Association is run with but a director, an assistant, a secretary, and an intern, while the Massachusetts CDC association has one more employee, a professional community organizer. Chicago Association of Neighborhood Development Organizations (CANDO), the nation's premier local economic development coalition, works its wonders with a professional staff of five. At the beginning of this study, the National Congress for Community Economic Development (NCCED), operated on a budget of around $600,000 with a staff size hovering around a dozen, but this national group grew rapidly.

Integrating the support sector are a wide variety of trade associations and coalitions. As table 8.1 shows, the NCCED, as the leading national group, brings together developmental activists, leaders from other coalitions and trade associations, funders, government, and technical assistance providers.

Although only an estimated 15 percent of all CBDOs are members of the NCCED, in this highly networked world, information quickly diffuses, often through the state- and citywide associations that themselves are members of the NCCED. For instance, Illinois had only twenty NCCED members including myself and nine CBDOs. But one member, CANDO, passed information from NCCED to its seventy CBDO members.

Statewide associations for CBDOs were set up in twenty different states, though their size and effectiveness were in constant flux. During the study, the Texas Community Development Association became active, while, with the help of the NCCED, the Oregon Association actually gained sufficient membership and technical capacity to sponsor a national convention. On the other hand, both the Michigan Association and the Wisconsin Federation for Community Economic Development deteriorated rapidly, with the offices of the Michigan Association shutting down.

Trade associations and coalitions accomplish much. They sponsor conventions that enable CBDOs to share information with one another, learn about new programs, and help socialize emerging organizations to the movement. At

**Table 8.1. Membership of the NCCED 1995**

---

Community Development Organizations—243 (62.3%)
    Community development corporations—184
    Community action agency (CAA)—52
    Minority development center—2
    Other community-level housing providers—5

Social Services Organizations Not Identified as a CAA—8 (2.0%)

Other Organizations from the Support Sector—68 (17.4%)
    Advocacy organization—1
    Alternative financial sector—3
    Citywide coalitions—5
    Research organizations nonuniversity -1
    State or regional association—15
    Nonuniversity technical assistance—30
    Technical assistance, university linked—13

Intermediaries and Benevolent Supporters—29 (7.4%)
    Churches (not church CDC)—1
    Financial intermediaries—15
    Foundations—9
    Public-private partnership organizations—4

Governmental Agencies—10 (2.6%)

For-Profit Sector—13 (3.3%)
    Banks, commercial (include bank CDC)—9
    GSEs such as Federal Home Loan Bank—2
    Other corporations—2

Other—19 (4.9%)
    Individuals not identified as technical assistants—8
    Trade or technical associations from other fields—2
    Not identified—9

---

these meetings developmental activists meet one another and learn that it is allowable to call upon these new acquaintances to ask for help on projects. Such help varies from answering a simple question on the telephone to broader arrangements in which an established CBDO partners with an emerging group on projects in the newer organization's community. Coalitions and trade associations intentionally work to bring about such CBDO partnerships, as an executive director of an association described:

The staff [of the trade association] does an extraordinary job of getting experienced developers, both minority and nonminority, [and] technical assistance professionals to come and serve on those committees. And then four or five CDCs get to work with those professionals. On some occasions they will borrow that expertise, even pay for it with their next project, but in many instances two or three CDCs will say, "Let's joint venture on something." . . . There are people that team up because of the state association.

State and local trade associations sponsor training programs on a wide array of topics including housing development, organizational management, and grantsmanship. Indiana's trade association received money from HUD to train CBDOs on how to work with HOME, a federal housing program. Training sessions also become the forums at which developmental activists swap "war stories" and further solidify their interpersonal support networks.

In addition, established trade associations play a significant role in public policy, through advocating for housing trust funds, lobbying statewide for funding for housing, or working to set up intermediaries such as the Ohio Community Development Finance Fund, described in chapter 5, and a similar organization in North Carolina. In Ohio and Massachusetts, trade associations successfully lobbied with state government to set up permanent financial support for the community development movement. As described in chapter 10, coalitions persuaded the city of Chicago to establish several new funding programs for development work. Associations run technical programs; CANDO, for instance, packages SBA loans and has managed a facade improvement project, while WIRENET in Cleveland is central to the city's industrial retention efforts.

Coalitions and trade associations prepare technical reports on new funding or regulatory programs and diffuse information on innovative projects. These reports span a wide variety of topics, from a generic overview of how to leverage funding to a detailed manual—what forms to file, when, what dates to show up to which meetings—that help CBDOs learn how to participate in scavenger sales (sales of tax delinquent property). NCCED ran one national conference on the theme of how CBDOs could resurrect local economies through human service projects, and, at that conference, released a technical report describing both general theories (paralleling those within the organic models) of why CBDOs should undertake human service work, as well as detailing exemplary human service projects accomplished by development organizations. The same year, the Community Information Exchange published a pamphlet that described techniques through which community-based development organizations can provide health care in neighborhoods of deprivation. In one significant report, NCCED detailed the problems that CBDOs had with intermediaries and made sure that LISC was aware of its content.

Other support organizations provide technical help for organizations that share a specific ideological bent. The director of a religiously based, rural CBDO remarked:

> When we did our very first extensive strategic plan . . . we hired . . . the Mccauley Institute. . . . It is a group that is both financially and structurally supported by the Catholic Sisters of Mercy, and the Mccauley Institute is specifically set up to do consulting for not-for-profit housing developers and they are particularly interested in those that have some type of church connection.

CBDOs work along with advocacy organizations such as Neighborhood Peoples' Action and the National Low Income Housing Coalition in direct action campaigns, especially on CRA issues, and in efforts to promote new forms of funding for affordable housing. In Illinois, SHAC—State Housing Action Coalition—began as an advocacy group for affordable housing, helped create a state housing trust fund, and now provides technical assistance to those using the fund. In Chicago, the Neighborhood Capital Budget Group pressured the city to set up a capital budget for neighborhood renewal. The National Community Reinvestment Coalition brings together both housing developers and advocates for affordable housing to stop bankers from gutting the Community Reinvestment Act.

To learn how to do deals, developmental activists attend training offered by the Development Training Institute or at workshops offered by the Pratt Institute, among other centers. Afterwards activists work with a wide array of organizations that help them stay abreast of changes in the field. Most trade associations, coalitions, and the specialized support organizations, circulate newsletters, bulletins, and technical reports, even actual research monographs. These publications describe funding opportunities, how to do deals, political changes that affect the community development movement, and successful advocacy efforts. They contain announcements about conventions and summaries of what happened at these meetings; on occasion, longer articles explore the core themes discussed at meetings. Bureaucratic matters are discussed, elections to office, or the retirement plan set up by the trade associations, as well as job announcements. The bulletins summarize technical reports prepared by the trade associations, such as the aforementioned study on using community social services to stimulate neighborhood economic development. The Woodstock Institute conducts and disseminates background research on CRA and Home Mortgage Disclosure Act (HMDA) compliance and provides information on redlining and other similar issues. At conferences, as well as during the interviews I conducted, developmental activists referred to the items covered in these publications.

Technical information can have a political impact and one achieved at a quite nominal cost. I asked a coalition director how his organization managed to produce a slick guide to housing activism that became the local bible for the city's affordable housing movement. His answer illustrates both the networking among support organizations and the effectiveness of the report:

> It is a bunch of smoke and mirrors. . . . I called my good friend Roger, who called the University of————and there is lot of networking here. . . . We hired a . . . guy who was doing some freelance editing around town for a number of years, to help us put the format together. And we had a staff person put all the data in and do the laser printing. But, you know, in terms of staff time and everything it cost us about $50,000 to do this book. We only got $10,000 from [Foundation]. . . . So we probably took a loss on the book that way.
>
> But for two or three months you couldn't open a newspaper and get an article about housing without them referring to the Housing Fact Book, so it was well worth it.

The National Low Income Housing Coalition spearheads advocacy work for affordable housing and keeps practitioners informed of changes in the field. C-Link offers affiliates of the Center for Community Change computerized updates of information. Handsnet is an extensive computer communication network for community and social service activists that covers issues ranging from housing and community development to AIDS-HIV research, welfare, and children's protection. Its approximately 5,000 subscribers gain access to a user-friendly interface that has an e-mail facility, as well as ongoing forums in different substantive areas of interest to social activists. In any one week, information will be provided of topics as diverse as "welfare-to-work programs," how to lobby against the "Istook nonprofit gag rule," or answers to technical inquiries on nonprofit management. Numerous organizations circulate action alerts (by fax or e-mail) that describe when to lobby for legislation of relevance to the community movement.

Specialized organizations such as the Property Management Resource Center provide nuts and bolts material on managing affordable housing, while offering seminars to teach CBDOs how to combat drug dealers in their apartments. In the upper Midwest, the Community Reinvestment Fund set up a secondary market for nonprofits and government housing organizations to sell loans made for affordable housing. The Pratt Institute and the American Institute of Architects formed programs through which architects helped community groups plan and design neighborhood revitalization. Specialized law firms and accountancy firms work closely with nonprofits on tax credit deals as well as suggesting how to structure accounting systems so that any profits made "disappear", before being taxed, by being absorbed in social service efforts.

Numerous consultants—Shore Bank Advisory Services, Brandwein Associates, or Rapoza, Inc.—work primarily for nonprofit developers, helping to write grant proposals, pulling together spread sheets, or guiding lobbying efforts. Consultants master the formalities for grant applications and enable development organizations, especially novice ones, to avoid bureaucratic mistakes in preparing applications. One consultant claimed his organization helped write applications that have obtained over 40 percent of all the money provided by OCS.

These consultancy firms have grown up with the movement and, in working with one group and then another transmit ideological perspectives throughout the movement, and then when hired by intermediaries, share these ideas with the funders. For instance, after the New Communities Corporation successfully developed the supermarket project, intermediaries, such as LISC, called in a consultant to help LISC establish a national program to set up inner-city supermarkets.

Consultants are far more than technical wizards at filling out forms; rather they pride themselves on helping even the most creative developmental activists test the feasibility of ideas and as such help reformulate ideas within the organic theory. In talking about his relationship with one of the nation's most innovative CBDOs, a consultant remarked:

> We did his OCS proposals . . . but those are [name of development activist]'s ideas. Those are all his; we don't force anything else. . . . We can tell them what makes more sense as far as funding goes and then we work with them.

Support organizations also partner with CBDOs or work to handle the overhead on a shared project. For instance, Chicago's Rehab Network, rather than the individual CBDOs, administered the paper work for the tax reactivation program, a program that allowed community-based housing providers to obtain tax delinquent property, but required mastery of numerous small legalistic details. Chicago's CWED worked with its member CBDOs to set up parallel community-based self-employment projects. In Cleveland, Wirenet works with several CBDOs in their industrial retention efforts, while the Cleveland Housing Network—CHN—acts as a housing intermediary, but one controlled by the CBDOs.

The workings of the Cleveland Housing Network (CHN) show how such support consortiums can help the individual CBDOs. CHN works with eleven CBDO members to manage what began as a lease-purchase program, but that expanded to include a direct housing sales program. A CHN official explained that the lease purchase program

> is basically a longer-term rental program using tax syndication, . . . where we purchase vacant/vandalized property. We rehabilitate them based on certain economic guidelines, in terms of ceilings we can't go over. We then lease them out for a period of fifteen years to families who are below the poverty-level. . . . We structure loans and financing so that at the close of that fifteen years the debt service is paid off and . . . you end up turning the house over to the family.

The separate community-based development organizations determine what properties to repair, while choosing future tenant-owners from their neighborhoods. CHN handles overhead matters, for instance, obtaining the tax credits, taking title to derelict property from the city, and sending out experts in evaluating building conditions and the quality of rehabilitation. The CHN negotiates with banks and claims, and, because of its size is able "to get concessions made by commercial lenders or savings and loans—who'll ever give us the best deal" creating "a very, very viable . . . financing product for that family."

The network structure allows the partnering CBDOs to maintain both independence and a large semblance of control in the projects, while at the same time gaining needed technical support. A housing director of a CBDO explains that her organization finds

> projects in the neighborhood that we want to do. Locally our acquisitions committee decides . . . what does it make sense to buy it for, what is [it] worth. How much work does it need? Then when [we] take the house to the Network acquisition committee, they're looking at how much of a risk is this. Can they really sell it? Can we really sell it for what we think we are going sell it for? Have we done our homework, do we have every possible rehab item listed, are the prices accurate? So it is like they are looking over our shoulders.

Community-based development organizations and the CHN do not always agree on what properties to repair, but unlike deals done with the intermediaries CBDOs maintain a great deal of autonomy. As the housing director continued to explain,

> the Cleveland Housing Network is a membership organization and would not exist without its member organizations, the eleven that participate. . . . So that there is an easy access to rectify problems . . . by the board members getting together and saying, "Okay, this policy stinks and it is going to be changed." . . .
>
> The other thing is that many of the staff that work at the Cleveland Housing Network came from member organizations so that you're not like dealing with some[one] comparable to like a planner at city hall or someone who works in community development who have no feel for what happens in neighborhoods, which[as] in . . . seven times out of ten it is the case with staff within the city. They [have] no idea what it is like to live in a neighborhood or to run a program in a neighborhood where the Cleveland Housing Network probably half the staff have come from neighborhoods. . . .
>
> Plus the directors of the community development organizations out in the neighborhoods aren't wimps either. . . . It's a marriage. . . . It's

like through confrontation and conflict resolution that a relationship gets better and consequently the same thing happens with the network as time goes on.

## THE EVOLUTION OF THE SUPPORT ORGANIZATIONS

The provenance of the separate support organizations differs greatly, but uniformly they emerge from within the movement itself. Several were set up to help CBDOs understand the arcane world of federal funding; others to teach about technical problems, for instance, how to manage affordable housing. The National Congress for Community Economic Development reportedly began as an excuse for the original Title VII developmental activists to party, but quickly evolved into a lobby group that also sponsored conferences on technical issues. Other groups emerged in response to an immediate political crisis and then took on other functions. The National Community Reinvestment Coalition was set up when the banking industry tried to gut the CRA, while citywide coalitions such as the Chicago Rehab Network came about initially to battle federal government cutbacks in housing.

Over time, support organizations change in form and function, from advocacy to technical assistance, and back to advocacy again. For instance, in Illinois, SHAC, the State Housing Assistance Coalition, began as a rump coalition of progressive housing organizations, primarily from the more radical housing organizations in Chicago. To effectively lobby the state legislature SHAC felt it had to show that affordable housing was much more than a Chicago issue and so began a membership drive that eventually signed up about seventy organizations, about half of whom were from downstate. But its mission remained unclear until its leadership attended a meeting of the National Low Income Housing Coalition, a group of advocacy organizations, and, at that meeting learned about housing trust funds, from a presentation made by the Center for Community Change:

> A bunch of SHAC members happened to be at a national housing coalition's annual conference and people went to one of the workshops that was on housing trust funds. And, . . . people said, "Hey, you know, we should get SHAC to do this." . . . So people brought it back, the proposal back to Illinois and SHAC's board, said, "Yeah, let's do it." . . . They put together a proposal, and then took it to the legislature.
>
> And, then, three years fighting for it! (laughter)

After the trust fund campaign succeeded, the government agency in charge of the fund hired SHAC to act as the technical assistance provider for the program. A protest coalition ended up being paid for by the very program it had aggressively lobbied for, though maintaining a belief in activism. As a leader of SHAC argued, if you "do development without organizing, You end up with some nice houses, but ultimately that's not your goal and that's not going to solve the problem."

In general, the support sector bootstraps itself with one organization spinning off another. Robert Zdenek, former president of NCCED describes (in Comstock 1992, p. 4) that on three separate occasions NCCED obtained grants from major foundations to help pay startup costs of state associations and to encourage these state groups to become involved in local public policy work. Interpersonal support networks reinforced the process. For instance, an activist from Massachusetts who had founded the Massachusetts Association of Community Development Corporations moved to Ohio and used her knowledge to help set up the Ohio state association.

Though many of the state associations were helped by the NCCED, each organization followed a trajectory of its own, affected by both the local political environments and the degree of coherence within the state's community development movement. The Wisconsin Federation initially was formed to bring together Milwaukee's CBDOs and to reconcile differences between CDCs and Citizen Action Program (CAP) agencies. At first, the federation was successful, lobbying the state government to provide capital to community organizations for housing programs, then later on for commercial and industrial incubators. But the internecine tensions persisted and later left the federation in disarray.

The problems with the Wisconsin Federation contrasted sharply with the successes in Indiana. The IACED—Indiana Association for Community Economic Development—had been run for years by a committed volunteer leadership with nominal financial support provided by the Ford Foundation. In addition, the IACED had received help from activists in sister movements. For instance, the state mental health association encouraged one of its employees to work with the IACED to lobby in support of state programs to house the mentally handicapped, while an employee of the CAP association, in effect, staffed the IACED during its early years.

Even when it was just a voluntary group, IACED conducted annual meetings, provided technical information to CBDOs, and, in a symbolically important move, presented awards to its membership for the projects they accomplished. Later, with some technical help from the NCCED, IACED obtained a substantial seed grant from the Lily Foundation that allowed it to hire professional staff. The new organization then asked help from the Ohio CDC Association about what programs to undertake and how. With staff in place, the IACED increased its efforts. It strengthened its annual meetings by inviting in well-known national activists, both to talk about philosophies of development and to update the membership on technical changes in the field. Quite early on, IACED won grants from the federal government to act as a training center for CBDOs who were applying for federal funding.

Ohio's CDC association was the most active trade association in the Midwest. The organization was started in 1984 to respond to the dismal state of affordable housing in Ohio, though being formed in a roundabout way. Ideas for the association initially came from the politically connected and activist urban center at Cleveland State, but funding for the group could not be found. Meanwhile, a citywide CDC association in Cincinnati provided a temporary home. Then working with the NCCED, the Cincinnati association obtained seed money from several foundations to provide technical support for the emerging state association.

However, the early days of the association were handicapped by a difficult relationship with the community action agencies as well as a lack of its own identity and purpose. Deciding it needed a defining purpose, the Ohio CDC association determined to focus on statewide lobbying and moved its office to Columbus. As previously described, the association was instrumental in forming the Community Development Finance Fund, while it played a core role in a coordinated effort with other housing, social and developmental advocacy organizations to make housing into a legal "public purpose" in Ohio.

Other support organizations came about to help shape the ideological direction of the movement. For instance, fearing that the Development Training Institute, the academy set up to teach about community-based economic development work, was too focused on technical concerns, graduates

> started having a whole series of discussions nationally around a set of standards and values that we felt needed to be developed. We realized . . . what held us together really was a set of values. . . .We do feel that first of all we have to put out that the field really does need to be value driven. And then that at least for ourselves we need to set up standards. . . . And it may or may not be accepted by the funders or the policy makers.

Such discussions resulted in the formation of the Development Leadership Network that worked to keep alive the ideological beliefs that could have been ignored within the plethora of technical materials taught at DTI.

In the remainder of this chapter, I shall trace out the history of the National Congress for Community Economic Development, the NCCED, and then describe the complicated interplay among trade associations and coalitions in Chicago and Cleveland. These histories show how support organizations evolve to help those in the community development movement respond to changing government and funding priorities.

### The National Congress for Community Economic Development

The evolution of the National Congress for Community Economic Development parallels that of the community development movement as a whole. In 1971 the large CDCs, initially funded under Title VII, each paid $5000 a year in dues to set up NCCED to provide CDCs with a collective voice to lobby for federal funds independent of the far more numerous community action agencies (Parachini 1980, pp. 70–71). The trade association slowly expanded over the years, adding other smaller organizations to its membership roles by luring them in with a $100 a year membership fee.

However, tensions occurred between the newer and smaller organizations and the initial members, tensions that were exacerbated by ethnic animosities. Members disagreed on whether or not NCCED should continue to work with more militant anti-poverty organizations rather than focusing primarily on development organizations (Parachini 1980, p. 182). Some of the older organizations retreated from active participation, formed their own subgroup, known as the "Eagles" and hired a lobbyist to work for them, rather than using the NCCED. An observer recollected:

> There was a split. NCCED back in the early to mid 70s had a big fight and the fight was over who were their clientele. Are their clientele a newer emerging [organizations] or was it the old Title 7 Special Impact groups? And it was also an Hispanic/black fight it was both . . . but anyway NCCED took the clear direction to work with as many CDCs as possible . . . and there was a split . . . there was a fight . . . [S]ome of the other older black folks had problems there was a lot of back and forth a lot of turmoil.

Disillusionment set in, leading many organizations to drop out of the trade association. Membership declined to forty from a previous high of one hundred (NCCED 1992) while some questioned whether the organization still served any meaningful purpose.

A reform effort began, lead by a Caucasian development activist who felt he could bridge the gaps between the ethnic groups, lure in newer CDCs and turn the mission of the NCCED about. He ran for president by building a coalition between the more active CBDOs and by crossing ethnic lines. The reformed organization hired a new executive director, chosen to bridge the gap between African-American and Hispanic developmental activists, and the organization entered into a long period of rebuilding.

Part of the rebuilding involved professionalizing the annual meetings to include information-laden seminars and constructive observational tours, rather than simply informal get-togethers. At the conferences, developmental activists share information, network, argue over goals and plan lobbying tactics, and in doing so have turned a disparate set of community builders into a movement for social change. Numerous plenary and breakout sessions describe, in detail, current and proposed legislation, as well as the techniques for lobbying for necessary bills. Plenaries often celebrate the sense of victory that comes about as the community development movement continues to survive within an unstable political environment. Panels balance technical and philosophical matters and are alternatively aimed at those most advanced in the field and to those who are new to the profession. In chapter 9, I will discuss how these meetings help frame what the community development movement is about.

Participants in the panel sessions reflect the geographical and racial diversity of the movement. An old-timer while addressing a plenary noted that

> I look out at the audience now and it has changed. The first CDC meeting I came to there was one white person in the audience. Everybody was black. This was a black movement. . . . As we started to look at what was happening in America the arms opened up and found out that not only Blacks were having trouble but Hispanics were having problem, Indians, Alaskans—all were having problems. This started to become the rainbow coalition. Eventually even disfranchised white communities we recognized had problems. So the rainbow coalition expanded.

It is a rare panel that does not contain speakers from different cultures, communicating that African-Americans, whites, Spanish-speaking, and Native Americans alike face problems of poverty and neglect. But the variety is not simply in the ethnicity, but in the diversity of the locations of the organizations, from isolated CBDOs in Alaska, to those located in New York City. Throughout the meetings speakers emphasis the commonality of the problems people from a wide array of places and from different ethnic groups share.

Conferences bring together workers in CBDOs and those from the support sector, as well as government. Funders get to meet and hear about the most successful of the CBDOs and are reminded why they should continue to support the community development movement. National figures from both the advocacy movements and development organizations routinely address conferences. Attendance has dramatically increased at the meetings. Just within the four years I observed, it increased from two hundred plus to five hundred and fifty and has continued to expand. Table 8.2 shows the conference brings together developmental activists with many others in both their support sector and the world of government and funders.

To further help CBDOs, NCCED publishes technical booklets that explain matters such as how to do a real estate financing or how to integrate social services, housing, and economic development into holistic efforts at community renewal. Several ongoing publications series keep members informed of funding and training opportunities, as well as what political actions are needed. To publicize the accomplishments of CBDOs to politicians and the broader public, NCCED routinely conducts surveys that measure the accomplishments of the community development movement.

**Table 8.2. Organizational Affiliation of Individuals Attending National Meeting**

Community Development Organizations—177 (45.9%)
    Community development corporations—149
    Community action agency—25
    Minority development center—2
    Other community-level housing providers—1

Social Services Organizations not Identified as CAA - 7 (1.8%)

Organizations from the Support Sector—79 (20.5%)
    Advocacy organization—9
    Citywide coalitions—10
    State or regional association—12
    Nonuniversity, technical assistance—38
    Technical assistance, university linked—10

Intermediaries and Benevolent Supporters—36 (9.3%)
    Churches (not church CDC)—2
    Financial intermediary—9
    Foundations—22
    Public Private Partnership Organizations—3

Governmental Agency—45 (11.7%)

For-Profit Sector—31 (8.0%)
    Banks, commercial (include bank CDC)—24
    Banking industry like FHLB—5
    Other corporations—2

Other—11 (2.8%)
    Chambers of commerce—2
    Individuals not identified as technical assistants—9

Multiple attendees from separate organizations possible. Fifty-nine not identified.

NCCED has become the point organization in the on again off again love affair between CBDOs and intermediaries. NCCED worked with intermediaries to convince them to become active advocates for the CDCs and has persuaded these better-funded organization to join the NCCED and pay quite steep dues. NCCED jointly lobbied with the intermediaries on legislation to benefit the affordable housing movement and to preserve CRA. Yet at the same time cooperation was occurring, NCCED, as the organization speaking for the CBDOs, produced a report, *Between and On Behalf: The Intermediary Role*, that highlighted the problems CBDOs face when dealing with intermediaries. The report explicitly rejected the intermediaries' efforts to impose their agendas upon the community-based development organizations.

During the study, NCCED expanded its lobbying efforts to aggressively push for new legislation supportive of the community development movement and did so in a way that would better integrate its diverse membership. NCCED sponsored focus groups with its membership and learned of the need for support for community economic development. As a participant described it,

> what we heard from those interviews was that there were a number of groups . . . in housing [who] . . . got involved in housing because there was . . . the need in the community and there were also institutions that had grown up help housing. . . . And that now groups were starting to want to get more involved in economic development. . . . Outside of the OCS money (a) there's not a federal home for CDCs (b) there is not a source of funding that is not project specific that would enable CDCs to develop ongoing strong economic development programs.

NCCED leaders discovered that this lack of funding for economic projects was creating tensions between CBDOs.

The trade association worked to formulate what eventually emerged as legislative proposal for the NCEPA (National Community Economic Partnership Act). In pushing for NCEPA, NCCED sought to push itself as the voice of the community development movement as whole. A board member explained:

> NCCED really wants to make a statement . . . that as a trade association it should become the lead [in] government policy development, in the entire field and that the practitioners need to take control more.

NCEPA was designed to increase funds for CBDOs doing economic development work, but did so in ways that neither subtracted from the money available for housing, nor allowed rivalries between established and emerging CBDOs from reappearing. In addition, NCEPA would provide a stream of federal funds available for CDCs that intermediaries could not touch. A member of NCCED's political lobbying committee explained:

> For the first time, we [would] have access to money that only nonprofits can go after. In the past, . . . certain pockets of funds, were set up to assist CDCs . . . [end] up going to the city, sometimes the state and sometimes to intermediary organizations.
>
> Intermediaries have become a major problem for CDCs . . . because few of us, any more, have direct access to the major national foundations. They give to an organization like LISC and say, "Now you all go see LISC. We don't have to be bothered with you." And those interme-

diary organizations have stepped in to take advantage of funds that have been available to the nonprofit organizations like us.

### The Chicago Triad

Arguably, Chicago is the nation's richest city in the sophistication of its non-profit support sector. Community-based development and other neighborhood organizations can get technical assistance from CUED at the University of Illinois or detailed help in doing direct actions from the NTIC (National Training Information Center), among many other specialized organizations. A wide array of information on the alternative economy is published in the *Neighborhood Works*, while the Property Management Research Center will teach owners of affordable apartments on the minutiae of property maintenance. Coalitions and trade associations abound, some fully staffed.

During the course of my study, five separate coalitions or trade associations of organizations were active. I focused attention on CANDO, Community Workshop on Economic Develpment (CWED), and the Chicago Rehab Network; in a later chapter, I discuss one metacoalition, the Neighborhood Capital Budget Group. I did not have the time to study the coalition of organizations involved in job training programs.

CANDO, the nation's largest citywide coalition of community economic development organizations, is considered as a middle of the road group willing to work with mainstream businesses. In contrast, CWED—the Community Workshop on Economic Development—is an activist coalition engaged in innovative economic development schemes to benefit the extremely poor, even if such efforts affront the establishment. The Rehab Network has brought together CBDOs that work to help upper-lower-class and lower-middle-class individuals become homeowners, those CBDOs that concentrate on providing affordable apartment housing, often for the near welfare poor, and those who build and maintained SRO (single room occupancy) buildings.

At the time of this study, CANDO had a membership of sixty-seven CBDOs (plus numerous local business associations), the REHAB network, twenty-nine CBDOs, and CWED, forty. Six CBDOs were members of all three coalitions, seven were members of both CWED and REHAB, and three were in both CWED and CANDO. In turn, the Chicago Rehab Network had close links to SHAC, a state housing advocacy organization, while CANDO had a nominal relationship with the Illinois Community Economic Development Association. Both CWED and CANDO were members of NCCED, with CANDO's staff being very active in the national organization, while REHAB was not even a member.

The emergence of the three organizations and the missions they chose, reflect the political forces in play at the time of their births. Just prior to CANDO's formation, the community movement in Chicago split between those who bought the Alinsky direct action traditions and those who felt physical development was the path to follow. Several individuals left their positions at the activist Neighborhood Peoples' Action to set up community economic development organizations to combat the city's emphasis on the downtown and politicians' continual indifference to the neighborhoods. As an original board member described it,

> CANDO was founded in the 1978–79. At that point . . . the city of Chicago was of a mind to throw a few bones to community groups like ours and appease groups like ours [but] keep us really out of the loop as far as major economic development policy issues.
>
> I don't think the city had a clue about major economic development . . . but basically the downtown development, the big deals, the stuff you know, the O'Hare expansions, all that stuff, was the big ticket stuff. And all of the neighborhood physical improvements and business area improvements and facade rebates and all of that stuff was "nickel and dime."
>
> . . . So in the early going it was confrontational, very beat 'em up; we walked in expecting city government to be unresponsive. Half of every meeting we had was with an expectation of the next negative press conference or forcing somebody to the table. . . . Everybody knew how to do that because most of them came from organizing backgrounds.

To gain the clout to get the attention of city hall, CANDO set itself up as a very broad-based coalition, including not only CBDOs but neighborhood business chambers of commerce. The initial membership of CANDO, unfortunately, reflected the city's racial polarization, with most of its founding members and its executive director being white in a city that was rapidly changing racially. However, by the time of this study, CANDO had built up a substantial multiracial membership.

CANDO's first victory occurred when it persuaded the city to contract programs to the CBDOs to improve the facades on neighborhood commercial strips. These programs both provided the CBDOs with an income stream as well as linkages to the community business people. After Mayor Washington's election, CANDO pushed for a citywide neighborhood industrial retention program and with Washington's support "we got it to the point where retail developers were tripping over each other to partner with CANDO member groups on retail strips to do things. That to me is a victory."

CANDO continued its lobbying efforts, for example, the coalition convinced the Daley administration to accept the idea of the CDFLOAT, an exotic financing technique to use unexpended CDBG (Community Development Block Grant) money for neighborhood programs; later on, as part of a broader coalition, CANDO helped persuade the city to establish a $160 million General Obligation Bond for neighborhood development projects. Other programs for which CANDO successfully advocated included a microloan project, a linked deposit program for neighborhood development, as well as a Planned Manufacturing District Zoning ordinance that preserved working-class jobs in parts of Chicago undergoing gentrification.

Though most visible in its lobbying, the bread and butter work of CANDO was still in providing technical support to its members. CANDO's staff helps constituent organizations prepare financial plans, pro formas for projects, while CANDO administers or coordinates loan programs for community economic development and runs a community trade fair. These services are accomplished with a professional staff of but five and a budget of $400,000 a year. However, since dues pay only 3 percent of CANDO's budget, the coalition must engage in direct fundraising activities and does come hat in hand to Chicago-based foundations.

In recent years, CANDO, as the country's largest citywide economic development coalition, has played a visible national role, in part by providing technical assistance to other coalitions throughout the nation. CANDO is an active member of NCCED, jointly sponsored tours and meetings with the national trade association, and has joined NCCED to lobby the federal government for changes beneficial to the community development movement.

The Community Workshop on Economic Development—CWED—was formed slightly after CANDO in response to three pressures—as a community reaction to prevent more harm from Reaganomics, to help CBDOs attempt more radical approaches to community economic renewal, and, in part, as a reflection of concerns that CANDO was simply too conservative. As described by one of its early leaders,

> CWED was formed in 1982 . . . with an advocacy agenda. It basically was a statewide coalition in reaction against the Kemp-Reagan enterprise zone concept . . . the concern of our member organizations was that enterprise zones is about development in a place but not development of a community.

The founders of CWED wanted to give voice to more radical sentiments for community-based development

> I think it is also fair to say that CWED was formed as an alternative to CANDO. . . . CANDO . . . ended up defining development as business development in chambers of commerce and that kind of thing. . . . And, so the founders of CWED were essentially trying to create an environment change to suggest as our logo says "Development as If Communities Mattered."

CWED was guided by an avowedly progressive ideology of social change, as an officer described it:

> CWED . . . has applied a single kind of a model to a wide range of applications in communities. And that model is . . . of democratic decision making and benefit to the folk who are supposed to be the recipient of public good, low-income . . . members. So Community Ventures [a partnership project done with CWED and some of its member organizations] said, "Let's have low-income community people develop, design, manage, and own their own business enterprises."
>
> We also . . . talk about how welfare recipients could transfer and eventually invest a stream of transfer payments in their business or job or employment opportunities. We had a women's project which was part of a national demonstration by the National Economic Development Law Project out of Berkeley, that allowed groups of women to control and develop and operate their own community economic development projects.

CWED unlike CANDO was willing to target its efforts to specific constituency groups based either on gender or ethnic backgrounds, rather than simply to neighborhoods in need.

When Washington was elected as mayor, CWED activists, who had actively worked in his campaign, ended up staffing the city's economic development and planning offices and were able to put in place the delegate agency program already described. But with many of its founders now in official positions, CWED was seen by some as part of the establishment, albeit a progressive establishment. After Washington's unexpected death, a reaction set in to CWED's experience in government:

> our board members said, "CWED is too close to downtown and not close enough to community. . . . Why don't we do some more work that is directly in partnership with our members in the communities."

In response, CWED worked with those CBDOs that were trying to implement radical approaches to solving inner-city economic problem:

> We have a public housing community economic development project now that looks at what are the particular opportunities and what are the particular obstacles to economic development in public housing. It involves resident management corporations and other community-based organizations and a wide range of local projects that have advocacy implications like rent ceilings, and removing obstacles to job training and job development.

As part of its outreach efforts, CWED joined with feminist advocacy organizations to support a micro-enterprise development program. CWED also began a campaign to convince foundations and government to recognize the difference between the costs needed to repair the damage in communities caused by societal neglect and the conventional economic expenses associated with the projects themselves.

Though starting out in opposition to CANDO, by the time this study began the two organizations were able to bridge their ideological differences. CANDO's publications contain articles written by the director of CWED as well as descriptions of joint projects involving CANDO, CWED, and Shel Trapp, the noted community activist. The two organizations worked together to sponsor a tour of Chicago's neighborhood economic development sites as part of an NCCED conference.

For a time, the Chicago Rehab Network found itself caught up in the rivalries between the separate coalitions each striving for the same pot of city funding. An activist from the Chicago Rehab Network told me:

> A couple of years ago, all the housing groups together [were] fighting the city for more CDBG dollars for housing. And we got a phone call from CANDO, right across the street. And, he says, the guy who used to be there he is now over at CWED. He said, "You guys over there are lobbying to cut our money."
>
> I said, "What do you mean? "
>
> "Well, you want to cut this program, that program, that program. That is our money."
>
> Well, we never called up the economic development groups and the industrial development groups before. We were in two different camps. We didn't communicate.
>
> When we started communicating; all of a sudden we found out, well we have a lot of the same issues. The need for more resources, the need for planning, and the need for some sort of accountability on the city's part. . . . We need planning. . . . So whether we were fighting for jobs, housing, economic development, commercial development, industrial development. Everybody agreed that those were three issues that we had as a citywide neighborhood coalition.

The Rehab Network not only has to bridge the gap between the separate coalitions, but also has the awkward mission of providing services to a diverse membership whose interests differ dramatically. Some of the CBDOs in the network focus their efforts on refurbishing SRO—single room occupancy—apartments, especially for the homeless, others provide affordable, rental housing, for extremely poor people, while still others work to build partially subsidized homes for lower-middle-income people, in an effort to provide stability to changing neighborhoods. Some of its members are merely builders, while others see housing as the wedge to bring about broader social change. Tensions are compounded by the ethnic and geographic divisions within the city. Community organizations working on the extremely poor west side of the city want the housing funds to be spent for deep subsidies for apartments for the very poor, while those in the northern and southern parts, in more transitional areas, demand money to maintain the affordability of their neighborhoods and prevent the exit of the remainder of the middle class. The Rehab Network has to walk a thin line of providing services useful to its membership, but not get caught in this competition. Sometimes these internal stresses simply paralyze the coalition's work, as when the coalition was unable to obtain a consensus on how to respond to the city's quite inadequate Community Housing Assistance Strategy, a report, mandated by HUD, that detailed what types of housing should be funded.

To help bridge these gaps the Rehab Network is structured as three affinity groups, respectively focusing on SROs, affordable apartments, and the single family network. For its advocacy and public policy work, the network focuses on work that either benefits the entire affordable housing industry, or on legal efforts that help some providers at no cost to others. For instance,

> the city of Chicago building code treated SROs like they treated the hotels downtown. . . . So the SRO network got together and we wrote a couple of ordinances changing the building code and all the people involved in SROs not just our members, the SROs operators around the city lobbied city council. And, last week, it finally passed the ordinance changing the building codes.

In efforts to hold together the coalition, the Rehab Network works in efforts that benefit its overall membership. For example, the Rehab Network allied with the Woodstock Institute to push for a Tax Reactivation program that enabled CBDOs to take possession of tax-delinquent properties. As the law was worded, though, situations could occur in which nonprofits might end up bidding against one another to acquire property. In response, the Rehab Network brokered the side-deals between the nonprofits to avoid such problems, a form of collusion that was very much a part of Chicago's real estate tradition. In chapter 10, I detail two other advocacy efforts that benefited Chicago's housing movement as a whole.

### Cleveland's Support Sector

The components of the support sector in Cleveland parallel those of the Windy City, though being far more limited in scope and effectiveness. The Cleveland Neighborhood Development Corporation explicitly tries to fill an niche similar to that held by CANDO. CNDC was formed 1981 to represent neighborhood economic developers, sponsor trade fairs, and set up training workshops for the developmental activists. CNDC helped to defeat efforts by the city to limit the use of CDBG funds in the neighborhoods and later on convinced the city to set up business revitalization districts as well as facade improvement programs to be run through CBDOs. Just prior to this study, CNDC almost died as a result of a failed trade show.

The organization then hired a new director, a senior employee of one of the oldest community-focused commercial development organizations, to help CNDC restructure and to embark upon new programs. CNDC increased its training programs, helped film a public relations video promoting local industrial development, and worked with the American Institute of Architects in a partnership through which architects, at quite nominal fees, helped design community renewal projects. The trade association increased its lobbying work, for instance, CNDC played a crucial role in convincing Cleveland's government to set up a microloan fund. This effort

> took [CNDC] a good nine months of bringing research and demonstrated success . . . [T]he industrial committee [of CNDC], . . . brought it to the attention of the Department of Economic Development. We just have kept beating on the city saying, "Look, this is a gap source of money that we can't get from anywhere. We continuously have businesses that are coming to us for small loans. They don't necessarily care how high the interest rate is, they just can't secure these dollars to keep their business going." . . . So the City finally responded. . . . I mean we had to push them very hard for any due recognition.

CNDC's meetings provided a forum at which developmental activists were able to speak with political and administrative officials from city hall who often attended. As described in chapter 5, CNDC played an important role in helping CBDOs battle NPI's effort to dominate the city's neighborhood development agenda. To strengthen the CNDC in its battle with NPI, its members decided to change the trade association's charter to allow housing development organizations to become voting members. The Cleveland Housing Network, the city's leading producer of affordable housing, quickly joined, as did one of the few remaining community development organizations still engaged in radical neighborhood organizing. The unity building effort was made easier after the CBDOs convinced the city to set up separate pots of money from CDBG to fund housing and economic development, thereby reducing internal competition within the community redevelopment movement.

Cleveland has no housing organization parallel to Chicago's Rehab Network, nor an active, left-wing economic development coalition. But what it does have are several organizations that are a hybrid model, halfway between being a

CBDO themselves, yet also acting to coordinate the work of separate development organizations. One organization, WIRENET, concentrates on economic matters, while the second, the Cleveland Housing Network, whose efforts were described on pages 196–198, works hand-in-glove with community-based development organizations in several housing programs.

WIRENET—the Westside Industrial Retention Network—coordinates community based industrial development work within an economically integrated part of Cleveland. WIRENET built upon work started by several advocacy organizations, such as Citizen Action, to preserve the industrial infrastructure and continued by several CBDOs. WIRENET brought together the work of these CBDOs, who, while maintaining close relationship with their neighborhood businesses, found that industrial development problems extended beyond the communities they covered. WIRENET persuaded the City of Cleveland to establish a program in which responsibilities to retain industries were delegated to community organizations, and coordinated by WIRENET.

> We did that because we felt that the City of Cleveland wasn't doing enough to retain industry. And, in fact, originally modeled the program on an initiative in an early warning system from Chicago. . . . But the reason that it works so well, is that all three of those organizations [that formed WIRENET] had well-grounded relationships with the industrial base in their particular neighborhood, and so we combined those strengths. . . . [A]ll of the local development corporations are still represented on the board of trustees, and yet it is a free-standing project that raises money on its own.

The support organization helps member groups provide services to the industrial community, runs a training program open to all businesses in its service area, and manages a private security patrol in the industrial corridor. Both the individual CBDOs and WIRENET itself are constituent members of CNDC, with the director of WIRENET heading CNDC's industrial retention committee.

The Cleveland Housing Network is a membership organization of housing providers that in partnership with individual CBDOs coordinates several programs to provide affordable housing. As described above, CHN works with a selected number of CBDOs that collectively run a complicated lease-purchase program to provide affordable housing. This program came together initially to carry out an ideological agenda of holistic renewal, quite similar to the organic theory, put forward by the Famicos Foundation after the burnings and destruction of the inner city in the late sixties. This Famicos model argued that neighborhoods would stabilize only after people owned their own homes and set up the lease-purchase model to accomplish this goal. The scale of work stayed quite small until the national intermediary Enterprise offered financial support in 1984. With Enterprise money, as well as funds funneled from local government,

Cleveland's community foundations, and eventually Neighborhood Progress Inc., the Cleveland Housing Network expanded both its membership and the amount of housing produced. In addition, it took on responsibility for several other housing programs indirectly funded through the city.

Toward the end of the study, the Cleveland Housing Network become a center of some controversy. Its policy of restricting membership created tensions with housing groups that were excluded. The rise of NPI further increased difficulties. Several of the member organizations of CHN were among the chief supporters of NPI, and CHN was itself one of the major beneficiaries of the increase in housing funds. Yet such support came with a cost. NPI insisted that CHN expand production, and in turn, CHN pressured its member organizations to do so. NPI argued that the community activists on CHN's board be replaced by developers and pushed the housing network to expand its efforts from the lease-purchase program targeted only at the very poorest, to a sales program that would allow people of higher income to purchase homes. My study ended with these tensions not yet resolved.

## FRAMING A COUNTERSTRUCTURE

I have described a wide variety of support organizations that while differing dramatically in form, function, and administrative depth, share several common features. Each of these organizations are creatures of the community development movement itself, dependent upon the political and financial support of the CBDOs rather than outsiders. Their boards, and often their staff, are composed of people who themselves have been developmental activists.

Support organizations intermediate between the community-based development organizations, the funders, and government, and by doing so, communicate the agenda of each to the other. Further, while providing services to the CBDOs, as consultants, partners, information gathers, or the like, the support organizations learn what the CBDOs want to accomplish and the reasons why. They become the depositories and communicators of the organic theory of development and, as shown in chapter 10, work to bring about the social policies implied by the theory.

The connections between support organizations and their members provide a dense, interpenetrating, overlapping set of networks that enable developmental activists to communicate with each other. These networks enable developmental activists to share ideas and ideological beliefs with one another and in doing so communicate both the content of the organic theory and the directions for action implied by the theory.

CHAPTER 9

# Creating a Common Culture within the Community Development Movement

> I went to my first [state] conference in February . . . and I've learned a
> tremendous amount. It has gotten me in touch with state funding
> sources, with policy planners and makers. Just a whole variety of
> things. The list is endless.
>
> —a director of the only CBDO in a small city

The last chapter described the services provided by a myriad of support organizations. In this chapter I examine how support organizations establish an infrastructure—of meetings, publications, and consultancy networks—that enables developmental activists to share ideas with one another about what community development ought to be about. It is these shared ideas, ideas that emerge from the organic theory, that developmental activists use to persuade government, intermediaries, and foundations to accept the CBDO's models for community renewal.

## PUBLICATIONS CREATE A SHARED CULTURE

Developmental activists collectively read a wide array of literature that presents not only mundane facts—a due date of a grant application—but also publicizes exemplary projects. Project descriptions include not only what was done but why, the rationales, the underlying theory, that guided the work. The descriptions written from the perspectives of the CBDOs help diffuse a lore, a shared framing, of what development can be about.

Trade magazines, especially those put out by the NCCED, the Center for Community Change, and several sponsored by supportive foundations portray complicated redevelopment efforts accomplished by exemplary CBDOs. In addition, the Fannie Mae Foundation widely publicizes the winners of its Maxwell Awards of Excellence and by doing so diffuses among the community development movement both images of success and their rationales. These discussions might frame the various welfare to work programs in terms of holistic models of redevelopment, or illustrate the moral imperative within the organic theory that redevelopment work must be done (and can succeed) even if the obstacles seem overwhelming.

Developmental activists read and write for publications such as *The Neighborhood Works* in Chicago, or *City Limits* in New York, or the nationally circulated *Shelterforce* that provide forums for active debates within the movement. An article in *City Limits*, later repeated in *Shelterforce*, argued on whether or not a CBDO should use policies of "tough love" when housing the formerly homeless or working with substance abusers, part of the concerns within the organic theory on balancing out individual and neighborhood empowerment. Writings prepared by Ronald Shiffman (Shiffman 1990), from the Pratt Institute, on holistic developed appear both in pamphlet form and in summaries in these journals and end up framing discussions of what holistic development does and should entail. Trade magazines circulate talks on the underlying philosophy of community-based development given by leading activists and theorists such as Mary Nelson from Bethel New Life or Pablo Eisenberg from the Center for Community Change, each explaining not simply what has been done, but providing intellectual rationales of why.

Briefer stories in newsletters put out by the coalitions and trade associations do brag about successes. But they also indicate that these successes come about because developmental activists belong to an coherent and forceful social movement, one with its own agenda. A typical issue of NCCED's *Resources* (Spring 1991), for instance, described how a coalition in Pittsburgh worked to make CRA more effective, examined a project in which African-American churches worked with CBDOs, while noting the successes achieved by the Ohio Community Development Finance Fund with CDCs throughout the state. Victories achieved by the coalitions and trade associations are shared: "Nearly $3 Million in Loans Approved," "Walnut Hills Redevelopment Foundation Holds Open House for Three Projects" (*OHIO CDC News*, June 1989). Such stories indicate the need for unity within the movement and the mechanisms through which niche organizations successfully function, while declaiming the "can-do" spirit of the movement. Further, the format of presentation encourages dialogue and sharing, with each story ending with a name of a contact person who can clarify points or provide further information.

The articles in CANDO's publications, for instance, are framed in ways that communicate the importance of CBDOs following a multipronged approach, integrating advocacy with development, as a way to target the cumulative problems that create concentrated poverty. A typical issue (Summer 1990) of CANDO's newsletter summarized the lobbying successes of CANDO—"City Council Passes Reform Land Sales Ordinance" and described the advocacy campaigns—the introduction of the CDFLOAT ordinance. It bragged about the services provided by the coalition—fairs, industrial development training, seminars on new government rules—and detailed successful projects accomplished by its membership. Lest the message be lost that different approaches to rebuilding community reinforce one another, the executive director of CANDO, in a signed editorial, described how Chicago's community development movement builds upon the protest traditions in neighborhood work begun in Chicago by Saul Alinsky.

Support organizations prepare lengthier documents to examine why specific approaches to community development are appropriate, explore the philosophies that guided exemplary projects, and discuss the technical tools needed to follow a particular approach. For instance, NCCED published *Human Services: An Economic Development Opportunity* (NCCED 1992), a booklet that argued for holistic redevelopment in which social service activities are joined to programs of economic change; another NCCED report detailed the importance of niche organizations partnering with other community institutions, illustrating the approach through the linkages that were emerging between CBDOs and African-American churches (Clemetson and Coates 1992). At conferences, panels are held to discuss these reports, and tours are conducted to visit the projects mentioned. Following the release of *Human Services* a postconference tour was conducted of the New Communities Corporation to see how that trend setting CBDO had linked programs of housing, social uplift, and job training to those of community renewal. Organic theory is spread through examples, stories, and narratives and is grounded in the reality of daily work.

The Center for Neighborhood Technology (CNT)'s *The Neighborhood Works* publishes articles, some of which examine value debates within Chicago's redevelopment community. An exchange was printed that included an argument between a mainstream nonprofit community housing developer and a radical housing and economic developer over whether banks by providing some operating support for CBDOs were buying off more militant tactics. During the course of my study, CNT released three longer reports on broader strategies of neighborhood development, one entitled "Working Neighborhoods: Taking Charge of Your Local Economy," another on strengthening local transportation, and a third on turning recycling into a profitable community-based business. Each study reinforced the idea of using physical development as a trigger for broader programs of holistic renewal and grew out of the organic examples of Chicago's practitioners.

Stories released by the trade associations publicize the successes, as well as the models followed in obtaining the successes, to government, funders, and the broader public. Every few years, NCCED reports results of a national survey of the accomplishments of community-based development organizations. These progress reports are given quite catchy titles—"Against All Odds" (March 1989), "Changing the Odds" (December 1991), and "Tying It All Together" (June 1995) —and are released to those in the movement and then circulated to major newspapers, funders, government officials and personally mailed to all supportive congress persons. Each report communicates four linked themes—the very miracle of bringing about housing and job projects in communities others have neglected; illustrations of exemplary successes most of which highlight how services and development are brought together by a niche organization; an accounting of the number of successes; and a message to outsiders that supporting CBDOs makes sense financially, since development organizations wisely leverage public funds. These reports end up being cited in foundation publications and in editorials in major newspapers, while their results are repeated in talks given by the developmental activists.

## CREATING A SHARED CULTURE THROUGH
## COMMON TRAINING PROGRAMS

The shared literature creates a common vocabulary and framing of what community development is about. These understandings are reinforced by what is learned at training programs, such as those sponsored by the Pratt Institute, the Management and Community Development Institute, or the most prestigious program, the Development Training Institute (DTI). These programs provide technical tools, but also act as socialization agencies for the practitioners in communicating values of the movement.

Many of the developmental activists I interviewed had been trained at the Development Training Institute. To qualify for the initial DTI program, individuals had to be executive directors of community-based development organizations and engaged in a major project that would become the "homework" done with assistance with DTI mentors. Attendees spend several weeks full-time attendance at DTI, and then undertake a yearlong project in their home communities (Development Training Institute 1992). While at DTI, developmental activists network with each other, share ideas and directions for the movement, and in addition, meet people from banks that are also sent to DTI for training (Metzger 1992, p. 88). After graduation, developmental activists become members of the DTI network that includes over four thousand community development practitioners, board members, funders, bankers as well as government professionals (Development Training Institute 1993, p. 9).

The formal training in the initial program set up by DTI focused on the philosophy of community economic development, accounting, economic development, real estate development, organizational effectiveness, as well as more specialized seminars in housing and commercial real estate and business development. In addition, attendance at DTI opens up a world of people to call and ask for help, as an enthused graduate described it:

> By going to DTI and NCCED those are the people you call because they are doing the projects . . . they are people who may have done pro-

jects but they are more educators . . . rather than actual practitioners.
. . . I still communicate with them.

Training is structured so that both technical information and the rationales for
following different approaches readily circulate.

Several graduates pointed how DTI dramatically changed their understandings, for instance by encouraging them to convince their boards "to creat[e] an
economic development agenda for the community," rather than simply work on
projects seriatim. A philosophy of holism is communicated. One described how
the training encouraged her to think as much about the why of what she did as
the how:

> They changed my thinking process. . . . Like, I feel like I was a very task
> orientated person—Let's get to the bottom line, cut the chase, . . . so
> they constantly surrounded me with process orientated people. The
> first session I thought I was going to kill some of them, because my
> whole thing is, I don't need for you to tell me how does my piece of the
> puzzle fit into the larger picture. . . . I need for you to . . . tell me the
> task that you want me to do. Tell me the bottom line, when it has to be
> done, how you want it to be done. That's all I need to know. . . .
>
> DTI was able to take me from a task-orientated person so that I
> have learned to appreciate what the process was all about. . . . I have a
> better balance . . . 'cause I think what process people do is let the
> process bog them down in completing the task. . . .

The results, though, were mixed:

> [I] did better with the neighborhood, did better with the CDCs, did
> horrible with my board, cause they were all task people. . . . They were
> all task people and now I'm talking process and now I'm talking about
> painting this big picture and . . . they just want to do housing. They
> want to do sticks and bricks. . . . They didn't want to deal with the peo-
> ple side. We just want to, you know, fix up all the houses.

Training programs evolve to reflect current practices. During the middle of
my study, DTI shut down and its president took a quasi-sabbatical, in part "to
somehow reconcile the ideology with the technical [while] maintaining the fervor and understand[ing] [of] broader principles." After consulting with many others in the profession, DTI's president launched a new program that was focused
more on how to build developmental leadership and to analyze local needs rather
the narrower technical aspects of doing deals.

Still some developmental activists felt that training programs such as DTI's
overly emphasized the technical in lieu of the ideological, and perhaps was deferring too much to the intermediaries. In response, they set up a loosely linked

support network, the Development Leadership Network (DLN). As described by an officer, these activists

> started feeling that at least at the grassroots levels that practitioners were having a smaller and smaller voice in setting the policy and setting the direction. And that we were often being seen by policy makers as the implementors of whatever was being set.

The Development Leadership Network

> was started by folks that had met each other at [DTI] and found that there were other people that kind of shared values with you, that you really could unite around those values and there was a lot of energy. . . . [T]hese were people you could trust. . . . [P]eople really got to know each other well enough to feel fairly strongly that they could connect on values. So we also realized that we could learn a lot more from each other than from consultants and even training programs.

The network expanded, set up a board and received its own nonprofit designation. Rather than restrict its membership to DTI graduates, DLN expanded to include practitioners who showed "unity with our values . . . that's . . . really what we're looking at, the bottom-line unity." Some of the shared values are specified in a "Statement of Values and Strategies" that contrasts the DLN approach to development with those put forth by the funders:

> We believe that economic democracy and justice, community and collective empowerment, and constantly striving to achieve greater democracy in the development of public policy, are values toward which our work should be directed.
>
> In any given project or initiative, profit goals should be subordinated to social, humanistic, and economic justice goals.
>
> Our decisions must be driven with a conviction that indigenous people should lead their communities as volunteers, staff, or board members of our organizations.
>
> Our approach must be holistic. For example, we shall link production with environmental considerations.

Further, community economic development is described holistically:

> Community economic development is the organization of a community's—and its institutions'—economic activities in ways that benefit the community as a whole. Community economic development leads to community and personal empowerment through strategies which encourage cooperation and interdependence, and which equalize resources among the community's rich and poor populations.

DLN encourages sharing of ideas among its membership, doing so through a newsletter and an annual meeting, often held in conjunction with the NCCED conference. DLN is not an oppositional group, but rather an internal support network that works to create a consensual framing of community development that includes progressive ideas for social change.

Ideas are also spread through personal networks of the developmental activists, especially those experimenting with innovative approaches. A CDC director who had experimented with the concept of individual development accounts, as part of an effort to empower people within empowered communities, first discussed the ideas with others in the movement in extended phone calls, and later set up a conference sponsored by the state trade association to explore the topic. When the founder of the New Communities Corporation won a MacArthur Foundation "genius award" he spent much of his time traveling the country as a Johnny Appleseed of community development to share, especially with newer organizations, what NCC had learned about programs of holistic renewal.

In addition, ideas from the organic theory are spread by the technical consultants many of whom are developmental activists themselves who are earning extra money by helping other groups. These organic theorists qua consultants teach technical matters, but in addition they spread the theories that development is more than bricks and mortar. In one case studied, neighborhood activists had come together to respond to the city's plans to build a massive sports facility in their community. This newly formed group hired, as a consultant, a successful developmental activist best known for integrating housing and commercial projects, who interpreted his mission as helping the nascent organization see beyond its immediate short-term concerns and to reflect upon systemic implications of developmental change. He summarized to me the arguments he made to the group that had hired him:

> I said imagine: "It's the year 2010. The [sports facility] is built. It [has] far exceeded anybody's expectations. It is extremely successful. . . . What happens at [your neighborhood]?"
>
> And everybody who was from [that location] said, "We ain't here. The [sports facility] causes all kinds of other development, causes gentrification, causes richer people to come in and we're pushed out." . . . What happens in Chinatown [adjacent to the neighborhood]? Everybody said, "Chinese are getting rich their making money hand over fist cause all those conventioneers and all those [sports] fans are going to Chinatown for dinner."
>
> What's the difference?
>
> The difference is that in one group of people you have a creation of production based on culture for export to an exterior market of consumers. And in the other one you're absent that strategy. . . . So what

we came up with was this. You build the [sports facility] You add a bond issue. You add onto the bond issue a big number. . . . And with that you do the following things: you revitalize the black metropoli[tan] historic district of [this location], which is our Harlem. . . . You also use part of this money from the bond issue to revitalize the historic blues district. . . . You expand beyond blues and the kind of entertainment. I mean you do hip hopping, rap too. I mean so that . . . it's really kind of African-American cultural entertainment center. . . . [T]he whole goal is to create a product for export.

The consultant suggested to the new group following a holistic renewal policy, one that carried out the models of community autarchy central to the organic theory, and then suggested a political tactic to bring it about. He transmitted the values, goals, hopes, and dreams, explicit within the organic theory of development, not simply techniques.

## CONFERENCES AS MILIEUS FOR SHARING AN EVOLVING CULTURE

Conferences sponsored by the national, state, and, on occasion citywide trade associations, bring together workers in CBDOs with their financial and technical supporters. At these meetings, developmental activists from across the nation chat, share war stories, and exchange both anecdotes and analyses of what has worked in their communities and what has failed. Participants arrange to visit each other's neighborhoods and continue mutual help by phone. At panels, and in private discussions, developmental activists collectively argue over the framings and definitions of what the community-based development movement ought to be about, on the respective roles of advocacy and development, on questions of whether ownership of property without providing social services is enough, among many other concerns. Conferences help bring together a disparate set of community builders and enable them to meld into a movement for social change.

My observations are primarily of those held by the National Congress for Community Economic Development. I attended, observed, recorded, imbibed, and, presented at these conferences, and on occasion joined in by providing advice to first-time attendees.

### Conferences and the Reinforcement of a Culture

The conferences held by the trade associations enable those in the community development movement to reinforce the image that they are together, teach newcomers about the culture of community development, and work out concerns over contending values. NCCED conferences contain plenary sessions, break out panels, working tours, as well as informal socializing. Contacts are made as people drink together, chat, and talk at luncheon tables. Either immediately before the meeting or shortly thereafter, those with the time and inclination join a tour to visit development sites near the city in which the convention is being held. A Chicago tour preceded a conference in Milwaukee, a tour to Newark to visit New Communities Corporation followed the meeting held in Philadelphia, and an exhausted dozen or so people joined the conference in Austin, Texas, having just toured the macquiloras and the colonias on the Texas-Mexican border, and discovered to their chagrin just how big a state Texas is.

Conferences help build bridges between the support sector and CBDOs. Representatives from support organizations make themselves available to explain whatever it is they offer while written material is distributed. In addition, complaints and tensions are aired. At one meeting, NCCED released a critical pamphlet *Between and On Behalf* detailing the difficulties CBDOs faced when dealing with the larger financial intermediaries, LISC and Enterprise. Still at that same meeting, LISC's president Paul Grogan addressed a plenary, LISC joined NCCED as a member, and became a sponsor for trade association activities.

Prior to the conference opening, an evening is spent at an informal reception. The next two and half days are packed with technical panels, plenaries that focus major concerns of the profession, usually those relating to changing federal programs, as well as half-day tours of local community development projects. At mealtimes, evocative speeches are held, frequently leading to exuberant responses. Willie Brown, then Speaker of the California House, brought down the house with his wry comments on how he got progressive community legislation through a somewhat recalcitrant legislative body.

Over drinks and meals, developmental activists informally meet one another and share with each other how their philosophies of social change are implemented. After the meetings these individuals phone each other for advice on projects, approaches, and ways for dealing with funders. Some form affinity groups that regularly meet. These personal networks do more than help people learn how to overcome technical problems; they allow developmental activists to understand that they are not alone but rather the problems they face as individuals are shared throughout the movement.

Plenaries provide an opportunity to thank sponsors and to honor supportive government officials and foundation leaders. Ranking officials from HUD have spoken, as well as leading administrators in public housing and foundation directors. Adele Simmons, president of the John D. and Catherine T. MacArthur Foundation, and a major funder of both community development projects and advocacy work, addressed the assembled, later followed by John Perkins, the president the Christian Community Development Association. Another time, the

President of LISC spoke on the need to build intersectoral links between public, private, and nonprofit organizations. At an evening reception, Chicago's Mayor Daley gave a stump address, and then was publicly praised by local developmental activists whose organizations had received city support.

Plenaries provide an opportunity to share pride in the very survival of the community development movement, in spite of working in an unstable political environment. Time is also spent at the plenaries to provide awards for successful projects and to honor professionals in the field. These awards do stroke egos, but of equal import, newer organizations learn about exemplars that can be imitated, as well as the philosophies that underlay the projects.

Some plenary and breakout sessions explore in detail current and proposed legislation in support of community work. Several meetings in a row discussed Kemp's ideas of tenant-resident management, while at the beginning of the Clinton administration, panels were held describing the implications of the empowerment zone legislation for CBDOs.

Plenaries also become the forums in which questions are raised and answered about where the movement has been and where it might go, virtually public debates on the values that shape the organic theory. Newcomers are often discouraged by the frustrations of development work. Understanding this, in public speeches leaders in the movement detail the travails they had faced and overcome and indicate that victories occur only after numerous false starts and defeats. One began a plenary by remarking,

> Before we say too much, we want to say that all of us have failed more times than we succeed and even when we people think that we succeed it has really been a bloody battle to get there. It's a learning experience. Most of us ended up doing things we never planned to do.

Most of the scheduled conference time is spent at formal workshops, each consisting of technical presentations followed by detailed questioning and answering. Topics range from those issues of building community support to narrow discussions of technical matters, such as lease arrangements, financial tools, what type of cleaning solvent to use. In 1985 a total of fourteen workshops were held, dealing with such matters as approaches to financing housing and businesses, explaining what federal resources are available, and focusing on commercial revitalization projects. By the time of the Chicago meeting, nine years later, twenty-nine workshops were held, in concurrent sessions, many in standing-room-only settings. In some sessions, officials from government were grilled about the funding for community programs, while other sessions discussed how CBDOs can partner with businesses or with churches. Numerous workshops focused on specialized types of projects, varying from commercial real estate to workshops on the management of micro-enterprises.

Panels balance technical and philosophical matters and are alternatively aimed at those most advanced in the field and at those who are new to the profession. In Texas, those attendees just starting their own CBDOs avidly took notes at a session on the Low Income Housing Tax Credit, which by then was a standard funding procedure for the established organizations. Yet, just three years earlier, many of the same issues had to be explained to the more established groups by a lawyer for the Center for Community Change. The same group of individuals that can cheer at rousing political speech by Willie Brown or Ernie Cortes on the moral obligations of developers is busy taking notes at a near full session explaining the minutiae required to fill out a Comprehensive Housing Assistance Strategy, one of HUD's many cumbersome attempts to rationalize its efforts.

Some panel topics, such as those describing government grants programs or forms of funding, are repeated in different years, simply because of the evolution in the regulations. Discussions were held on how to manage mixed-income housing or how neighborhood security work affected development. Several workshops focused on emerging tools of the trade—electronic communications—or techniques for applying for an OCS grant—the major source of federal money for community economic development—run by the same consultant who charged fees for such information in private work. Representatives of support organizations often speak on specialized topics, varying from how they package funding to quite technical presentations on how to resell loans.

Other discussions take place at roundtables, some at early breakfasts, during which half a dozen people share their experiences on specialized topics. One I attended was concerned with how to link programs to improve inner-city education with projects to build neighborhood assets; another involved developmental activists swapping behind the scenes tales of how they enticed state agencies to join in with them on their community work through "the foot in the door approach. The toe in the door." Collectively these breakfasts constitute workshops in implementing the organic theory.

Most conference panels become as much peer-to-peer exchanges as they are formal presentations. It is the concrete experiences of the actual organizations who have been there before that is of most interest. Practitioners share their experiences with one another and try to enable others to emulate what they have done, even though there is potential competition for the same pool of grants. Speakers from successful organizations communicate how their famous projects carry out a holistic philosophy, rather than simply concentrating on the physical development work. A major housing and shopping center developer described how

> over the last twenty some years we have been involved in employment training as well as economic development, social services and housing because of the particular needs of our constituency. And one of the

most recent things that we have combined using economic development and using more specifically the Job Training Partnership Act. We
operate a comprehensive employment training program . . . and also a
couple of older worker programs . . . the airport was adding a huge wing
. . . and we pushed though . . . to get minority participation and some of
the vendors for that new wing.

The presentations indicate the need to be aggressive in asserting the CBDO's
agenda. In the airport story, big business objected to giving contracts to a community group, opposition that was only overcome through the advocacy work
conducted by this CBDO.

In the narratives presented at panels, speakers trumpet their accomplishments, doing so in a story form that contrasts the ultimate success with the initial
difficulties in packaging a deal all the while arguing for the need to persevere. At
times, the stories are told in ways that evoke the older Br'r Rabbit tale, showing
how the smaller CBDO out thought their funders. For instance, a community
developer detailed how he set up an incubator in the largest building around,
rented a small office in the building and placed his organization's logo over the
office. Was it his fault, he asked, when the local newspaper assumed his organization was the owner, and never inquired to learn that his CBDO only had a master
lease?

Conferences communicate underlying messages that help frame future work.
For instance, throughout the sessions, community-based development is portrayed as an industry that is maturing and that can accomplish important tasks.
Yet, at the same time that developmental activists portray their organizations as
flexible businesses, proud to own property, and run in the black, they also talk of
being part of a tradition of social change with close affinity to those involved in
neighborhood change and those leading battles for social justice.

Problems and tensions are frankly examined: Can and should a community-
based development organization get involved in management and end up having
to demand rent payments from those being served? Can a CBDO make money in
owning rental apartments? Studies say probably not, yet an argument is made by
those who have succeeded in doing so. Can a CBDO build homes that are affordable, yet at the same time work to support labor in its efforts to maintain Davis-
Bacon legislation? Overall, how well can a CBDO carry out its multiple roles as a
business and a social agency?

How and whether to lobby was a subject of discussion at numerous workshops and plenaries. At one such meeting, after recognizing the legal constraints
on nonprofit lobbying, a director of a state association concluded, "If we don't
lobby, we don't exist, though we call it legislative education." At a subsequent
luncheon, speakers argued that politicians who resent the lobbying aren't going
to support the community development movement anyway.

Conference workshops often end up as vibrant debates on the direction of the movement—can advocacy coexist with development?—or exhortations to continue to fight the fight, or, more recently, mini pep rallies to support lobbying efforts. The speeches made at conference sessions often are dramatic and quite moving and clearly are based on much thought and effort. I asked a leading developmental activist why, in spite of the work involved, he so willingly volunteered to speak. He described that these speeches provided a chance to show that community development is about much more than real estate construction:

> I believe this is a movement and . . . if all we were about was real estate development then I don't think a lot of us would participate. . . . Many of us do see that what we're doing is we're part of the movement and we're part of a movement that isn't satisfied with how social policy is being played out. . . . We have a sense that we can build new systems that begin to address poverty. . . . It is important to make sure that you're not only connected but helping nurture the movement.

He shared with others his understanding of the organic theories of change.

At one memorable lunch, Ernesto Cortes, the organizer for the activist Industrial Areas Foundation, gave a speech showing the linkage between development and advocacy, providing a finely honed definition of what an activist-based development should be about. He argued that physical development is not enough:

> Unfortunately . . . the only kind of capital that we think is important is financial capital and we fail to recognize a very important point and that is financial capital can only be productive to the extent that a society or a culture or community has invested in human capital and invested in what economists call social overhead capital.

He continued to explain that social capital is

> really nothing more than and nothing less than the robustness of the relationship that exists in the communities. Whether or not a community has relationships of trust, whether or not there are networks of relationships between people to sustain the culture, to develop young people and to transmit values.

For Cortes, the reasons for doing the bricks and mortar projects is to enable such capital to be built. Questions followed the speech, asking how to link advocacy to development, and how to balance out the fervor required in social movements with the necessity to compromise to obtain project funding.

His speech was received with standing applause. But now the ways in which organic theory emerges became apparent. Msgr. William Lindner spoke next. Lindner the founder of NCC, one of the nation's most successful CBDOs, praised the work of Cortes, arguing that "we are very much tied to an Ernie Cortes and his thinking." But then he built upon Cortes's idea of social capital to argue that the poor should own their own community, that is possess the material capital, a core part of the organic theory of community-based development. According to Msgr. Lindner, empowerment for the poor comes about when people and communities are in control of property:

> You begin now to create your own kind of resources and your banks for resources. . . . [T]he community now can control so much of its future because it really controls its development corporation and it really controls a lot of the resources that you need to see something.

He concluded by arguing that community power comes about when developers work with both advocates and social service providers. While not disagreeing with Cortes, Lindner reframed the discussion to show how developmental activities bring about empowerment in a different way.

Conferences help socialize new members both to the NCCED and to the development field. Special luncheons are held for those attending for the first time while older members take newcomers under wing. New members busily take notes, and as they learn that the norm is to ask detailed questions, do so, and are rewarded by patient and informed answers. Much information is shared with newcomers and the old alike about the values that guide the movement and the problems that beset activists.

At one dramatic plenary session in Boston, leading activists sat in front of a packed auditorium and were grilled by those in the audiences on the tensions that divided the movement. Topics ranged from whether small CBDOs could even make a dent against poverty given the massive threats faced by urban America, the compatibility of advocacy and development, to what constitutes "community" within community development, and whether or not CBDOs spend too much time chasing the dollars, rather than working with the community. In this public dialogue, issues such as whether owning and managing property distracts CDCs from their missions of social change, and how well CDCs can cope with urban ethnic fragmentation in their communities, or handle corruption in their profession were actively debated.

Comments were quite blunt even though the meeting was being taped. Issues of corruption were frankly discussed, or when asked about competition in the movement, a speaker answered:

> Politics in our community [movement] is as vicious as it gets anywhere. . . . We are all advocates. Then there's money in the drawer. Then there's jobs. Where those jobs go and who gets them and who keeps them and who survives them. . . . We get pretty bloody. What you are seeing here is the survivors.

But then he continued by arguing on the need to overcome such disruptive competition and indicated how sharing information enabled CBDOs to do so.

Reflexive self-criticism also occurs. A leader in the field pointed out how CBDOs should not forget their origins as part of a broader community change movement:

> When we begin to talk about the whole notion of advocacy versus development, because that is the issue we are actually struggling with . . . I believe what happens to most of us who begin to see ourselves as tenured [CBDO] directors also begin to take ourselves a little too seriously. . . . I honestly believe that when we revisit and get into a corner and say we just did this housing development and it looks good and it feels good and I'm happy with [it], everybody is happy with it, "Boy oh boy, am I great!" All we have to do is turn that corner and go back to the community and say, "How do you feel about what I just did?"
>
> I challenge you to do that. . . . Measure yourself by those who formed you and those who gave you the message of moving forward, and I think you will find that you will have to balance them both. You will have to continue to advocate . . . for that community on behalf of that community while continuing your economic and housing development.

People respond to questions on the dilemmas faced with quite practical advice that, as suggested by the organic theory, CBDOs cannot ignore the realities of concentrated poverty. For instance, at a panel on getting mortgages from banks, questions were raised on what to do about the weak credit ratings of poor minorities. Being fully supportive of people who had been victims of discrimination is core to what the field is about, yet the CBDOs want to assure they or the banks get the loans repaid. The response recognized the tensions involved, the obligation to help the poor, but do so in a financially responsible way:

> If we were going to insist that we only want people with unblemished credit records we wouldn't be able to make any loans. . . . So what we have to do is try to distinguish between which of the problems are indicative of the people [who] really have no intention to retaining their loan and which of them I think that are not that substantial. . . . If we're going to do a loan, you got to work with the folks and try to massage it into something that is bankable.

Panels and plenaries communicate far more than the overt information presented. It is a rare panel that doesn't reflect the ambivalence felt by many CBDOs, as they try to balance out the fact that they are businesses, proud to own property, and run in the black, but also part of a tradition of social change concerned with more fundamental issues than the bottom line. A director of an economically successful CBDO explained that they do the work they do to try to overcome the structure of the economy in which the "rich get rich and the poor get poorer," while others argue on the need to create the social capital that enables the poor to participate in the economy, yet at the same time pointing out that a bankrupted CBDO can accomplish nothing.

In many ways it is the latent content of the meetings that is as important as the manifest discussions. The ways in which exchanges take place, the subtexts contained within the information, and the very fact that the meetings bring together a diverse group of organizations operating in a financially competitive environment, help build a community that can speak to the broader public with a common voice. Newer developmental activists and those in the smaller cities learn they are not alone and that even the most successful CBDOs are in the same uphill battle to convince government and the foundations that the effort to combat concentrated poverty is a worthwhile endeavor. Those from the smaller organizations learn that the behemoths in the field face the same environment of concentrated poverty and reinforcing social ills, and to get resources they must negotiate with a foundation world that might want to help, but doesn't quite understand, while dealing at the same time with recalcitrant government agencies. The latent message is that we, big and small, urban and rural, in spread-out Phoenix and concentrated Chicago, are in this fight together, and it is a common fight.

Further, the message is made clear that there is no one cookie-cutter approach to development, so that individual innovation is to be tried. New construction is the norm on the west side of Chicago, simply because there is so much empty space from burnt-out, torn-down buildings, while in the north side of Philadelphia innovative techniques for (literally) holding up old buildings have been developed to reduce the costs of providing affordable housing. What is taught, is that there are no simply resolutions to the numerous tradeoffs that are required to renew hope within impoverished communities.

Participants gain confidence that the answer "it depends" is not simply a cop-out. Different settings, and local history and city governments require separate responses to what at first seem to be similar problems. In some cities, community developers, direct action organizers, and those in community action agencies work hand in glove with one another, while in other places relations, if they exist at all, are quite acrimonious. Knowing that sometimes housing should precede commercial renewal and others times the reverse, can reduce the internecine squabbling that occur in locales between organizations that promote one or the other approach.

Through the arguments that occur in the corridors at meetings, in the small seminars, and in the larger plenaries, on the values and goals of the field, participants slowly work out a broader and shared model of a holistic approach to community-based development. This broader model then shapes how these developers collectively speak to funders and government, as the developers present a more unified view of what their work should be about. The shared consensus, a common "framing" of what community development is about, helps create an ideological definition for the field.

## The Conference Tour

Central to the socialization that occur in the conferences are the exchanges that take place on the tours. These tours become part of the lore of the continuing convention, a lore that evolves into almost a cultural myth for those who come back year after year, and in some way gives identity to the movement.

Tours combine visits to innovative or complicated holistic projects with trips to a few ordinary housing efforts. For old-timers, a visit to a apartment refurbished through a tax credit deal teaches little that is new, but for those new to the profession such projects are the meat and potatoes of what their startup organizations must learn to do. For an established CBDO, a visit to New Communities Corporation can prove to be an inspiration. During such visits, I watched experienced developmental activists take notes on the restaurants and the daycare facilities, especially those for AIDS babies, and later learned that some attempted similar projects.

Tours provide insights on how to cope with those problems, not taught in classes or in training academies, that can spell the difference between failure and success. Participants learn, for instance, that LISC can be more readily stalled on a loan repayment than can a city's development department, or that eliminating the charge for a water tap on fee is a nontrivial concession that a city can make that lowers the cost of providing affordable housing. They see first hand how a project can be set up to accomplish multiple purposes—a soup kitchen within a refurbished transient hotel—and by doing so leverage money from different sources.

There is a pleasant camaraderie among the participants on these tours—competing for the too few meat pies served with freshly brewed Sam Adams beer in a CBDO-sponsored incubator in Boston in which both the baking and beer firm began, or the surprised looks at discovering an in-door golf-putting range in a building owned by an inner-city CBDO. But even the fun provides learning—jocularly expressed rivalries over ethnic foods, triggered by shared meals that feature a variety of ethnic flavors, or visits to multicultural food stores—turn into conversations on how to use ethnic resources as a base for neighborhood renewal. Purchases made at community arts and crafts stores, or of Native American jewelry, turn into ideas of what can be built at home and stimulate similar projects.

Most of all, the tours are intense learning experiences in which those in the movement help one another to learn and grow. At each site the questioning is deep and pointed and those being questioned answer with a seeming frankness and openness, both on the technical details and the underlying reasons why things were done. On several sites that I visited twice, once as an individual researcher and later as part of a tour, the developmental activists were far more willing to talk about "short-cuts" and failings in front of the larger tour, than they were in our private conversations. On one occasion, a staff person for a CBDO seemed to be sidestepping questions on how the organization placated funders on an economically marginal project. The executive director intervened and in a direct fashion revealed sub-rosa negotiations needed to keep projects afloat.

The learning is enhanced, as those on the tour add in their experiences to the insights provided by the hosts. Such conversations enable new developmental activists to understand the variety and potential in the development world. At one site, the spokesperson described how his organization got funded for a 159-unit Nehemiah Grant project. Getting this large grant was impressive, but the number of homes being built would exceed the total affordable housing production done in many cities, discouraging others from even thinking about applying for similar funding. But a person in the audience, herself a well-known national figure, immediately interjected that her CBDO

> got one of the smallest Nehemiah Grants this year; we received a grant for seven units at $15,000 each. The formula is the exact same, the land was given by the city, for a dollar. And I just want you to know that when you are looking at something this massive don't assume you can't go home and do the very same thing. . . .If you got three lots on a corner, you probably could compete for a Nehemiah Grant . . . Please believe, we are not recreating the wheel out here. Understand, that two houses can be done this way or 250 homes can be done.

And, by doing so encouraging smaller CBDOs to apply for the funding, reasserting the moral obligation in the organic theory of attempting what others fear to try.

A subliminal message is given to those on the tour, since to visit a developmental site, you, naturally enough, have to get there. And, in this case, getting there can be much of the learning. Whether visiting the high-rise slums in Chicago or Newark, the blocks of abandonment in Philadelphia, or the dusty dryness in the colonias, developmental activists learn that poverty and neglect have multiple faces beyond the locales and ethnicities that they each serve.

On the bus rides on the tours, activists swap stories and tell tales on what works and what might not. Driving by an inner-city shopping center, those on the tour learn that when a bank started to renege on the financing, the community activists reminded the bank that the CBDO was associated with a church having a membership in the thousands, implying threatened advocacy efforts. A bus parked outside a school quickly moved as the speaker pointed out the gun holes in the adjacent buildings from the ongoing gang warfare. Yet across the street a landowner refused to sell his property to the CBDO, realizing that if the community-based development organization's project were to be successful, his property value would dramatically increase. Bullet holes and land speculation, hope and enthusiasm, but sensible inner-city caution.

An incredible variety of projects are explored, from simple efforts to repairing homes, to what appeared in Newark to be an entire new inner city being built by the New Communities Corporation. On one city tour, we visited a community center doing housing, a car repair-garage-cum-day-care center qua microenterprise generator, a streetscape developer and a large incubator. Elsewhere people wondered why there even was a CBDO since the street visited seemed to be a vibrant commercial strip. The developmental activist then narrated how his CBDO resurrected the community area. The very normalcy of the present-day appearance was the victory of the organization.

On a two day intensive presession in Chicago, we saw homes and businesses established by Bethel New Life, several incubators including one for artists, buildings converted from dope houses to affordable housing. We visited with a self-management project in public housing that itself had spun off a CBDO. We were driven around a totally redone commercial area during which a developmental activist described the complementarity between housing and commercial renewal. We passed through several projects that appeared to have failed, one held back by the breakup of a for-profit partner, the other handicapped by quarrels between four neighborhood development organizations. At lunch, talks were given on how CBDOs joined with neighborhood associations to lobby for programs to maintain Chicago's industrial corridors. Another meal was spent hearing about how to work with churches as co-developers. During the drives between the widely scattered locales, and places in Chicago can be an hour apart even during periods of low traffic, the tour guides—heads of two of the activist coalitions— explained what their coalitions did, and interpreted how the background politics of the city affected what CBDOs could achieve.

Many of the projects visited demonstrate holistic development efforts, in which housing supports commercial development and social services are integrated within physical development. The most dramatic case was the work done by the New Communities Corporation (NCC), which ranged from large-scale affordable apartments, a job center, and a community supermarket, to restaurants, transitional apartments for the homeless, several day care centers, job training programs, and most moving of all a day-care center for babies born HIV positive. To sit on the floor of the day-care center and cradle these babies, while learning how to fund such projects, cannot but help to motivate developmental activists to continue their struggle, and provides them with reasons to try.

Questioning on tours quickly homes in on quite technical matters, as people ask such brasstack questions as "when you talk about starting that development fee to the non-profit parent corporation, how do you handle the issues of unrelated business taxable income in that when the fees are generated?" Answers are given that are better left unheard by public authorities. In informal asides and over drinks and food, managers of one CBDO noted how the city tried to sabotage their work and then elaborated on the machinations needed to do an end run around a recalcitrant local government.

Descriptions on the tours repeatedly took on the cant of what has been termed a story (Rubin and Rubin 1995, pp. 232–34), a rendition given to emphasize the important moral lessons that can be drawn. Stories show the need to be clever and, perhaps, cut corners. After eating a meal in the headquarters of NCC, in a restaurant tastefully laid out in what had been a church building and whose gourmet food attracted downtown business people to eat outside of their enclaves, the speaker described how a "miracle" occurred that made the facility possible.

The restaurant, as well as the main offices of NCC, are built in a refurbished church, but as the plan for the restaurant emerged, troubles occurred, as there was inadequate parking and no room for expansion except on a spot occupied by small abandoned priory building for which the city had been delaying to issue a removal permit. As the story is told, the monsigneur prayed for a miracle in front of his active congregation in another church, and one weekend, by gosh, folk appeared with tools, and by Monday the building was miraculously gone sans official permission.

On another tour I again heard repeated to the assembled group the same story that I was told on a personal interview (Rubin 1994). The developmental activist explained why his group did both housing and commercial work since

> we recognized . . . there wouldn't be any bakeries if there weren't people who could afford baked goods. And if there weren't any bakeries, there wouldn't be children growing up learning there were people who baked. So there really was kind of a holistic effort to try to figure out commercial develop[ment], but not just so that we could revitalize some old junk buildings but so this could really become a new main street for a very eclectic multiracial, multi-ethnic neighborhood.

This story was an icon for models of holistic, neighborhood redevelopment.

Core to the tours were the talks provided by those people who had brought about the projects. The beginnings of most of the talks were rehearsed presentations that I have no reason to suspect were not the same renditions given to visiting city or foundation officials. But the tones changed, either in response to focused questioning by those in the audience, or perhaps out of an obligation to share with those within the field booby traps to avoid and tricks that enable CBDOs to succeed. Some exaggerations do appear. On a tour, one speaker indicated that his organization would probably pull out a profit of a half a million dollars plus from one deal that I later learned turned out to be half as much. Still even this story reflected the ethos of the field to fight even if it seems like nothing is working, as the developmental activist described it: "We've received only one check so far . . . so we are a little behind. But that is what groups like ours are supposed to be for."

Problems with funding are discussed again and again; a question, "Could you go through the financing again and where you stand in terms of your debts" gets such a detailed answer only an accountant, or the head of a highly leveraged community development organization could understand. Quite human difficulties are described, for example, what to do about a Chinese restaurant that had stayed open while a building was being refurbished to be an African-American arts incubator. The financially wise and humane decision was made not to evict the Asian owner. Answers are frank: one developer for instance, described how he had been totally deceived by a business person on his board, who claimed that a business was a permanent fixture of the community, only to remove the firm in its entirety. Questioning is pointed: those on a tour asked why one organization had men in their mechanics shop and women running the day-care center. When subsidy figures are provided, someone in the audience is bound to add them up and if they don't properly total, questions are asked of why, usually eliciting further descriptions of as yet unmentioned funding.

Important clarifications are requested, as when one speaker mentioned that the housing project succeeded because the local churches pressured the city government. The speaker was interrupted by a question from the touring group wondering how such pressures are brought about. The answer reflected the realities of local politics and the ways in which niche organizations can be effective in encouraging others to join in:

> During election time . . . all [the elected officials] need to see is those twenty men [the ministers] and they will move . . . , given the fact that any two or three of those ministers can get 200 people on a day's notice down to city hall. You don't have to say that but they know it. But at the same time, you are not coming in and asking anything outrageous. You are asking them to become a partner and this is what you need to do in order to be a partner.

And, on tours, even the tensions within the movement itself are discussed. A coalition director described rivalries between different development organizations as one of the groups started a large-scale effort to upgrade a retail shopping strip:

> What happens when there are multiple organizations all targeting similar kinds of changes at a community, . . . but coming at it from completely different perspectives, focusing on completely different tools, from organizing to housing development, to business development, to service and advocacy. . . .Well, you can imagine the concern and the interest of the other three community development organizations in

the neighborhood [over the strip]. The organizing group and the housing group said, "What is this going to do to our housing values? Are . . . we going to see our constituents displaced and have no reason for being here?"

At the same [time], the social service agency took a look what is this going to mean for employment for our people for our people. "What is this going to mean for business opportunities for some of the entrepreneurs that we work with?" And they started to say, "Well, we are in favor of this if . . . it includes a firm first source hiring agreement for those residents. We are in favor of this if there are real business opportunities for low-income entrepreneurs in the community."

The speaker continued by detailing the pedagogical lesson of what those on the tour could learn about:

how each group looked at the development, how they looked at it as a threat to the community, how they looked at it as an opportunity for the community, how they instituted some community structures that build in tensions, even between organizations, and how ultimately they did . . . cooperate at least to some extent on the project.

What to the activists in this city was a quite precarious situation was translated by those running the tour as a set of experiences from which others could learn and perhaps avoid similar problems. In addition, it was an object lesson of the need to think holistically.

Tours reinforce among their participants that they can and should help one another, that developmental groups can work out their own strategies for change, and provide an inkling that the goal is to persuade, perhaps manipulate, the funders to buy into the agendas of the community groups themselves. The tours, and the conferences, reinforce the awareness that developmental activists are working from a shared set of beliefs about what should be done and why.

In addition, the tours and conferences themselves strengthen the sponsoring coalitions and trade associations. Successful conferences mean that more members sign up and a stronger force comes into being. Further, since government officials, intermediaries, and bankers also attend the meetings, these funders learn that the trade associations and coalitions do speak for the developmental activist. The trade associations and coalitions build on this image of unity in their campaigns to pressure these funders to support the community development movement. How this occurs is discussed in the next chapter.

# CHAPTER 10

# Traditional and Coalition Advocacy

CDCs [have] become that front for downtown [funders] by . . . not bit-
ing the hand that feeds them. Shit, bite it once and a while. At least,
nibble at it.

—an old-line activist turned developer

How do you organize all those turf-oriented people to come together
collaboratively to respond to some common issues 'cause they really
ought to be very concerned about how will my organization fare in
this. And what's in it for me?

—a coalition director

In the competitive world for public funding, efforts are required to persuade
those in public office to support nonprofit housing developers. As the head of
an activist trade association explained,

[the movement] has to be pro-active, setting the partnership [with fun-
ders] from the direction of the community-based organizations. . . . So,
instead of always participating in somebody's else's thing, we need to
set up our own projects and invite them to participate in what we are
doing.

However, aggressive actions on the part of community-based development organizations that depend on government for funds can be problematic. As an activist
warned,

you should never bite the hand that feeds but if you know you got to
bite that hand you shouldn't go them for food.

To reconcile these problems, community-based development organizations advocate and pressure through their trade associations and coalitions.

Coalition lobbying and direct action campaigns are often successful. During
the study, I witnessed campaigns to defend CRA, another that convinced Congress to make the Low Income Housing Tax Credit a permanent part of the tax
code, as well as a near success to set up NCEPA, federal funding targeted toward
the community development movement. In Chicago, developmental activists persuaded the city to reprogram funds from downtown to low-income neighborhoods

237

while providing substantial sums for affordable housing. In Ohio, a combined CDC—Housing Advocate-Community Action campaign succeeding in changing state laws, both making housing into a public purpose eligible for subsidies, and adding a line to the state budget in support of nonprofit developers. Overall, in the words of a coalition director,

> as a new or old programs are being designed and evaluated, implemented, . . . we have a respected place at the table, helping to design and implement and evaluate and change the program. I mean if you have to boil it down, that's what all advocacy campaigns that we work on are about.

## FROM CONVENTIONAL TO COALITION ADVOCACY

In their involvement in advocacy and lobbying, coalitions and trade associations carry on a tradition of the community development movement. As Goetz and Sidney (1995, p. 5) report, many CBDOs are "an outgrowth of other ongoing community-based activities [including] opposition to urban renewal plans, Community Reinvestment Act challenges, tenant organizing." Other studies show that "50 percent [of the CBDOs] engaged in community organizing and 25 percent did tenant organizing" (Goetz and Sidney 1995, p. 5), while a third of the CBDOs do advocacy to support the Community Reinvestment Act (Center for Public Finance and Housing 1994). Even successful developers maintain links to the community organization tradition.

> [T]here was just as much organizing activity among the older [CBDOs] as among recently formed [CBDOs], suggesting that these groups are not less likely to organize residents as they grow. (Goetz and Sidney 1995, p. 6)

Organizing has enabled developmental activists to gain seats on the boards of public-private funders that allocate developmental money. A developmental activist who had been a community organizer, said that as a result of protest activities:

> I sit on the reinvestment board of [four banks]. . . . And I sits on . . . the economic development board of the city of [name ]. So, I sits (chuckles).
>     I watches all the money to make sure the underserved communities get their fair share. . . . I know better what their needs are [better] than those guys with those fancy ties and shirts on that sit at the board.
>     . . . I don't back up. They see me coming, I'd like bite my fingernails, but I am a hard nose. And I like numbers. I'll sit there all day and quote the numbers. . . . They are not used to having community people

pull the bullet. . . . Because I get the statistics. I know what go on. I go out into those communities. . . . I got time for that because it is empowering the black community, the poor community, the community that no banks is going to deal with.

Being at the table might can mean having sufficient power to pressure government to back the CBDOs when neighborhoods are harmed by businesses or banks. In an iconic case, a national firm had negotiated a grant with the city and, in return, promised to maintain an older plant. The director of that neighborhood's CBDO, though, had been hearing rumors of the plant's shutdown:

We had gotten one anonymous letter sloppily typed from a worker that said, "I fear that this that and the other thing is coming." . . . The letter . . . was sent to the mayor. The mayor's office gave it to the commissioner of economic development, . . . who gave me a phone call and sent the letter to me and I confronted the [plant's] president with it. He categorically denied it and said, "By the way send me a copy of the letter" and he, not only did he deny it but he said, "Why would we shut down when we're so profitable?"

Shortly, thereafter the plant shut down, firing all its employees. The director of the deceived CBDO was disillusioned:

I was really burned out . . . and dispirited by the whole notion that I could have been so naive to think that this conglomeration of businesses really gives a shit about the community and every ounce of leftist literature that I was reading was feeding into this insecurity cause. . . . I was starting to think business people were greedy and didn't give a shit.

But with the support of the city government, a coalition of community organizations led a massive protest against the shutdown. This coalition employed Alinsky-style tactics, gained some concessions, including the donation of the abandoned building, but the shutdown remained. The city made resources available for reemploying the displaced workers and offered generous incentives to help the CBDO do something with the abandoned building. With the guarantee of local support, the CBDO was able to get a federal grant to reopen the building, though now housing businesses that paid far less than did the initial employer.

Some coalitions have close enough relationships with those in government that government itself takes the lead in pressuring the banks. In one case, a pro-neighborhood faction was trying to convince bankers to set up a fund to pay for affordable housing. Many of the banks were quite willing to cooperate, but some seemed recalcitrant. In the words of the ranking government official who was conducting the negotiations:

I call these friends of mine [in the community movement] and I say, "Look, why don't you picket the bank president's house and here is where he lives and here is his annual report." . . . So I spent a year and a half on the phone every day with a variety of community groups working on beating up the banks while negotiating with the banks acting like I was trying to protect them from the community organizers. I was playing kind of both sides against the middle role, but my heart and the mayor's heart was clearly on trying to get the banks to come to the table.

A place at the table might be institutionalized through the creation of a Housing Trust Fund, especially one in which community housing advocates or developers allocate the money. Campaigns to establish the funds are undertaken by broad-scale coalitions of neighborhood organizations, housing advocates, and community-based development organizations, frequently coordinated by the Center for Community Change. As an example, SHAC, the advocacy coalition in Illinois, had worked from 1987 to 1989 to convince the legislature to pass a Housing Trust Fund paid for by a nominal income stream from a real estate transfer tax. During the campaign, opposition occurred:

The realtors didn't want to increase the real estate transfer tax and the white ethnics in the House don't want THEM in their districts, so they're not going to vote for affordable housing.

In response, SHAC bused people to Springfield and working with other social activists to conduct noisy protests. A participant remembered:

We had these signs, "Free the Human Services Hostages." But the legislature came out and started yelling at us, "Don't be our conscience!" We said, "Then don't be assholes and at least call some of those [bills] for a vote." They closed the blinds so they didn't have to look at our signs.

Encouraged by this pressure and with the support of the majority leader and the legislative Black Caucus, the bill passed.

Some tactics followed are redolent of those used by traditional protest groups. A development activist shared his experiences in persuading a bank to loan money:

The bank wasn't happy with the way we approached them. We showed them all this data and statistics and etc. And, at the time, a group of churches, about twenty churches along with us, . . . "we want to sit down and put a program together." And the bank declined and they did not want to talk about putting a reinvestment program together.

We proved to the local bank that we had the data. And the data was from the Woodstock Institute, surveys that we did in the community and all that different type of data that we brought forward that they was not reinvesting.

And it got so that it began to be a three-ring [circus] 'cause what we had to do was bring out the peoples. And we brought busloads of people into the bank lobby, into the streets, around the bank. We had churches to call up and tap the bank line. The bank couldn't communicate to business for three days. The bank was developing a new bank. . . . We sent busloads of people over there to stop the contractors. The contractors couldn't do any work. So we just shut down the whole operation.

We said, "You don't want to talk with us poor people with a legitimate plan. We don't come to fight, we come to talk." The bank wasn't used to sitting down and talking with poor, low-income people. . . . Just because we're poor doesn't mean we ain't got nothing to say. You know. And it came to a point that the protest began. Like I say, we pulled the churches in and we were organized, and we pulled the churches in and the community was in. And we shut the bank down for a few days. . . . And, finally it came to the point where they decided that they would have me put together a draft of what we want.

This protest and other similar actions encouraged banks to negotiate a citywide community reinvestment package to be run under the supervision of a board that contained community activists.

Other action campaigns forcefully remind government of its obligations in poor communities. In one case, direct actions were used to persuade both government and a charitable group to keep a hospital open until the CBDO could acquire sufficient funds to buy and redevelop the property. The tactics described by the developer were reminiscent of those used in the civil rights era:

[W]e had a pray-vigil around the hospital right at the critical moments and before all this had been negotiated. And got enough folks out, got twenty churches out, and got enough folks out to have a hand to hand around the whole square block of the hospital with candles. And then once we made the whole human link around the hospital and prayed, you know, God would help keep the hospital open.

Elsewhere, a statewide coalition responded to cutbacks in funding for affordable housing by holding the

first annual neighborhood fax-in . . . community organizing for the '90s. We found out that there were two fax machines in the [state] house; two in the Senate and one in the governor's office. And we inundated those

SOBs. We set out so many faxes. . . . We get a phone call . . . "the governor just called, the governor's office just called and they're listening . . . knock it off!!" and . . . it had only been two hours and we said, "Well, gee, you know, we're really not capable of doing that. We've turned them all loose."

In another state, a coalition, working with a supportive solon performed virtual street-theater to pressure the state legislature to continue a program that

helps nonprofits that work with handicapped individuals. . . . [W]e brought out a fellow who has cerebral palsy . . . I mean he could talk but you couldn't understand him. He had an interpreter who could understand him and then she would tell you what he was saying. You saw somebody who definitely was unemployable.

Instead, he owns a business now that employs eleven people. . . . It's a small newspaper, community newspaper. . . . And he is an entrepreneur. . . . We brought him in to testify and once people saw that. I mean their mouths dropped. No one said a word against him in both houses.

Though direct actions do occur, more often, "community organizing for the '90s" involves day in day out efforts to lobby, though done in ways that stay within the legal limits for nonprofits. Lobbyists for the movement frame to those in government what community development is about in terms that public officials can accept. A coalition director explained that

we don't call it a grant program; we tell the legislators, this is an investment which brings back dollars to the state. We show the truly small amounts of money that we get in grants and then we show them our ability to access federal dollars back in to the state grants to do construction or economic development and some of the figures. We can even get Republicans to agree to some of the investment programs.

## COALITION ADVOCACY

But advocacy by individual CBDOs can prove problematic. For developmental activists, putting together deals is time consuming, leaving few hours and less energy to lobby, advocate, or organize. A coalition head explained to me:

[I]t is very difficult [to advocate] because the folks in the large institutions have the luxury of time and money to do this kind of work. . . . Whereas our members are expected to do all the work that they are supposed to do at the community level with horribly low wages and horribly low resources. . . . And then to also participate in [the coalition]. And . . . fight these citywide fights.

Worse yet, the very targets of the campaigns are often the funders whose support is needed. For instance, activists recognize that HUD should be attacked because of its horrible inefficiencies that create obstacle piled on top of obstacle for the affordable housing movement. Yet HUD remains Washington's strongest bureaucratic advocate for community renewal and the largest source of funds for housing.

Instead of the individual CBDOs leading direct actions, the work of lobbying, advocating, and ultimately protesting is undertaken through coalitions and trade associations that "tr[y] to fight those fights on behalf of our members." Sometimes all that is needed is gathering information and ensuring that this data is strategically placed into the policy process. For instance, studies done by the Center for Community Change, or the Woodstock Institute that document the extent of mortgage, and more recently insurance, redlining have become the weapons of choice to persuade officials that financial institutions, are not living up to the Community Reinvestment Act. An official from Woodstock remarked:

the fact that we publish by community, by seventy-seven community groups—[loan originations] by gender and race and income. The banks know what stuff [the CBDOs] have there and . . . the banks have corrected themselves. . . . But the fact that the information's out there, that it's available, and it's useful I think is partly what is responsible for the banks doing whatever community lending they do.

Advocacy coalitions often come about as those in the community development movement join with housing or social service advocates to create metacoalitions. Joan Pogge describes how the antiredlining coalition in Chicago, one that eventually forced the First National Bank to reinvest in poor neighborhoods, brought together three different sectors of community activism:

Gale Cincotta was a leader of the original redlining fight. . . . Mary Nelson was executive director of Bethel New Life, one of the most productive community development corporations in Chicago. . . . Jim Capraro, executive director of Greater Southwest Development Corporation, was a national pioneer in commercial and industrial revitalization. The combination of perspectives that included community organizing, low-income housing development, and commercial and industrial revitalization was key to shaping an agreement. (Pogge 1992, p. 137)

Such coalitions gain strength by becoming part of national networks, that in turn help establish local affiliates. For instance, Illinois' State Housing Action

Coalition initially gained its skills through training programs provided by the National Low Income Housing Coalition.

Multipronged efforts do work, with each participant contributing its own strengths. To combat efforts to gut the Community Reinvestment Act, direct action housing advocates joined with builders to form the National Community Reinvestment Coalition. On another occasion, NCCED, LISC, and advocates for affordable housing came together in the campaign to make the Low Income Housing Tax Credit permanent. Specialists from the development organizations helped draft legislation, the activist National Low Income Housing Coalition rallied its members to lobby elected representatives through out the nation, while the Alinsky-style Neighborhood Peoples' Action activated its national membership and was able to "get 150 calls into Washington in an hour and [to get] congressmen [to] change these votes."

A purpose of coalition advocacy is to diffuse the blame for direct actions and by doing so protect those in the CBDOs from retaliation. A speaker at an NCCED conference described, "in coalitions you rotate so everyone does not have to take the hit." The director of a citywide coalition elaborated:

> My board president [from a CBDO] will not go the mayor's office and sit down and say, "Look, God damn it [hits the table], you better put some more money into housing right now or we are going to call a press conference blasting the fact that city did less than a 100 units of housing last year." But he will call me up and say, "You get your butt over there and do it.". . . My board president has a three million dollar deal sitting there for the mayor to sign off on.

Sometimes more buffering is required, since the public officials are well aware that a coalition director is really speaking for a CBDO, which still could be subject to retaliation. In these cases,

> there is a strategy you're finding more, especially with this [more conservative city] administration in office. People are creating [pause], I tend to call them shell coalitions. And a shell coalition stand[s] up and say [shouts] "Mayor so and so." And so you [the mayor] get mad at that coalition and mad at that staff person [who is] executive director of the coalition.

Shell coalitions protect the individual CBDOs from retaliation by setting up a two stage remove between those who need the money and those who lead the public demonstrations. As an instance, in Chicago, the Neighborhood Capital Budget Group (NCBG), brought together housing advocates, economic developers, and housing developers, who in turn ran a campaign to redirect the city's capital budget, a daring action as it constituted a direct threat to Chicago's politics as usual. The activists in the NCBG were chosen from the coalitions, rather than the individual development organizations, providing buffering for the individual CBDOs.

Coalition advocacy becomes part of a continuing effort to change the political opportunity structure (Tarrow 1994). These efforts can be seen in both Ohio and in Massachusetts in which the state coalitions step by step improved the environment for community development.

Until 1989, the Ohio state constitution did not consider housing as a public purpose, thereby denying needed funding. In response, the state CDC association obtained a foundation grant to research state laws on public purpose, joined together with several advocacy organizations and successfully pressured the legislature into passing a constitutional amendment making housing a public purpose. As part of this continuing campaign, the CDC association persuaded the legislature to approve $4.35 million as a budget line item to support community-based development organizations. To bring about this end, the coalition built bridges between legislative liberals wanting to help those in need and conservatives who appreciated the self-help, capitalist approach within the community development movement.

Such legislative action are strengthened when the statewide group can orchestrate the efforts carried out by the individual CBDOs. For instance, the Massachusetts Association of Community Development Corporations—MACDC—convinced the state legislature to set up dedicated funding for the community-based development organizations. To bring this about, MACDC first circulated a list of accomplishments of the development groups district by district to the legislators. Then, the MACDC worked with individual CBDOs to make sure they explained to their own legislators of the importance of the projects done in each district. Development activists were advised to

> contact . . . your legislator. Write him or her a thank-you note. Send them annual reports. Send them newsletters. Send them press clippings. . . . Invite them to meetings so they'll know who your group is. . . . And what we do in Massachusetts . . . is we put together a legislative briefing every year. . . . We . . . have it at noon and serve lunch. . . . I'm talking tuna fish sandwiches and potato chips. . . . And when they come to briefings, they see in the room lots of CDCs, lots of community people, lots of their other colleagues who are there as well counting heads.
>
> And . . . the reason there are other senators and representatives in the room at that legislative briefing is because the local CDC have called their local senators and their local reps, and said, "Hi, we're gonna be in Boston, are you coming to the briefing?" "Are you going to hear about our issues?"
>
> What we do is we put together a briefing packet. . . . We have factsheets on each of the budget items that are important to us. . . .

We're making this as easy as possible. . . . We have a very simple brochure that tells you what it is that CDCs are. We call this "CDC making a difference in your community." And it basically says what a CDC is and how its working and all that. We have this item . . . which is questions [that] policy makers frequently ask about community development corporations. . . . Why do we need CDC? They're not project developers. Why aren't CDCs self-sufficient? . . . And most importantly, we have a sample of news clippings of our members activities from all around the state. Urban areas, rural areas, general news articles about CDC, photographs.

### *Tensions in Maintaining Advocacy Coalitions*

Maintaining advocacy coalitions, though, is very far from easy. The very structure of funding forces CBDOs to compete for the same money, requiring the coalition to bring potential rivals together. Activists argue that it is better for the CBDOs to figure out a fair allocation of money rather than be played off against one another by those in office. But interests do differ and allies in the community development movement can disagree on which federal programs to back and how strongly.

For instance, during the campaign to make the Low Income Housing Tax Credit permanent, more radical individuals argued that the LIHTC is "Feeding the Sparrows by Feeding the Horses" (Hartman 1992, p. 12), that is, arguing that LIHTC primarily helps rich investors reduce their taxes, provides fees for lawyers, but only aids the poor indirectly. In contrast, representatives from the intermediaries saw the LIHTC as "good policy, good politics" (Grogan and Roberts 1992, p. 13) that ensured that private investors would make sure that projects were built up to high standards (Grogan and Roberts 1992, p. 13).

Putting together metacoalitions can involve tense bargaining. A metacoalition was formed between the National Neighborhood Coalition, the Council of La Raza, LISC, Enterprise, the Low Income Housing Coalition, the Center for Community Change, NCCED, and DTI to work out strategies toward the Cranston-Gonzales Housing Bill. Observers described the coalition bargaining sessions as "real 'pissing matches'" with the developers like LISC pushing for the maximum amount of money to be made available for the nonprofits, while the advocates from the Center for Community Change were most concerned to ensure that the funds reached the lowest income groups.

## CAMPAIGNING COALITION STYLE

Coalition advocacy campaigns require constant attention to a changing political environment, a need to balance contending agendas of the constituent members of the coalition, and decisions on how best to incorporate tactics from a protest tradition within a developmental model. The three efforts detailed—preserving CRA, the failed campaign to create the NCEPA (National Community Economic Partnership Act), and a series of linked efforts in Chicago to increase the budget for development—illustrate these components of coalition advocacy.

### *Ongoing Efforts to Preserve CRA*

In the last decade the major continuing advocacy effort among housing and developmental activitsts has been to preserve the Community Reinvestment Act against right-wing attacks and bank recalcitrance to participate. As of the beginning of this study, successful CRA campaigns in Boston, Chicago, Pittsburgh, Milwaukee, and elsewhere have had tangible results: "$18 billion in reinvestment commitments have been negotiated in over 70 cities around the country" (Squires 1992, p. 12). Most of these efforts came about as mainstream advocacy organizers joined together with those in the community development movement to directly pressure banks, often following tactics such as those described on page 240.

As the financial health and corporate form of ever-merging banks change, so does the local CRA environment. Developmental activists vigilantly monitor the environment. In one case examined, a bank had been quite helpful to CBDOs, but then as a developmental activist and leader in the local coalition described it,

> the [bank name] got in major financial problems. . . . New management came in—they basically looked at this community development stuff and said, "Forget that. We got bigger problems to worry about" and so they really disappeared. They were gone from the community development market. . . . And all of their institutional knowledge about community development was either laid off or forced out or was gone.

In response, the citywide developers coalition had to "get a little more aggressive with them" and did so indirectly through pressuring the city. The bank

> came up in 1991 for city depository review . . . and the [development] consortium as a group opposed their designation as a depositor. . . . So the consortium said, "Well, if the city depository designation is going to mean anything, then this would be the case where you say, . . .". As a result of that . . . the city council gave them a probationary depository for six months and said, ". . . Well, that did get———Bank's attention, because you are talking about a lot of money. . . . It worked very well. . . . They came up with a new home mortgage program that was really the most progressive program. . . . They revamped their small

business division, put some good people in charge of it, and gave them
the authority to do something.

In a similar effort, in Cleveland, the city joined in with the community CRA
coalition to pressure Banc One to sign a major CRA agreement.

Nationally, the entire Community Reinvestment Act remained under attack
by a consortium of smaller and middle-sized banks spurred on by the antiregulatory
wing of the Republican Party. In response, several separate housing and community
development coalitions established a metacoalition—the National Community
Reinvestment Coalition—NCRC. NCRC maintains full-time pro-CRA lobbyists
in Washington, spotlights those banks that are playing fast and loose with CRA,
and publicizes CRA ratings of all banks. NCRC circulates studies done by the
Federal Reserve Banks that detail the persistence of racial discrimination in housing lending, and by doing so counters the banks' arguments that discrimination
based on race no longer occurs so CRA can be abandoned.

When faced with conservatives' 1994 efforts to gut the CRA, NCRC lead a
counter fight. Its director and staff worked the Hill, legislator by legislator, convened several national conferences in Washington of supporters of CRA that
then lobbied the Hill, and circulated numerous action alerts to encourage developmental activists and housing activists to make contact with their elected representatives. As of this writing, the NCRC effort has been successful. Though some
regulations have been streamlined, the heart of CRA remains. Bank lending data
still must be made public and banks that unfairly disinvest can be sanctioned.

### The NCEPA Campaign

In contrast to support for housing, very little federal money is made available for
community economic development work. CDBG funds can be used for these purposes, but the CDBG pot has numerous supplicants to feed, while money from
the Office of Community Services is very limited, perpetually threatened with
elimination, and available to many organizations other than the CBDOs. Leaders
in NCCED discussed the problem at both board meetings and workshops with
political consultant firms. The decision was made that NCCED should spearhead
an effort to create a source of federal money for community economic development and try to create for the community development movement "a home of
our own and vehicle . . . over which we had substantial control."

In structuring the campaign, NCCED's leaders anticipated tensions that
could occur between older established CBDOs and emerging organizations. Under
the proposed bill, established CBDOs would have separate access to a large revolving loan fund for high-risk economic development projects. At the same time, the
bill would provide "emerging" CDCs opportunities to compete for operating

grants and technical assistance money of up to $75,000 a year, money for which the older CDCs were not eligible. These newer CBDOs would become eligible for loans up to half a million dollars from a second revolving fund to carry out their economic development projects. However, these projects would be done with the technical assistance provided by the established organizations, hired with set-aside money to mentor newer groups through their first projects.

To help with the lobbying campaign, NCCED hired an experienced political consultancy firm that previously had worked for the old-line established CDCs. At NCCED's national conferences, representatives from the consultancy firm ran several workshops on lobbying strategies. During these discussions, both NCCED board members and the professional lobbyists stressed to the membership the benefits that would come about by having a dedicated source of funding. NCCED's board members made a personal commitment to the lobbying, with each member promising to fund part of the $175,000 required for the effort by raising at least $1,000 each. In addition, state associations promised to raise $1,000 each, while a gap of about $40,000 came from foundation grants.

To accommodate both the disparate interests of its own membership and pressures from Washington bureaucratic and legislative politics, changes were made in the proposed legislation. NCCED preferred setting up an independent agency to run the program, but accepted the need to place the program in either HHS or HUD. Deals were made so that NCEPA would not overlap with the provisions in the bill to support community development finance institutions that was being simultaneously considered.

The formal bill was introduced by Senator Kennedy in October of 1991, but only after NCCED had used its national network of CBDOs and state trade associations to encourage numerous other legislators to sign on. The established CDCs

> really focused on doing lobbying on the Hill. [For] some of the more mature CDCs it's part of their everyday work [to] work their congress-people. And they, the congresspeople are aware of who they are. They are pretty big players in terms of the politics locally. . . . When they're in Washington they usually make it a point to drop by to talk to a staffer and say, "Well, you know we're doing this ground breaking and this is what we're doing here and here's where the child-care center's going." And so that's sort of part of their work they see as keeping the federal elected officials involved and in tune with what they're doing locally.

Eventually the lobbying lead to the bill's having over fifty legislative sponsors and though there was "no groundswell" in Congress for the bill, there was little public opposition either.

Pushed by the uprisings in Los Angeles, NCEPA legislation moved rapidly through Congress and ended up as part of the Revenue Act of 1992, which unfortunately was vetoed by President Bush. With Clinton in office, there was little political opposition to NCEPA, though also little support from the White House, since President Clinton was concentrating on empowerment zone legislation. Still, NCEPA was reintroduced and added as a rider to the 1994 Crime Bill, again with no major opposition. When the Crime Bill went down to legislative death, as part of the broader battle between Clinton and Congress, NCEPA simply died. NCCED dropped its efforts to continue to promote the legislation and turned to other efforts.

## Coalition Activism in Chicago

In Chicago each of the major development coalitions, CWED, CANDO, and the Chicago Rehab Network (as well as the Jobs Network that I did not study), have engaged in separate advocacy actions. These campaigns receive technical support from CUED, a community-focused research center at the University of Illinois–Chicago, the Midwest Center for Labor Research, the Center for Neighborhood Technology, and, most important for work in affordable housing, the Woodstock Institute.

Prior to the period I studied, the coalitions had succeeded in pressuring the state for legislation that allowed local governments to deed tax delinquent property to nonprofits; other successful efforts based on CRA pressures established community lending programs. In another campaign a metacoalition—the Community Land Use Network—convinced the city council to streamline the procedures for selling city land to community groups. The campaigns I examined reflected continuity with this activist past.

The willingness of different sectors to work together came about as part of the unsuccessful fight to stop the Hasbro Corporation from closing the Playskool plant. What had occurred was that on the promise to keep the Playskool plant open within a working class community, HASBRO, an international conglomerate, received a subsidy from the city. In spite of this support, the company reneged and shut down the plant. In response, an elaborate coalition was formed ranging from Alinksy-style community groups, technical activists such as the Midwest Center for Labor Research, as well as participants from the community development movement. In spite of clever tactics—signs questioning how one could close a toy factory near Christmas—the protests failed, though they did coerce the company to provide some compensation for the displaced workers. Both the company's perfidy and the campaign itself became an icon for the community movement and, in the words of a developmental activist, caused "the whole economic development community in Chicago . . . to sort of sit up and take notice and really question what economic development is about, what industrial retention is about, and what kinds of social goods we expect as a result of public investment."

The ability of both neighborhood organizers and development activists to work together was shown in a more successful campaign to create a zoning category—Planned Manufacturing Districts (PMD)—to protect working-class jobs from gentrified housing. Upscale housing had been introduced in areas that encroached upon manufacturing districts, and factories that could not afford the increase in rents and taxes caused by the gentrification were fleeing (Ducharme 1991). As a leader in the advocacy effort rhetorically asked,

> Are you going to put in luxury townhouse for white folks or put in industrial jobs that are going to have more of a benefit for the population of that community?

Under the leadership of a community economic developer who was a board member of CANDO, coalitions of developers and neighborhood groups publicly demonstrated and personally lobbied the city to create the new planned manufacturing zoning classification. The coalition circulated newsletters and press releases detailing how planned manufacturing districts would help maintain the industrial infrastructure within the city. Reports prepared by university research shops that estimated how many jobs were created for each manufacturing position retained were widely circulated. Unfortunately, the leading urban affairs newspaper columnist in the city actively opposed the idea of PMDs, apparently causing the city to hesitate in supporting the coalition's proposal.

The developmental activist spearheading the campaign explained the underlying logic for the campaign:

> [T]here are five hundred acres in these three districts [that] are important . . . because of the existing industrial base. . . . So we are interested in keeping these industries and these jobs and getting more industrial development. . . . About 75 percent of the workers in these jobs are city residents; about 65 percent are black and Hispanic. The average wage of the jobs in this area is $28,000 a year plus benefits. And these are the kinds of jobs that the city really can't afford to loose anymore of and should be using the space to build on for its development in the future.

The coalition held rallies and brought out the troops, though much of its work involved participation in the minutiae of zoning hearings. The activist further described the effort of both development groups and neighborhood organizations:

> [We had] to organize the [local] companies to go to the public hearings that were conducted every time somebody was trying to change the zoning on an industrial property from manufacturing to either commercial or residential. And we began to organize them to go and oppose these zoning changes . . . and it got us to the point where at least the one alderman who was feeling most of the heat on this began to feel

like he really wanted to find the solution to this problem. And we were also getting some tacit cooperation from the city's Department of Economic Development; they had not come out with any kind of a policy in favor of retaining an industrial base in this area. But they were allowing us to do research with them and explore the issue. . . .

And when we finally got the first alderman to agree that something needed to be done . . . the whole situation kind of changed around as he asked the city to work with us. . . . And we spent a number of years creating enabling legislation that would allow us to have what are called Planned Manufacturing Districts and then going through community planning processes in three wards. . . .

Now the last passed under the Daley administration. He campaigned against this ordinance and we managed to change his mind on it. . . . [W]e've always focused on helping the administration understand that good policy and good politics could go together on this. And we built a large coalition of industry owners, unions, workers, community groups, and a lot of different organizations involved in economic development around the city to support this effort.

Collectively the PMD campaigns, the older CRA efforts, the tax reactivation effort, the Playskool battle among other issues taught those in the community development movement that their efforts could succeed, based on "the dissemination of ideas and the adoption of similar policies by a large number of organizations . . . facilitated by the frequent interaction of key actors" (Wiewel and Alpern 1993, p. 132). A climate had been established in which those in the community development movement recognized the value of coalition advocacy.

With the base for cooperation established, leaders from CWED, CANDO, the Rehab Network, and others got together to start the Neighborhood Agenda Campaign, a coalition advocacy effort to focus public attention on the reinvestment needs within the poorer communities. As part of this broader approach, CANDO successfully pressured the city to accept CDFLOAT, while the Chicago Rehab Network initiated a successful Affordable Housing Campaign. The most controversial activity was an effort to convince the city to establish a general obligation bond for capital funds for neighborhood revitalization.

**The CDFLOAT Campaign.** Through both lobbying and mild advocacy tactics, CANDO convinced the city of Chicago to allow community-based development organizations to use unexpended money from CDBG—the CDFLOAT—for interim development financing. Two of the active members of CANDO's board had learned from national contacts about the possibility of floating unexpended CDBG money, but individually had failed to persuade the city to accept the scheme, apparently because of a combination of bureaucratic inertia and technical ignorance.

CANDO's board decided the CDFLOAT would make an ideal public policy issue, as it seemed a win-win idea.

> The first benefit to the city is that [these are] projects that they probably would like to put public subsidies in anyway because they save the project costs on construction financing. . . . And, two, the city could charge some interest on this loan and earn new income and their only obligation is to make sure that the income earned on the program also went to CDBG-eligible activities.

With the help of a consultant, CANDO explored the technicalities of the idea, paying for the work with a small grant from a foundation that was encouraging the community development movement to become involved in public policy work. CANDO then worked out presentations for the city's development cabinet that included a "dog and pony" show on what the community-based development organizations had accomplished, a full-fledged written description of what CDFLOAT would entail, as well as a bureaucratic design for carrying it out. Further,

> some of our members were involved in the community development advisory committees [for CDBG] . . . so they would push the idea. Some of our members would go talk to their alderman about the idea with us, without us. So it was worked in different ways.

But little progress was made in selling the idea, as several city bureaucrats kept stalling by adding technical obstacles to the proposed procedures. To overcome these obstacles required a "small way of embarrassing the administration." As the leader of the campaign remarked,

> I was able to get access to the city's draw down rate at the HUD regional office. . . . And we had our most productive meeting with the city once they knew I had seen they had $150 million sitting in D.C. and they were still drawing down 1989 money in late 1990 and we had been correct all along in our assumptions.

When the program was finally passed, the mayor claimed credit for it and appeared at a ribbon cutting for a senior citizen apartment building that had been made possible by the CDFLOAT.

CDFLOAT became part of the broader Neighborhood Agenda Campaign in which CANDO, as part of a metacoalition of neighborhood organizations, worked to end the undercapitalization of programs to redevelop neighborhood infrastructure. The campaign was conducted in a far more confrontational matter than the CDFLOAT effort, causing some dissonance among leading members of CANDO.

**The Neighborhood Capital Budget Campaign.** The capital budget campaign was carried out by the Neighborhood Capital Budget Group—NCBG—initially a shell coalition set up to aggressively pressure the city to increase infrastructure projects in the neighborhoods rather than concentrating most such funds downtown. Some individual community groups were members of NCBG; however, its primary structure was that of a coalition of coalitions that included CANDO, the Chicago Rehab Network, the Community Land Use Network, the Chicago Jobs Coalition, CWED, and the Chicago Coalition for Affordable Housing. After four years of pressure and informational tactics, NCBG was able to convince the mayor to issue a $160 million general obligation bond for capital projects. Of this sum, almost eighty million were to be spent for community focused economic development such as industrial parks, with much of the rest targeted for infrastructure repair (CANDO summer 1992).

The Neighborhood Capital Budget Group campaign followed a multipronged strategy. Using the metacoalition to rally the troops, NCBG held mass meetings, very much in the traditions of the Alinsky community congresses, at which demands were publicly put forth for reinvestment in the neighborhoods. This congresses produced a plan based on community input for what projects should be done. In addition, holding the congresses in each ward activated citizen supporters throughout the city.

The next stage involved NCBG's publicizing the severe deterioration of infrastructure in the neighborhoods, while questioning why most of the city's capital expenditures were concentrated in the downtown area. In making this argument, the coalition turned technical statistical information into a weapon of social activism. As described by one of the organizers,

> We took the city's capital budget on four years ago and just tried to figure out who got to make the decisions, what's in the darn thing, how do you read it, and how could you make it better. That [effort] evolved . . . us utilizing the technique of geographic-based reporting. We said, "Well, gee, this document is so complicated to get any accountability over it at all, you need to break it down by some meaningful unit of geography so people can readily identify and track what the city is doing where."
>
> So we took the unit of the ward because . . . people had an opportunity to demand accountability over elected officials . . . to say that one ward is getting more money than another ward means something. . . . People . . . say, "Oh, you know we live in the 49th ward and how much money are we getting? We pay these property taxes, we pay these water and sewer user fees, what are we getting back?' We have all these things in our neighborhood that don't work very well or that are broken and need fixing or are deteriorating and contributing to blight—

we want them fixed!" . . . There's an issue of equity in terms of how
public dollars are distributed. . . .

. . . We are about to break down the third successive capital plan
by ward and ranking from highest to lowest whose getting the most
money and whose getting the least money. . . . And that was the importance for the people in Rogers Park and East Edgewater said, "I'll be
damned! You know, we have no business being 50th on the list. . . . We
deserve better than this." And that's for them to organize themselves.

The diffusion of the information on the huge imbalance in the expenditure of
redevelopment money activated separate neighborhood organizations. Data analysis blurred into activism:

I mean, we are unabashedly advocates and we don't pretend to be objec-
tive researchers but, I mean, common sense is common sense. The bottom line is if you're only spending a few million dollars every five years
on an area as large as a ward, there's no way in hell you're gonna maintain the infrastructure—not in an old city like Chicago. When one
ward is getting twenty times more money than another ward, it's pretty
hard to justify the difference on the basis of need. When you have just
two wards out of fifty getting over 25 percent of the total capital spending, it's pretty hard to justify.

The efforts of NCBG translated an intentionally obscure city capital budget
into terms that both citizens, and many of the aldermen, could follow. Then,
armed with this information, NCBG got the attention of elected city officials,
through newspaper articles, through direct action campaigns in which people
were assembled at city hall during council meetings, and through pressure from
the neighborhood organizations on the alderman. The battle was fought by

flooding the commissioners office, flooding the budget office, testifying
before city council. . . . That kind of stuff you know getting a story
placed in the Chicago Sun Times about you know a project that is
going to not happen because the city doesn't have this [money].

Old-line protest tactics were used, though modified by the need to communicate
the technical analysis:

Phone calling, letters, legislative public hearings, media campaigns, we
also issued a study. We contracted with a Ph.D. economist and had him
demonstrate what the jobs economic impact would be on the city's
economy if the city were to do a GO Bond. Then we went public with
those findings in a major press conference where we had over eighty
people from different neighborhood groups across the city. Downtown at
10:00 in the morning we marched to city hall after the press conference

and two months later the mayor . . . called for the issuance of a GO Bond.

Support from the local press was used to pressure the mayor:

> [The] Chicago Sun Times carried front-page articles about our ward-by-ward rankings [of infrastructure reinvestment]. I mean that is something that Daley understands. He does not like bad press. It created a public discourse. It created a public debate. . . . And we came up with a model ordinance that said that there should be annual public hearings required, early disclosure of the capital budget, a citizens' advisory commission to the mayor to advise him on policy and legislative matters and to monitor the implementation of the capital program.
>
> We've gotten all those things implemented because the mayor was threatened that a whole bunch of alderman were listening and might just pass an ordinance with even more teeth in it than we wanted.

Concurrent with the press campaign, coalition members showed each of the separate alderman how unfairly the capital budget was divided. The NCBG encouraged

> community groups . . . [to] demand that [their alderman] and the head of the planning department come out and take a walking tour of their neighborhood to look at the capital improvement needs. . . . [The community groups] were being coached on by the coalition—We want a citizen advisory body. We want early disclosure to plans. We want ward by ward breakdowns. And we just flooded the budget office with requests for this. . . . We asked people to go meet with their alderman and issue an aldermanic report card on whether or not their alderman was smart about public works.

The pressure convinced the alderman to support the coalition's GO proposal and agreements were reached with the city. Still, NCBG wanted to ensure that the initial agreements were to be kept.

> Our next challenge is to really find out where the GO Bond dollars go. And very shortly we're gonna be doing a mailing to all the Community Protest Organization (CPOs), the CDCs in neighborhoods that are slated to receive GO Bond funded capital projects next spring, and say to them you've got to be the eyes and ears. You've got to get on the city's tail to make sure that these promises are carried through.

During the period during which NCBG was pushing for the General Obligation bond, the city transit authority, announced plans to repair the severely deteriorated elevated structures on which the public train transit ran. Poorer neighborhoods feared that the shutdown of the train lines would be used as an excuse to permanently replace them with less convenient bus service. Activists from the Neighborhood Capital Budget Group met with community organizations within these communities and used the fears about the train lines as a lever to motivate further community organizing. By doing so, the coalition linked the traditional issues of neighborhood organizing to the bricks and mortar programs pushed by those in the development movement.

**The Affordable Housing and Jobs Campaign.** In frank imitation of the capital development actions, the Chicago Rehab Network began its "Affordable Housing and Jobs Campaign." The plan for the campaign came about at a Rehab Network retreat held to discuss a background strategy paper prepared by the activist research center, the Center for Urban Economic Development. This paper was written in response to concern among activists on how to unite the contending elements within the affordable housing movement. This campaign lasted for a year and half, resulting in Mayor Daley's leading the city council to pass an ordinance that placed $752 million into affordable housing that provided 17,000 rehabbed units, a third of which would be affordable for the very poor, added money to the Low-Income Housing Trust Fund, and created new jobs as part of the home building program (Ervin 1994).

To carry off this complex advocacy effort, the Rehab Network solicited help from the Midwest Academy, an old-line Alinsky-style protest and training organization, to orchestrate community demonstrations and to provide technical advice on what other actions to take. Marches were conducted in front of city hall and attention called to the proposed ordinance with a massive postcard campaign. The campaign created a coalition of "Endorsers" including 260 organizations and coalitions, tenant and block associations, religious and ethnic advocacy organizations, and the citywide United Way agency. It then formed an active negotiating team including Rehab Network officials, several affordable housing providers, as well as a representative from the University of Illinois at Chicago Circle, backed by a larger strategy team that brought together people from banks, foundations, and the Federal Home Loan Bank, as well as community activists.

The campaign included heavy media barrages to inform city politicians on the need for housing:

> Yesterday we had a press conference at city hall with six other alderpeople introducing a major piece of legislation that calls for a creation of a billion dollar, five-year housing investment fund for the city of Chicago. And this was an ordinance which we actually wrote.

The media campaign was bolstered by a technical report on the lack of affordable housing in the city released at a strategic time by the University of Illinois.

With the support of the media and the sign on by numerous organizations, the Rehab Network escalated its demands to "generate a billion dollar affordable housing investment fund for the city of Chicago over the next five years . . . a billion, BILLION! We're . . . thinking big." The campaign developed its own momentum, and midway through had to fight off efforts of the city to sidetrack the coalition when Mayor Daley presented his own plan that provided about $200 million in support of mixed-income housing (Ervin 1994). Rather than buying this compromise, the Rehab Network increased pressure on the city and released, in video form, an embarrassing report accusing "the Department of Housing of 'cooking the books' by counting repairs . . . to existing low-income units . . . to increase the number of units it claimed to have created" (Ervin 1992 p. 9).

Many of the alderpeople supported the proposal; others needed persuasion, a persuasion that came about based on the realities of Chicago's ethnic politics. Taking the role of the aldermen, the coalition director played out encounters he had with these officials:

"Yeo, my folk—northwest, southwest side—don't want no low-income housing in the neighborhood." Because you say low-income housing you're thinking black, you're thinking Hispanic and most importantly you're thinking CHA [Chicago Housing Authority].

Okay, well what you have to do is we have to go and educate alderpeople and say, "Okay, how many senior citizens do you have in your community who own their own homes, letting them deteriorating around them because of fixed income?" A lot of them have them and they all go to vote, too, by the way. . . . "How many of them need some sort of small loan or grant and they can't go to the bank because they're on some fixed income or they've got to mortgage their house through home equity loans or you know go in debt for the rest of their lives? All of them have that problem."

See, what we have to do is define affordability in such a way that everyone sees that it meets their self interest and it does because I'll give you white, black, or Hispanic, everyone's in that same category in the city of Chicago, period.

To counter fears about the expense of the plan, the Rehab Network worked out a complicated proposal detailing how funds could be obtained; it included money that the city would have spent on housing anyway, supplemented by outside sources that the city did not know were available, such as an internal loan component from CDBG.

As passed, the ordinance dramatically expanded the pot of money for affordable housing, and with the commitment to the Low-Income Housing Trust Fund, provided the crucial capital required to carry out all but the most economically marginal deals. The final ordinance also required public reports to be made to assure that the city lives up to the agreement (Ervin 1994 p. 10). The campaign ended up as a win-win situation for the diverse membership of the coalition. Its success was publicized in a widely distributed flyer that proclaimed:

VICTORY

"One Step Forward, One Mile to Go"

## REINFORCING IDEOLOGICAL NETWORKS

The examples in this chapter show how by working through coalitions and trade associations, developmental activists influence the broader environment for community-based development. No sea change in public policy has come about, but the campaigns have had an impact, with more local funds going to affordable housing, the institutionalization of the tax credit, the preservation of the Community Reinvestment Act, and the overall recognition that nonprofits are part of the renewal game.

Some of the campaigns are simply about keeping money flowing. A termination of the LIHTC without a replacement would devastate the affordable housing movement. But much of coalition advocacy is about obtaining the very resources that support the leveraging tactics described in chapter 7 through which CBDOs give direction to what development projects are about. For instance, the small sums provided by Housing Trust Funds enable CBDOs to undertake a more ideologically driven social mission, not simply construct buildings, while the very purpose of the NCEPA had been to obtain such seed money for the movement.

Coalition advocacy is about pressureful persuasion. For coalition advocacy to succeed, internal consensus on both values and tactics is required among the developmental activists. Builders must talk with advocates and in doing so flesh out ways of reconciling disagreements. Persuasion is most effective when developmental activists frame the discussion in ways that reflect the beliefs within the organic theory that empowerment comes when the poor own property and development is focused on places in need. Coalition advocacy provides the mechanism that transforms the ideas that emerge from the organic theory into public policy.

CHAPTER 11

# Structuring Complex
# Interorganizational Systems

It is to theory, and the empirical validation of theory, that activists
must look for guidelines in working through the dilemmas they
confront.
                                    —Prudence Posner, *Dilemmas of Activism*

So you have to go through the experience and test the theory with the
experience and then determine what is valid. But you've got to go
through the experience before you know how things work and how
things don't work and how they might work.
                              —Director of combined neighborhood association
                                    and CDC thinking about a new city policy

In chapter 2, I presented a preliminary sketch of a model describing how weaker
organizations within a societal sector gain influence over more powerful entities. In this chapter, I elaborate upon the model in light of the narratives, stories,
and insights of the developmental activists. I shall limit the discussion to the
community development movement since that is the case for which I have gath-
ered the data. But the pattern presented, in which an organic theory that emerges
from the experience of activists then influences funders, would seem applicable
to other societal sectors undertaking social change, so long as four characteristics
are present:

1. *Bargaining occurs within a complicated, but not hostile environment.*
   Contentions between the smaller organizations and the funders are
   over the means to a shared end, not over the value of the end itself.
2. *Ideas count and are actively and vigorously debated.* The action organizations are not simply carrying out an established technology.
   Rather both funders and action organizations are experimenting
   with a wide variety of contending approaches.
3. *The variability of the environments in which work occurs provides a nat-
   ural laboratory to test out different approaches.* Practitioners share and
   debate insights into what works and what does not. But initial
   practices take place in widely dispersed locales.

261

3. *Support structures develop and persist.* Support structures for the smaller organizations create the forums for reshaping the ideas that grow out of an emerging organic theory. This counterstructure intermediates between the smaller organizations and the political and funding environment.

## THE INTELLECTUAL FRAMING OF THE THEORY OF THE NICHE ORGANIZATION

As described in chapter 2, the framing for this study and the theoretical questions posed mesh with ideas from new institutionalism theories (Powell and Dimaggio 1991). New institutionalism theory suggests that to understand interorganizational influence the scholar should view a societal sector as a single entity, rather than as an aggregate of separate organizations. Further, new institutionalism theory indicates that within this sector ideological direction is shaped by the actions of the larger and better funded organizations. The new institutionalism model points out various methods through which the wealthier organizations control the weaker through patterns of coercive, mimetic, and normative influence. The details of how this comes about have been discussed in chapter 2.

The first part of this empirical study shows the presence of such top-down pressures. Chapter 3 describes why CBDOs are vulnerable to top down influence. To bring about the projects in neighborhoods that face profound social burdens, CBDOs require money that can only be obtained from government, foundations, and the intermediaries. Of equal import, developmental activists—torn between the worlds of advocacy and business, the need to build and the obligation to provide social services—face deep ideological tensions on what development work ought to be about. In their efforts to reconcile these tensions, the actions developmental activists take can be influenced by the pressures from the funders, irrespective of the CBDO's own sense of what is needed. Chapter 4 demonstrates how through both coercion and imitation, CBDOs end up adopting programmatic approaches that respond to a changing political environment. In addition, chapter 5 details how the changing fashions among foundations and intermediaries strongly influence what CBDOs attempt. Top-down influence is certainly present.

But the remainder of the empirical material belies many of the suggestions within the new institutionalism literature and offers an alternative understanding. The smaller organizations are shown to be far from powerless; for instance, they are able to bring about programs of holistic redevelopment even against pressures from funders for production to scale. Community-based development organizations build housing but also push for holistic, community empowerment.

Further, numerous examples are shown of how funders end up adopting ideas that emerge from the CBDOs rather than simply imposing their own beliefs.

The descriptive chapters detail how through selective leveraging of resources, not only do the CBDOs get the needed funding, but do so in ways that seem consistent with their own ideological beliefs, rather than ideas imposed from above. The material on the coalitions and trade associations, as well as the discussions of coalition advocacy, show how the smaller and weaker action organizations shape the ideology of the broader movement. Most important, the ideas within the organic theory that emerge from the daily experiences of the developmental activists themselves are discussed among the activists, and end up framing the image of what development is and ought to be about among all the actors within the societal sector.

What the descriptive study indicates is that what counts is not simply raw power (economic or otherwise), but the ability of smaller organizations to frame the issues in ways that then can be transmitted along interorganizational networks, networks that are created by the coalitions and trade associations. Further, direct confrontations between the weak and the more powerful over resources and the direction of the movement are rare. Rather argumentation over what should be done and why takes place through on-going incremental "micro-negotiations" (Mansbridge 1995, p. 31). It is through these micro-negotiations that the larger organizations are influenced as they slowly allow the experiences of the developmental activists to shape their own agendas.

It is the flow of images, beliefs, and ideas, not simply economic resources that shape what movements can be about (Snow and Benford 1992, p. 137; Snow et al. 1986, p. 464; Polletta 1998, p. 139; Williams 1995, p. 127). Power emerges as people share stories with one another and provide narratives that make plain, to both the small organizations and the large alike, possible solutions to common problems (Klandermans 1992; Polletta 1998, p. 141–42, 152–54). These solutions are implicit within the organic theories that emerge from the experiences of the developmental activists, shape what their organizations attempt, and, in turn, influence the perceptions of the funders.

Within a societal sector, missions, goals, directions, and relationships are constantly reenacted. My model argues that three structural characteristics of the societal sector permit CBDOs to gain such influence. First, the very diffuseness of the sector enables CBDOs to incrementally leverage ideas. Second, through a process of speciation, newer CBDOs come about, often bringing into the sector alternative ideas that originated from organizations less centrally involved in the world of community-based development. And, finally, the wide variety of local cultures within the societal sector permits an array of development models to coexist in separate areas, weakening the ability of the larger, but more distant, organizations to impose an intellectual hegemony.

*Strategic Leveraging Through Linked Negotiations*

Within the dyadic relationship, it would appear that funders, intermediaries, or governmental organizations automatically dominate the individual CBDOs, as the smaller organizations find it easier to attempt projects that the funders readily accept. But, in practice, as funders and CBDOs negotiate about individual projects, small concessions are made by the funders to the ideas suggested by the development groups. These small concessions made in separate locales incrementally influence what occurs elsewhere.

Through the information that is spread by word of mouth, publications, and stories shared at conferences, developmental activists in other locales learn about the concessions made. Most often these concessions come about as developmental activists build upon their experiences, formulate them as part of their organic theory, and convince funders in their cities to accept the small changes implied. These concessions, now framed as part of the organic theory, become the starting point of CBDO-funder negotiations in other locales. For instance, a CBDO in one city might capitulate to pressures from LISC or government officials, to establish a commercial core of conventional firms within the neighborhood. But as part of this project, the CBDO persuades the funder to include a first-source hiring agreement for community members. This concession—part of the organic theory suggesting the need to link individual to community empowerment—readily diffuses, providing CBDOs elsewhere with the ability to begin their negotiations with other funders by assuming a first-source hiring agreement is normative. Small victories in one place are reframed to become the normative elsewhere.

On occasion, a CBDO might persuade a foundation or those in the public sector to support an exemplary project, one that directly reflects the ideology of the community group itself. If successful these projects become the exemplars that define the organic theory and as such are readily copied by others. These projects are visited and talked about and, as such, become part of the continuing narrative that defines the broader culture of community development, a narrative in which both CBDOs and funders partake. For instance, alternative funding programs such as Housing Trust Funds, experiments with sweat equity programs, holistic programs such as the day-care-cum-home-building-qua-community efforts came about because of the ideological persistence displayed by a single CBDO just to try out the approach. Funding is initially obtained as those in government, the foundations, or intermediaries do recognize the problems the communities face, realize other efforts have not succeeded in bring about change, and accept the need to experiment with the CBDO's idea.

In this way larger organizations end up adopting ideas originated by the CBDOs. For instance, as a result of continuing CBDO pressure to go beyond building affordable housing, LISC slowly accepted the need for holistic programs of community empowerment, almost a sea-change from its initial mission, and one that reflected the importance of ideas from the activists themselves.

As exemplary projects succeed and then are reconstituted as part of the shared narrative of success, CBDOs elsewhere are better able to persuade foundations, intermediaries, and governments to accept the innovations. Larger funding entities then emulate what is now considered normative, without feeling they are capitulating to the pressures from the smaller organizations they are funding.

## Speciation

Community-based development organizations emerge in separate locales in response to community deterioration, unemployment, or other local problems, often coming into being with little awareness of the existence of funders (or even other development groups). These newly emergent groups reintroduce into the sector a wide array of understandings, their formative ideologies, about how to approach the renewal problem. In some areas, CBDOs came about because of a religious mission, others to implement a leftist ideology in support of communal living, while many emerge in response to a feminist agenda to combat gender-linked poverty. These organizations are motivated by more than simply a desire to build.

Still, to obtain support for capital projects, even these ideological organizations must respond to the funding environment, whether to a production model put forth by a LISC or simply the organizational restructuring needed to carry out a LIHTC deal. But these ideological organizations will not capitulate beyond the point that defines their initial reasons for coming into being. Feminist job training programs are set up to be as much about giving people confidence as they are about finding the jobs. Organizations that run such programs, while requiring resources from the major funders, will withdraw from such relationships if their ideational agendas are threatened.

As such, these ideological organizations do die and vanish from the scene, and are more likely to do so when they defy the larger funders. But while alive they influence other groups in the movement to think of alternative approaches to social change. For a time, ideologically driven organizations interact with the established CBDOs, reminding those in extant organizations what the movement initially was about.

## Local Cultures

The image of a societal sector is that of a cascading network of interlinked organizations whose actions collectively frame a definition of what the sector is all about. But specialized subcultures emerge within this broader sector, subcultures that reflect an intensity of interaction peculiar to one geographic locale or among those organizations that share a specialized mission. These subcultures become self-reinforcing reservoirs of alternative ideas emerging from the CBDOs of what the broader sector ought to be about.

Subcultural bonds come about because of shared historic and functional affinity among certain CBDOs. Title VII CDCs, no matter how far their current efforts now diverge from their initial missions, still share a thirty-year history—a history of contestations over policies toward the poor, of changing funding climates, and so on. The leaders of these older CBDOs share ideas with one another and then these ideas diffuse among other development groups within the localities from which these older organizations come.

Subcultural bonds exist between CBDOs influenced by the same powerful funders. Neighborhood Progress in Cleveland, the Neighborhood Revitalization Program in Minneapolis, and the Fund for Community Development in Chicago each created subcultures of development groups. Locally the CBDOs might appear to be dominated by these funders, but the very variety of what each funder wanted—the production model in Cleveland versus the neighborhood approach in Minneapolis—keeps alive a variety of ideas.

Other CBDOs are part of functional networks—advocates for feminist empowerment, incubator developers, and so forth—that link these organizations to social change groups from nondevelopmental sectors, providing ideas and support for a wide variety of alternative approaches. For instance, an emerging CBDO in central Cincinnati is mentored by several of the city's older CBDOs, receiving information on the technicalities of housing development and as such is influenced by the funders. Yet, at the same time, this small organization is tied into national networks, in this case those that work to empower disadvantaged women. This smaller emerging CBDO articulates to the more established development groups the goals of feminist empowerment, and in doing so helps create a local culture that integrates ideas of feminist empowerment with the dominant production ethos within that city's community development movement.

In general, linkages to other societal sectors occur—to the older traditions of direct action advocacy, or to the organizations promoting agendas of empowerment of women—in ways that lead to a cross-fertilization of both technical ideas as well as ideologies. Some housing development organizations are also members of the activist Neighborhood Peoples' Action. Organically shaped experiences cause developmental activists to discover the complementarity between advocacy and development work, strengthening their beliefs in the part of the organic theory that supports holistic models.

The very redundancy, as well as the density of networks, within a societal sector enables shared learning and change to take place in which developmental activists build on their experiences to strengthen their commitment to a bottom-up model. Information on a successful project readily diffuses, while the wide geographic dispersion, and separation of the subcultural arenas, permits the broader system to both tolerate failure and learn from it. Both the demise of several CBDOs in Minneapolis and the altered purposes of others within that city, become object lessons to the national movement of how an ideological thrust to promote citizen participation at all costs can harm the poor.

Subcultures provide a persistent source of alternative ideas of what the sector is about that can differ from that of the dominant ethos pushed for by the funders.

## HOW THE SMALL AND WEAK FIGHT BACK

I have suggested three ways in which the ideas of the smaller and weaker organizations can persist and ultimately shape the images held by the richer and more powerful: through the selective promulgation of organically suggested innovations from one locale to the next; through the speciation that allows newly emergent organizations to present alternative ideologies; and through the persistence of alternative ideologies that come from the linkages that CBDOs maintain to other societal sectors.

But how do these ideas diffuse and how are they given voice? I suggest two mechanisms: First, as niche organizations, CBDOs garner resources in ways that strategically combine the contending interests of the funders, directing the overall projects in directions that are consistent with those desired by the CBDOs themselves. In addition, in efforts to obtain the technical support required, CBDOs have brought into being coalitions and trade associations that end up creating an institutional counterstructure that gives voice to the smaller organizations.

Second, activists in the community development movement have worked out a shared ideology—the organic theory—that comes about as they translate their experiences in daily work into the defining ethos of the movement. Funders, lacking first-hand experience, absorb these ideas from the successful developmental activists. An organic theory diffuses throughout the societal sector, providing an agenda for change that emerges from below rather than being imposed from above.

### *Niche Strategies*

Power imbalances between organizations in the community development societal sector are quite apparent. If HUD programs with their billions of budgets were only accessible to build homes for little green people, proposals would probably be written to that effect (though grants would also be sought to paint the poor green); or when LISC decides to fund supermarkets, the larger CBDOs who are into commercial development quickly see the wisdom of building such markets (but then set up their own employment programs within the inner-city neighborhoods involved). Or, if to get a grant requires having an outside audit, outside audits will occur.

But such illustrations of dominance do not imply that the smaller organizations are powerless. Smaller organizations create networks, reify them as coalitions and trade associations, and use the ideas put forth by these endogeneous supporters as bargaining tools when dealing with the funders. For instance, technical reports issued by NCCED on how to merge social services with physical development projects enabled CBDOs to convince funders to expand efforts beyond that of the mere production of physical products.

Further, as niche organizations, CBDOs capitalize on ideational spaces provided when the separate funders each support different images of what changes are needed. The CBDO itself creates an integrative project that piece by piece satisfies the separate funder's agendas, but, in the aggregate, represents the developmental activist's own image of what community development ought to be about. As shown in the chapter on leveraging, the interstitial gaps between the agendas of the funders constitute points of vulnerability from which the smaller organizations work to redefine the goals of the broader sector in ways more compatible with the ideas of the developmental activists.

Niche organizations master the art of bootstrapping resources by using initial indications of support to convince subsequent funders that more support should be forthcoming. But more is being done than simply gaining money. Each time funding is sought, the niche organization convinces the more powerful that the larger organization's own agenda is being accomplished, but that this agenda must be modified, in small part, to mesh with that of the other funders. By working to persuade a multitude of funders that such meshing is required, the CBDOs themselves end up bringing into place their own models of what development work should be about. And, later when this project succeeds, funders elsewhere are more willing to emulate the idea, and by doing so adopt the framings of the CBDOs as their own.

It is through this piecemeal merging of resources and step-by-step redefinition of the project through which niche organizations shape the image of the societal sector. This macrostrategy is strengthened through the microtactics that niche organizations use in their bargaining with the individual funders. One such tactic involves a bargaining from weakness in which the strength of the niche organization comes about by the very fact that it is small. Such an organization might die, but for those who care, an ideological steadfastness is not an insignificant value and can cause individuals in the smaller group to actively contend against agendas of the funders that they cannot accept.

Another approach is that of ostensible compliance in which the smaller organization doubly frames what its work is about, once to reflect what it is the funders want, and once again in ways that are more consistent with the ideas emerging within the organic theory. To both show the funders that the CBDO is producing housing, yet at the same time to work to empower those whom the CBDO helps is not all that hard to finesse. A funder is pleased when apartments or commercial space comes on line, but then the CBDO sets up a tenants' council in the apartment houses or insists upon local, first-source hiring for the commercial spaces created, or works hard to assure that minority entrepreneurs become the tenants of the incubators or recipients of revolving loan funds. The funders are satisfied by the physical changes made. But those in the community development movement recognize that what they have brought about is a positive step in the broader process of holistic change to empower tenants, minorities, or low-income women, in which the physical construction projects are but a means to this broader end.

### Coalition Strategies

Smaller, niche organizations discover that they share collective problems and needs, yet also learn that others in the movement have the knowledge and skills to answer persisting questions. To share this knowledge with one another, developmental activists create trade associations and coalitions that provide a forum for exchanging ideas.

These coalitions and trade associations, as creatures of the CBDOs and not of their funders, are reasonably independent of government and the intermediaries. As such, they can aggressively speak out for the overall movement. They can bring direct pressure on government and funders both to increase resources available to the community development movement and to do so in ways that carry out the agendas of the CBDOs.

Further, the very logic of conducting coalition work ends up strengthening the linkages between those in one societal sector and those in related movements. Community developers of necessity must deal with housing advocates. The need to cross boundaries between different societal sectors introduces into the community development movement ideas from sister spheres, ideas that offer counterpressures to those of the development funders. For example, in fights to preserve CRA, community-based development organizations join together with coalitions of housing advocates to pressure banks. At the same time, these CBDOs might be feeling pressure from their funders to pay less attention to the extremely poor and work on housing for the slightly more affluent. To economically survive, a CBDO might feel the need to comply with its funders, but developmental activists will think twice, lest if by complying with the funders, the CBDO were to chance losing the support of the housing advocacy organizations necessary to keep CRA alive.

*Organic Intellectuals and Interorganizational Spanning*

The strategies of the niche suggest a structural mechanism through which smaller, core organizations can get their say. But, as both the new institutionalism and new social movements literature point out, contestations are not only over structures, but over ideational framings. In this battle, developmental activists have an advantage. The larger organizations have the wealth to push for their own agendas, but these organizations lack the insights that come from carrying out a mission that is informed by real world experiences within the communities of need. Instead, funders find these insights in the narratives and stories of the developmental activists who, as organic theorists, end up framing both for themselves and eventually their funders what the sector is all about.

From their daily experiences in rebuilding poor communities, developmental activists, of necessity, learn the extent to which their goals and values can be accomplished within the resources available. They discover the need to bring about holistic renewal, and how programs to benefit individuals can speak to broader community issues. Then, through personal conversations, at trade association and coalition meetings, at training sessions, and through shared publications, organic theorists share and refine these formulations with others in the field. They share stories of success that become the cultural icons of what the movement is about. These ideas and understandings percolate up to the funders, intermediaries, and, at times, to the governmental agencies, who then see the successful efforts of the developmental activists as the schemes they must adopt to make themselves appear to be successful. The bottom line is that the funders and the intermediaries need to show success, either to please politicians or their own contributors, and the projects suggested by the organic theories provide a way to achieve these successes.

The organic intellectual becomes the agent, the mechanism, through which those in the smaller organizations transmit their ideas, build consensus, and, create sufficient solidarity to persuade others to adopt their definition of what the sector is about. This ideology is transmitted along the interorganizational networks presupposed by both new institutionalism and new social movement theories. The organic theory brings together the goals for what should be achieved, as well as experientially induced reasons why specific actions are appropriate for accomplishing these goals. An organic theory begins with a normative understanding among the developmental activists of the way things ought to be—a hope for greater social equity or the fundamental belief that people should feel secure in their everyday life.

An organic theory is shared with others in the societal sector, both to argue for the legitimacy of the underlying goals and to test out from a broader experience base whether what was learned from one endeavor speaks to larger goals. Is the community development movement about building homes, or is it about restoring hope in neighborhoods of deprivation, a more contentious enactment of what the movement is about? The answers merge different perspectives learned by the separate CBDOs, for instance, as one group convinces another of the ability to both construct homes for the poor and then to build upon the physical projects by setting up tenants' councils that have a social impact of empowering the broader community.

Organic theories are then reshaped from the heuristic lessons learned from practice, as developmental activists modify their actions in ways that both enable a project to succeed, yet keep alive core goals and values. A public discussion among organic theorists on how to build an inner-city supermarket moves from the details of funding to suggest ideas of how to shape these projects in ways that empower poor individuals by giving them the dignity of having choice in where they shop while at the same time empowering the neighborhood by increasing its economic autarchy. These induced theories that have been shown to work are then communicated to the funding organizations.

Building upon the reality of daily struggle and contestations, an organic theory brings about a set of realistic goals that can be accomplished, or that are, at least, worthwhile to try. Rather than worrying whether physical development work is compatible with empowerment, or whether to focus on programs that benefit individuals or the community as the whole, organic theorists have discovered ways of helping empower individuals in ways that enable the overall community to come out ahead.

The very act of sharing an organic theory helps developmental activists battle pressures from the funders to hire only those who are most technically trained. Even if such hiring comes about, discussions of organic theories at staff meetings of the CBDOs, at retreats, or at trade association meetings, communicate these values to the technical personnel. A radical developmental activist explained to me how such discussions caused his technical staff to reflect on what they were about beyond simply building homes. During these discussions with staff members and the community,

> we focus a lot on whether or not what we do is truly progressive. . . .
> Are we just dividing up the pie a little different? Or are we participating in some way, in some measure, in a fundamental change . . . that really calls into question the ways that decisions are made, the way control is exercised, the way resources are allocated? We look carefully at what we do to see if we are doing the latter or not. And, because if we are just doing the former, maybe we are just helping this lousy system work a little bit easier, to get by a little better. . . . We ask ourselves: Are we doing something qualitatively different? Is there some fundamental change that comes out of what we do?

The ideas within an organic theory gain circulation within publications read by developmental activists, academics, and their funders alike. For instance, the

New Communities Corporation puts out a series of pamphlets on both the practice and theory of community development, while a director of a smaller organization shared with me an internal document circulated to those in his organization. This document "The Role of the Development Organization in the Movement for Progressive Social Change at the Community Level" puts forth an organically induced theory arguing what community economic development should be all about. For organic intellectuals, coalition or trade association meetings become an opportunity to reinforce the shared belief that what they do is more than simply building homes or industrial plants.

Theory emerges in conversations during which individual organic intellectuals reason with one another about why specific actions are appropriate for accomplishing the movement's goals. The language used, though, is not one of social theory, but rather of evoking concepts through well-told stories and narratives of success. Developmental activists describe the physical buildings and support structures their organizations have created, and the tricks they use to obtain the funding, but do so in ways that the lessons become obvious—that redevelopment is about undoing social injustices, not simply hammering nails. The ideas shared convince others, both developmental activists and the funders, because they are communicated through narratives that are based on a firm grasp of what is possible. Organic theorists do not try to rationalize away gang problems and the scourge of dope as they design development projects. They accept that the apartments they build must be set up with rules and mechanisms that guard against these social dysfunctions.

In framing their ideas, the organic intellectuals take into account what other, more established, entities will accept—an image of some socialist utopia that is clearly unacceptable to funders becomes transformed into a set of participatory boards within a community that have a say on which projects are done and which are not. As ideologues, some developmental activists might want to bring about collective ownership, as organic intellectuals who must balance out social realities with the ought, these individuals settle for the idea of participatory community boards, an approach toward local autonomy that is more acceptable to the economic mainstream.

By creating theories that explain why they do what they do, organic theorists engage in "frame alignment" (Snow et al. 1986, p. 464) to define, in their own terms, rather than those of outsiders, what their societal sector can and should become. Through such explicit engagement in conceptual policy debate, organic theorists recognize that "the language of policy . . . not only depicts but also constructs the issues at hand" (Fischer and Forester 1993, p. 1). This enacted consensus becomes the image, the framing, presented to the funders, government, and the general public.

Building an organic theory is self-consciously a political act in which social activists argue for their image of change and work to persuade others of its legitimacy. These ideas, their self-reflections on motivations and goals, provide a conscience for community developers, a directing and guiding force, not always followed, but something to strive for, moving developmental activists beyond being community carpenters. Organic theorists create an ideological shape for their movement that at the same time enables funders to support successful projects of physical renewal. It is the images that are shared in the narratives of success that are absorbed by the funders and subsequently accepted as their own. As such, influence in framing what the sector is about percolates from the weak to the strong.

## A CONCLUDING NOTE

The image that is shared is of the hope for the possibility of rebuilding neighborhoods to help the poor living there. Doing deals and building projects are important but so is creating the hope that the renewal task is possible.

To walk through neighborhoods of deprivation, seeing abandoned homes, burnt-out blocks of stores, and visible signs of gang activity, and to remember what the neighborhood was like but a generation or two in the past, can cause the weak of heart to throw up their hands in resignation: we cannot get there, so why try? But step-by-step actions guided by a CBDO bypass this initial despair. Improved homes encourage neighbors to remain and rebuild and, even some that have fled to return to regain ethnic and community roots. New home owners and stable tenants become customers for the stores that CBDOs help reopen and with luck the cycle of decline reverses.

Community-based development organizations bridge the gap between the harshness of market-driven capitalism and the obligations imposed to help those in need. Hope comes about by leveraging public financial resources and by building on the economic, social and cultural assets in place, even within neighborhoods of apparent deprivation (Kretzman and McKnight 1993). The goal is to have those in the community themselves guide redevelopment (Clavel, Pitt, and Yin 1997, p. 435).

CBDOs learn, as government seems slow to understand, that renewal is about compensating for past inequities but doing so in ways that make financial sense for the present. A subsidy is required to clear out the burnt-out lot on which a supermarket will be built; the physical damage in the community is a collective social responsibility; but unless the supermarket pays its ongoing operating expenses, including the extra security costs often necessitated in renewal locations, the project will go belly-up. The CBDO ties together a social mission with capitalist realities.

Community-based development organizations leverage a diverse array of social and economic resources, and adapt to changing political climates, yet do so in ways that keep in mind the core agenda of empowering those within neighborhoods of deprivation. To provide balance and direction in their work, developmental activists have worked out an organic theory of change that puts forth a moral premise that community developers have an obligation to work in neighborhoods that others have abandoned. The theory explains how social goals can be integrated to physical development in ways that enable the poor and poor communities to gain ownership of assets, though at the same time insisting that those empowered accept the responsibilities to maintain what they have gained. The theory points out that renewal comes about through a holistic strategy, uniting development with social services, while not shunning advocacy. Finally, the model recognizes that while helping people is vital, place does count and those trapped in poverty because of discrimination or language barriers will best be helped if CBDOs work to build economically autarchic communities.

Still, developmental activists recognize that working alone the community development movement cannot provide a solution for problems of concentrated poverty. Problems that have taken generations to create cannot be solved overnight and by one magic bullet, especially when many in our society still want to brush the problems of the poor aside. Yet, catalyzed by the efforts of community-based development organizations, neighborhoods of deprivation do fight back against the forces that have lead to housing abandonment and job loss.

Community-based development organizations provide the hope to combat the self-reinforcing cynicism that has lead to the abandonment of many neighborhoods. They follow a pragmatic ideology of a humane capitalism for social change that community members, as well as politicians of both conservative and liberal leanings, can accept. CBDOs become the symbol that it is both psychologically and economically possible to reverse the damage that has been done to the nation's poorest communities.

Community-based development organizations are not about leading an in-the-streets revolution, but they are about increasing social equity and demonstrating that a market economy still can have a heart. By reshaping the underlying symbols of a capitalist society to serve a social need, community-based development organizations end up renewing hope in neighborhoods of despair.

# Appendix

## Learning to Hear and Hearing to Learn:
## Discussions of Research Methodology

It has been a very interesting conversation with you because . . . in the course of the conversation it's given me the time . . . to reflect . . . on what we are doing and how we are doing it.
> —Comments made by a developmental
> activist after the second interview

*Renewing Hope* is an interpretive essay that explores questions of how social change organizations function within complicated networks. In this appendix, I describe the provenance of the research, some of the assumptions I brought to it, and discuss my approach to interpreting the words of others.

## ITERATIVE, FLEXIBLE, AND CONTINUALLY EMERGING DESIGN

My initial goal had been to contrast the premises of the community development model with those underlying neighborhood advocacy work. To learn the vocabulary of the developmental activists, I attended conferences and talked with several prominent in the movement. These initial inquiries dramatically reshaped the work, as I learned about the pressures on the CBDOs to conform to the will of funders, the differences in the local environments in which CBDOs worked, as well as the elaborate support structures available. I rethought the project in its entirety to focus on of how contrasting task environments and support structures shaped the way in which developmental activists went about their work.

All together, seventy-three community-based development organizations were visited in six midwestern states. Only one individual denied my request for an interview. After an initial interview, several organizations were dropped from the study, as their level of activity was so low, and one organization refused a second interview. To follow up on environment problems, I interviewed city officials, those in intermediaries, support organizations, as well as foundation personnel. I routinely attended meetings of the National Congress for Community Economic

Development, observed and participated in sessions, and recorded (or purchased) tapes of the sessions. Each NCCED conference included minitours in which I participated. I also participated in two extended pre- and post conference tours.

I learned that community-based development organizations in several cities were faced with strong "environmental disturbances" caused by Chicago's Fund for Community Development, the turmoil in Cleveland with the advent of Neighborhood Progress Inc., Indianapolis's new partnership program, as well as the tensions from Minneapolis's Neighborhood Revitalization Program. These disturbances became extended case studies on how environmental changes impacted the work of the CBDOs.

Most developmental activists were interviewed formally at least twice, plus numerous informal conversations were held at encounters at NCCED meetings. All together, 204 formal interviews were held among forty-one support organizations and six dozen CBDOs in seventeen locations, varying from a half an hour in length to one that lasted from 8 a.m. to 7 p.m. Still, I consider my sample size an "n" of but one, that is, what I was doing was obtaining separate and complementary views of a single, growing movement.

The recorded and transcribed data base ran over two million words and were supplemented by a dozen boxes of documents. I transcribed about a third of the interviews myself and hired people to help with the rest. Once transcribed, the interviews were coded into Orbis, a marvelous software program that helps in the analysis of qualitative data and that is included as part of the Nota Bene word processing package.

Table A.1 summarizes the who, what, and how much of this study.


## HEARING DATA

My interviewing followed the loosely structured, interpretive model described in *Qualitative Interviewing: The Art of Hearing Data* (Rubin and Rubin 1995). With this model the researcher defines the overall scope of the interview [community development, not presidential politics], the interviewee, labeled as a *conversational partner*, provides the specific focus of the conversation. The job of the researcher then is to listen carefully enough to hear what people have to say so as to be able to follow up on the topics of import to the conversational partner. What the interviewer hears, learns, and reports is from the perspective of the conversational partners, not from some imposed model.

In the initial interview the researcher asks a series of main questions to determine what issues the developmental activists themselves want to share with others. Such main questions are worded in ways that suggest the overall interest of the research, but do not limit the possible responses. Follow-up questions pursue the specific interests and understandings of the individual conversational partners.

## Table A.1. Description of the Sample for the Renewing Hope Project

*Cities Studied*

    *Sites with Multiple Community Organizations*
    Chicago—15 organization
    Cincinnati—8 organizations
    Cleveland—10 organizations
    Grand Rapids—5 organizations
    Indianapolis—7 organizations
    Milwaukee—9 organizations
    Minneapolis—9 organizations

    *Sites with Only One Community Organization Studied*
    Goshen, Indiana—1
    Green Castle, Indiana—1
    South Bend, Indiana—1
    Tell City, Indiana—1
    Athens, Ohio—1
    Lima, Ohio—1
    Marion, Ohio—1
    Lily Lake, Wisconsin—1
    Madison, Wisconsin—1
    Oshkosh, Wisconsin—1

    73 organizations total

    *In addition records were shared and informal discussions held with*
    New Communities Corporation
    Hispanics por la Causa

*Coalitions, Trade Associations Whose Officials Were Interviewed*
CANDO
Chicago Rehab Network
Cleveland Housing Network
Cleveland Neighborhood Development Corporation
CWED
Development Leadership Network
Indiana Association for Community Economic Development
Indianapolis Coalition for Neighborhood Developers
Massachusetts Association of Community Development Corporations
Minneapolis Consortium of Nonprofit Developers
National Congress for Community Economic Development
Neighborhood Capital Budget Group
Neighborhood Development Corporation of Cincinnati
Ohio CDC Association
State Housing Action Coalition—Illinois
WIRENET—Cleveland
Wisconsin Federation for Community Economic Development

Table A.1. (continued)

*Funders, Support Sector Organizations Whose Officials Were Interviewed*
Center for Community Change
Center for Neighborhood Development—Cleveland State, Cleveland
Center for Urban Economic Development—U. of Illinois at Chicago
Chicago LISC
Community Development Finance Fund Ohio
Community Reinvestment Fund
Consultant Firms
Development Department City of Chicago
Development Offices City of Cincinnati
Development Department City of Cleveland
Development Offices City of Minneapolis
Development Training Institute
Gunn Foundation
Housing Development Official City of Boston
Housing Development Officials State of Indiana
Housing Development Official State of Illinois
Indianapolis Neighborhood Partnership
Indianapolis Office of Federal Home Loan Bank
Joyce Foundation
MacArthur Foundation
National LISC
Neighborhood Progress, Inc. Cleveland
Neighborhood Revitalization Program—Minneapolis
Rapoza Associates (lobbyists)
Woodstock Institute

*NCCED Meetings Observed*
Austin
Boston
Chicago
Milwaukee
Philadelphia
San Francisco
Washington, D.C.

*Postmeeting Observational Tours*
Chicago
Newark, New Jersey

*Aggregate Information Collected*
Transcribed Notes Exclusive of Documents: 2,072,442 words
Number of full formal interviews with recording: 204
Plus transcripts of events on tours, and partial transcripts of sessions at conferences of
    community-based developers
12 boxes of backup materials

In the second interviews, my mere appearance itself functioned as a de facto follow-up by reevoking previous concerns. As often as not, the conversational partner, without my even asking, began to elaborate on themes he or she had started the previous time. Other interviews were more explicitly structured to cover problems with intermediaries or explore the content of the organic theory with individuals who had not initially introduced the concepts.

The third round of interviewing focused on obtaining specific information needed to complete the stories that I had heard. For instance, I interviewed people from foundations to better understand their side of the encounters with intermediaries, or on another occasion, spent several hours questioning about the nuts and bolts of managing affordable housing.

With full permission, I recorded the interviews. Several interviewees felt awkward swearing on tape, but otherwise did not seem hesitant to discuss most issues openly. I was only once asked to turn off the tape, and then only for a few minutes.

## CONSTRUCTING MEANINGS FROM STORIES AND NARRATIVES

In the interpretive/constructivist approach followed, evidence is inferred from the logic of the stories, events, and narratives and not from the coded frequency of some pre-ordained category. The researcher builds up a portrait of the world being studied, one incident and one extended narrative or story at a time. The narratives presented by the conversational partners might or might not be literal descriptions of events, but rather are seen as a "collective story" through which cultural meanings are shared (Richardson 1995, p. 208). In the book, I present much of what I learned in the words of the developmental activists themselves, recognizing what I am communicating is their perspectives, not some written-in-stone truth.

## REACHING, JUSTIFYING, AND PRESENTING CONCLUSIONS

Within a qualitative paradigm, the process of coding data, of making inferences, of adducing theory, and of presenting evidentiary narratives are part of a continuous and linked whole, and not, as they are in positivist research, separable stages. Validation is inferred from the richness of the narratives and stories that are communicated in which their truth emerges from how well they reflect the voices of those being studied. "Validation" is more a process of convincing others about the credibility of what it was the researcher saw and heard than a disembodied procedure for demonstrating some abstract, external reality (Kvale 1995, p. 25–26).

Validation becomes an ongoing process to reflect upon what was heard and seen rather than a search for a measure of statistical precision. However, the credibility of the research is increased when the researcher can show that core concepts and themes occur across a variety of cases and in different settings. So, for instance, that part of the organic theory describing how assets are linked to empowerment was separately suggested by a Caucasian male whose organization was running both housing and job programs in an ethnically mixed neighborhood of a larger city; repeated in conversations with a African-American activist in a smaller city; supported by a leader of a housing organization in a very large city who was still engaged in advocacy; while a slightly modified version was presented by a feminist in a rural area whose work was in establishing systems of networks rather than bricks and mortar projects. In addition, complementary comments were made at NCCED meetings and found within the literature shared by the developmental activists.

The final analysis depends on how well the material communicates to both those in the arena being studied and to other scholars in the field. To test out how well I was "hearing" what was being said, I circulated both draft and published manuscripts to those in the field. Most agreed with much of what I was saying, though suggested that I had left out the "dark side" of the field. Or as another test of how well my ideas stood up, one paper was widely circulated and quoted at some meetings of the practitioners, while a draft of a manuscript describing the relationship between intermediaries and CBDOs was used, to my surprise and embarrassment, by developmental activists as part of a fight between CBDOs and their funding intermediaries.

Two-thirds of the way through the study, I presented some of my findings at a seminar at an NCCED meeting. Activists in the audience elaborated upon some of the ideas, provided different examples, but did not attack core themes. Perhaps they were being courteous, but my observations of such meetings in which discussions are quite frank suggests otherwise.

A qualitative researcher is never sure of how much his or her personality affected what was seen and heard. My own enthusiasm for the community development movement could have in unknown ways distorted my understandings. I do try to clearly indicate in the text what are my interpretations and what it was the developmental activists said, comments that I left as much in the words of the developmental activists themselves as far as it was editorially practicable.

However, on rereading I note a bias. The quotations chosen more often than not communicate the enthusiasms of the developmental activists and their convictions that what they are attempting is possible, a feeling with which I agree. If that bias has come through, it does so because it is what they taught me and it is the lesson I want to share.

# Notes

## 1. WORKING IN THE NICHE

1. Background descriptions of the community development movement can be found in a wide array of writing, ranging from detailed evaluation studies to laudatory propaganda pieces. These writings included Berger (1992), Clay (1990), Lenz (1998), Parachini (1980), Peirce and Steinbach (1987, 1990), Perry (1987), Shavelson (1990), Vidal (1992), Zdenek (1987), among other.

2. Her results, however, probably exaggerate the accomplishments since she intentionally focused upon organizations that were "larger, more complex, and more accomplished than the average CDC" (Vidal 1992, p. 1).

## 4. RESPONDING TO THE PUBLIC SECTOR

1. This section was synthesized from Blaustein and Faux (1972); Goetz (1993); Halpern (1995); Koschinsky (1998); Parachini (1980); Peirce and Steinbach (1987); Perry (1987); and Zdenek (1990).

2. With lobbying efforts on the part of the nonprofits, substantial sums of money for housing programs have been restored, but such events took place after the conclusion of this project.

3. Others have examined the NRP program (Fainstein 1995; Goetz and Sidney 1994,a,b,c Nickel 1995). My conclusions have been tempered by their observations but my comments are based on my own interviews, observations, and documentary research.

# Bibliography

"Applications Due for CDC Designation under EZ Bill." *Development Times* 3 (April 1995): 1.

Berger, Renee. *A Place in the Marketplace: Making Capitalism Work in Poor Communities.* Washington, D.C.: National Congress for Community Economic Development, 1992.

Blaustein, Arthur, and Geoffrey Faux. *The Star Spangled Hustle.* New York: Doubleday & Company, 1972.

Brady, James P. "Arson, Fiscal Crisis and Community Action." *Crime & Delinquency* 28 (April 1982):247–74.

Bratt, Rachel G., Lanley C. Keyes, Alex Schwartz, and Avis C. Vidal. *Confronting the Management Challenge: Affordable Housing in the Nonprofit Sector.* New York: Community Development Research Center, Graduate School of Management and Urban Policy, New School for Social Research, 1994.

Buechler, Steven M. "New Social Movements Theories." *The Sociological Quarterly* 36, no. 3 (1995):441–64.

Carroll, William K., and R. S. Ratner. "Master Framing and Cross-moving Networking in Contemporary Social Movements." *The Sociological Quarterly* 37, no. 4 (1996):601–26.

Caudros, Paul. "Death of a CDC." *The Neighborhood Works* 19 (September/October 1996):10–13.

Center for Public Finance and Housing. *Status and Prospects of the Nonprofit Housing Sector.* Report to the U.S. Department of Housing and Urban Development Office of Policy Development and Research. Washington, D.C.: Community and Economic Development Program, Urban Institute, 1994.

Clavel, Pierre and Wim Wiewel, eds. *Harold Washington and the Neighborhoods: Progressive City Government in Chicago, 1983–1987.* New Brunswick, N.J.: Rutgers University Press, 1991.

Clavel, Pierre, Jessica Pitt, and Jordan Yin. "The Community Option in Urban Policy." *Urban Affairs Review* 32 (March 1997):435–58.

Clay, Phillip L. *Mainstreaming the Community Builders: The Challenge of Expanding the Capacity of Nonprofit Housing Development Corporations*. Cambridge, Mass.: Department of Urban Studies and Planning, Massachusetts Institute of Technology, 1990.

Clemetson, Robert, and Roger Coates. *Restoring Broken Places and Rebuilding Communities: A Casebook on African-American Church Involvement in Community Economic Development*. Washington, D.C.: National Congress for Community Economic Development, 1992.

Cohen, Rick. "Getting Your Piece of the New Federal Home Funds." *Shelterforce*, 14 (May/June 1992):14–17.

Comstock, Donald E. *Linking Local Successes: The Achievements of State Community Economic Development Associations in the 1980s*. A Report for the National Congress for Community Economic Development. The Phoenix Group, Inc., 1992.

Development Technical Institute. *Training Plan for the National Internship in Community Economic Development: Class of 1992*. Baltimore: DTI, 1992.

———. *Leadership and Management Program for Community-based Development: Training Plan 1993–1994 Program Year*. Baltimore: Development Training Institute, 1993.

Dimaggio, Paul J., and Walter W. Powell. "Introduction." In *The New Institutionalism in Organizational Analysis*, eds. Walter W. Powell and Paul J. DiMaggio, 1–38. Chicago: University of Chicago Press, 1991.

———. "The Iron Cage Revisited; Institutional Isomorphism and Collective Rationality." In *The New Institutionalism in Organizational Analysis*, eds. Walter W. Powell and Paul J. DiMaggio, 63–82. Chicago: University of Chicago Press, 1991.

Dreier, Peter, and Bruce Ehrlich. "Downtown Development and Urban Reform: The Politics of Boston's Linkage Policy." *Urban Affairs Quarterly* 26, no. 2 (1991):191–216.

Ducharme, Donna. "Planned Manufacturing Districts: How a Community Initiative Became City Policy." In *Harold Washington and the Neighborhoods: Progressive City Government in Chicago, 1983–1987*, eds. Pierre Clavel and Wim Wiewel, 221–37. New Brunswick, N.J.: Rutgers University Press, 1991.

Enterprise Foundation. *Seeds of Change: 1992 Annual Report*. Columbia, Md.: The Enterprise Foundation, 1993.

Ervin, Mike. "Building Blocks: A Step-by-Step Organizing Campaign Leads to New Funding for Housing." *The Neighborhood Works* 17 (February/March 1994):7–10.

*Executive Summary: Report on Indianapolis Community Development Organizations*. (Indianapolis, Neighborhood Housing Program) Indianapolis, 1990.

Fainstein, Susan S., Norman Glickman, Clare Gravon, and Clifford Hirst. *An Interim Evaluation of the Minneapolis Neighborhood Revitalization Program*.

Center for Urban Policy Research–Rutgers. New Brunswick, N.J.: Center for Urban Policy Research, 1993.

Fainstein, Susan S., Hirst Clifford, and Judith Tennebaum. *An Evaluation of the Minneapolis Neighborhood Revitalization Program*. Final Report of the Center for Urban Policy Research. CUPR Policy Report No. 12. New Brunswick, N.J.: Center for Urban Policy Research, Rutgers, 1995.

Ferman, Barbara. *Challenging the Growth Machine: Neighborhood Politics in Chicago and Pittsburgh*. Lawrence: University Press of Kansas, 1997.

Fischer, Frank, and John Forester. "Editors' Introduction." In *The Argumentative Turn in Policy Analysis and Planning*, eds. Frank Fischer and John Forester, 1–17. Durham, NC: Duke University Press, 1992.

Friedland, Roger, and Robert R. Alford. "Bringing Society Back In: Symbols, Practices and Institutional Contradictions." In *The New Institutionalism in Organizational Analysis*, eds. Walter W. Powell and Paul J. DiMaggio, 232–63. Chicago: University of Chicago Press, 1991.

Giloth, Robert, and Wim Wiewel. "Equity Development in Chicago: Robert Mier's Ideas and Practice." *Economic Development Quarterly* 10 (August 1996):204–16.

Giloth, Robert, Charles Orlebeke, James Tickell, and Patricia Wright. *Choices Ahead: CDCs and Real Estate Production in Chicago*. Chicago, Ill.: The Nathalie P. Vorhees Center for Neighborhood and Community Improvement, 1992.

Gittell, Ross, and Avis Vidal. *Community Organizing: Building Social Capital as a Development Strategy*. Thousand Oaks, Calif.: Sage, 1998.

Glazier, Jack D., and Peter Hall, M. "Constructing Isomorphism in an Interorganizational Network." *Humboldt Journal of Social Relations* 22, no. 2 (1996): 47–62.

Goetz, Edward G. *Shelter Burden: Local Politics and Progressive Housing Policy*. Philadelphia: Temple University Press, 1993.

———. "Local Government Support for Nonprofit Housing: A Survey of U.S. Cities." *Urban Affairs Quarterly* 27 (March 1992):420–35.

———. "There Goes the Neighborhood? The Impact of CDC-build, Subsidized Multifamily Housing on Urban Neighborhoods." *Shelterforce*, 18 (May/June 1996):20–21.

Goetz, Edward G. and Mara S. Sidney. "Revenge of the Property Owners: Community Development and the Politics of Property." *Journal of Urban Affairs* 16 no. 4 (1994a):319–334.

Goetz, Edward G., and Mara S. Sidney. *The Impact of the Minneapolis Neighborhood Revitalization Program on Neighborhood Organizations*. Minneapolis: Center for Urban and Regional Affairs, Hubert Humphrey Center, 1994b.

Groenbjerg, Kirsten A. *Understanding Nonprofit Funding: Managing Revenues in Social Services and Community Development Organizations*. San Francisco: Jossey-Bass Publishers, 1993.

Grogan, Paul S., and Benson F. Roberts. "Debating the Low-income Housing Tax Credit: Good Policy, Good Politics." *Shelterforce*, 14 (January/February 1992):13, 15.

Halpern, Robert. *Rebuilding the Inner City: A History of Neighborhood Initiatives to Address Poverty*. New York: Columbia University Press, 1995.

Harrison, Bennett. *Building Bridges: Community Development Corporations and the World of Employment Training*. A Report to the Ford Foundation. with Marcus Weiss and Jon Gant. New York: The Ford Foundation, 1995.

Harrison, Bennett, and Marcus Weiss. *Workforce Development Networks: Community-Based Organizations and Regional Alliances*. Newbury Park, Calif.: Sage, 1998.

Hartman, Chester. "Debating the Low-income Housing Tax Credit: Feeding the Sparrows by Feeding the Horses." *Shelterforce*, 14 (January/February 1992): 12, 15.

Hebert, Scott, Kathleen Baron Heintz, Chris, Nancy Kay, and James E. Wallace. *Non Profit Housing: Costs and Funding Final Report, Volume I: Findings*. Prepared for U.S. Department of Housing and Urban Development Office of Policy Development and Research. Abt Associates with Aspen Systems. Washington, D.C., 1993.

*Indianapolis Neighborhood Housing Partnership Strategic Overview*. 1990.

Jezierski, Louise. "Neighborhoods and Public-Private Partnerships in Pittsburgh." *Urban Affairs Quarterly* 26 (December 1990):217–49.

Keating, Dennis W. "Community-Based Housing Development in Cleveland." College of Urban Affairs, Cleveland State University, Cleveland, Ohio, 1989.

Keyes, Langley C., Alex Schwartz, Avis C. Vidal, and Rachel G. Bratt. "Networks and Nonprofits: Opportunities and Challenges in an Era of Federal Devolution." *Housing Policy Debate* 7, no. 2 (1996):201–29.

Klandermans, Bert. "The Social Construction of Protest and Multiorganizational Fields." In *Frontiers in Social Movement Theory*, eds. Aldon D. Morris and Carol McClurg Mueller, 77–103. New Haven: Yale University Press, 1992.

Koschinsky, Julia. "Challenging the Third Sector Housing Approach: The Impact of Federal Policies (1980–1996)." *Journal of Urban Affairs* 20, no. 2 (1998):117–36.

Kretzman, John P., and John L. McKnight. *Building Communities from the Inside Out: A Path Toward Finding and Mobilizing a Community's Assets*. Chicago: Center for Urban Affairs and Policy Research, Neighborhood Innovations Network, Northwestern University, 1993.

Krumholz, Norman, and John Forester. *Making Equity Planning Work: Leadership in the Public Sector*. Philadelphia: Temple University Press, 1990.

Kubisch, Anne C. "Comprehensive Community Initiatives." *Shelterforce*, 18 (January/February 1996):8–11.

Kvale, Steinar. "The Social Construction of Validity." *Qualitative Inquiry* 1 (March 1995):19–40.

Lemann, Nicholas. "The Myth of Community Development." *The New York Times Magazine*, January 9, 1994, 26–31, 50, 54, 60.

Lenz, Thomas J. "Neighborhood Development: Issues and Models." *Social Policy* 19 (Spring 1988):24–30.

Linder, William, and Gerald Shattuck. "New Communities Corporation: An Alternative Community Development Model in Religious Context." Community Development Series Paper 100. Newark, N.J.: New Communities Press, 1991.

Lipsitz, George. *A Life in the Struggle: Ivory Perry and the Culture of Opposition.* Philadelphia: Temple University Press, 1995 (orig. published 1988).

Local Initiatives Support Corporation. *1993 Annual Report.* New York: Local Initiative Support Corporation, 1994.

———. *Local Initiatives Support Corporation: LISC Working Partnerships for Neighborhood Development 1991 Annual Report.* New York: Local Initiatives Support Corporation, 1992.

MacArthur Foundation, the John D. and Catherine T. *1991 Report on Activities.* Chicago: The John D. and Catherine T. MacArthur Foundation, 1992.

Macdonald, Heather. "The Resolution Trust Corporation's Affordable-housing Mandate." *Urban Affairs Review* 30 (March 1995):558–79.

Mansbridge, Janet. "The Politics of Engagement: Challenging the Mainstream." In *Feminist Organizations: Harvest of the New Women's Movement*, eds. Myra Marx Ferree, and Patricia Yancey Martin, 27–34. Philadelphia: Temple University Press, 1995.

Marquez, Benjamin. "Mexican-American Community Development Corporations and the Limits of Directed Capitalism." *Economic Development Quarterly* 7 (August 1993):287–95.

McDougall, Harold. Black *Baltimore: A New Theory of Community.* Philadelphia: Temple University Press, 1993.

Medoff, Peter, and Holly Sklar. *Streets of Hope: The Fall and Rise of an Urban Neighborhood.* Boston: South End Press, 1994.

Metzger, John T. "Remaking the Growth Coalition: The Pittsburgh Partnership for Neighborhood Development." *Economic Development Quarterly* 28 (February 1998):12–29.

———. "The Community Reinvestment Act and Neighborhood Revitalization in Pittsburgh." In *From Redlining to Reinvestment: Community Responses to Urban Disinvestment*, ed. Gregory D. Squires, 73–108. Philadelphia: Temple University Press, 1992.

Meyer, David S., and Nancy Whittier. "Social Movement Spillover." *Social Problems* 41 (May 1994):277–98.

Meyer, John W. and Brian Rowan. "Institutionalized Organizations: Formal Structure as Myth and Ceremoney." In *The New Institutionalism in Organizational Analysis*, eds. Walter W. Powell and Paul J. DiMaggio, 41–62. Chicago: University of Chicago Press, 1991.

Meyer, John W., John Boli, and George M. Thomas "Ontology and Rationalization in the Western Cultural Account." In *Institutional Environments and Organizations: Structural Complexity and Individualism*, eds. W. Richard Scott and John W. Meyer, 9–27. Thousand Oaks, Calif.: Sage, 1994.

Mier, Robert, and Richard D. Bingham. "Metaphors of Economic Development." In *Theories of Local Economic Development*, eds Richard Bingham and Robert Mier, 284–304. Newbury Park, Calif.: Sage, 1993.

Mihaly, Mary. "Who's Running the Neighborhoods?" *Cleveland Magazine*, April 1993, 26–30.

National Congress for Community Economic Development. *Changing the Odds: The Achievements of Community-based Development Corporations.* Washington, D.C.: NCCED, 1991.

———. *Between and on Behalf: The Intermediary Role.* Washington, D.C.: NCCED, 1991b.

———. *Human Services: An Economic Development Opportunity A Manual for Economic-based Enterprises.* Washington, D.C.: NCCED, 1992.

———. *Proven Partners: CDCs Coming of Age.* 1990–1991 biennial report. Washington, D.C.: NCCED, 1992.

———. *Human Services: An Economic Development Opportunity: A Manual for Economics-Based Enterprises.* Washington, D.C.: NCCED, 1992.

———. *Tying It All Together: The Comprehensive Achievements of Community-Based Development Organizations.* Washington, D.C.: NCCED, 1995.

———. *NCCED: Strategic Plan 1995–2000.* Washington, D.C.: NCCED, 1995.

Neighborhood Progress, Inc. *1993–1995 Policy Recommendations.* Cleveland, Ohio: Neighborhood Progress Inc., 1992.

Nichols, Lawrence. "Social Problems as Landmark Narratives: Bank of Boston, Mass Media and 'Money Laundering'" *Social Problems* 44, no. 3 (1997): 324–41.

Nickel, Denise R. "The Progressive City? Urban Redevelopment in Minneapolis." *Urban Affairs Review* 30 (January 1995):355–77.

"OMB Plans to Eliminate OCS Grants to CDCs." *Development Times* 4 (January 1995):1, 5.

Parachini, Jr., Lawrence F. *A Political History of the Special Impact Program.* Cambridge, Mass.: Center for Community Economic Development, 1980.

Parzen, Julia Ann, and Michael Hall Kieschnick. *Credit Where It's Due: Development Banking for Communities.* Philadelphia: Temple University Press, 1992.

Peirce, Neal R., and Carol F. Steinbach. *Corrective Capitalism: The Rise of America's Community Development Corporations.* New York: Ford Foundation, 1987.

————. *Enterprising Communities: Community-Based Development in America.* Washington, D.C.: Council for Community-Based Development, 1990.

Perkins, John M. *Beyond Charity: The Call to Christian Community Development.* Grand Rapids, Mich.: Baker Books, 1993.

Perry, Stewart E. *Communities on the Way: Rebuilding Local Economies in the United States and Canada.* Albany: State University of New York Press, 1987.

Persky, Joseph, David Ranney, and Wim Wiewel. "Import Substitution and Local Economic Development." *Economic Development Quarterly* 7 (February 1993):18–29.

Pogge, Jean. "Reinvestment in Chicago's Neighborhoods: A Twenty Year Struggle." In *From Redlining to Reinvestment: Community Responses to Urban Disinvestment,* ed. Gregory D. Squires, 133–48. Philadelphia: Temple University Press, 1992.

Pogge, Jean, and Maria Choca. *The Long Term Future of Resources for Chicago's Community Development Corporations.* A Report to the John D. and Catherine T. MacArthur Foundation. Chicago: Woodstock Institute, 1991.

Polletta, Francesca. "'It Was Like a Fever . . . ': Narrative and Identity in Social Protest." *Social Problems* 45 (May 1998):137–59.

Posner, Prudence. "Introduction." In *Dilemmas of Activism: Class, Community, and the Politics of Local Mobilization,* eds. Joseph Kling and S. Prudence, 3–20. Philadephia: Temple University Press, 1990.

Powell, Walter E., and Paul J. DiMaggio, eds. *The New Institutionalism in Organizational Analysis.* Chicago: University of Chicago Press, 1991.

Richardson, Laurel. "Narrative and Sociology." In *Representation in Ethnography,* ed. John Van Maanen, 198–221. Thousand Oaks, Calif.: Sage, 1995.

Rich, Michael J. *Federal Policymaking and the Poor: National Goals, Local Choices, and Distributional Outcomes.* Princeton, N.J.: Princeton University Press, 1993.

Robert A. Rapoza Associates. *Section-by-Section Analysis of the National Community Economic Partnership Act.* Compiled by Alison Feighan. Washington, D.C. Rapoza Associates.

Rubin, Herbert J. "'Shoot the F——ing Intermediaries, Especially LISC': Theories of Intermediation for Community-Based Development." Paper presented at the 25th Annual Meeting of the Urban Affairs Association. Portland, Oreg., 1995.

————. "Renewing Hope in the Inner City: Conversations with Community-Based Development Practitioners." *Administration and Society* 27 (May 1995):127–60.

————. "There Aren't Going to Be Any Bakeries Here If There Is No Money to Afford Jellyrolls: The Organic Theory of Community-Based Development." *Social Problems* 41 (August 1994):401–24.

Rubin, Herbert J. and Irene S. Rubin. *Qualitative Interviewing: The Art of Hearing Data*. Thousand Oaks, Calif.: Sage, 1995.

Salamon, Lester M. *Partners in Public Service: Government-Nonprofit Relations in the Modern Welfare State*. Baltimore: John Hopkins University Press, 1995.

Scott, W. Richard. "Institutions and Organizations: Toward a Theoretical Synthesis." In *Institutional Environments and Organizations: Structural Complexity and Individualism*, eds. W. Richard Scott and, John W. Meyer, 55–80. Thousand Oaks, Calif.: Sage, 1994.

———. "Unpacking Institutional Arguments." In *The New Institutionalism in Organizational Analysis*, eds. Walter W. Powell and Paul J. Dimaggio, 164–82. Chicago: University of Chicago Press, 1991.

Scott, W. Richard, and John W. Meyer. "The Organization of Societal Sectors: Propositions and Early Evidence." In *The New Institutionalism in Organizational Analysis*, eds. Walter W. Powell and Paul J. DiMaggio, 108–40. Chicago: University of Chicago Press, 1991.

Shavelson, Jeff. *A Third Way: A Sourcebook of Innovations in Community-Owned Enterprise*. Washington, D.C.: The National Center for Economic Alternatives, 1990.

Sherradan, Michael. *Assets and the Poor: A New American Welfare Policy*. Armonk, N.Y.: M. E. Sharpe, 1991.

Shiffman, Ron. "Uprooting Poverty through Community Development." *City Limits* 15 (November 1990):8–11.

Smith, Steven Rathgeb, and Michael Lipsky. *Nonprofits for Hire: The Welfare State in the Age of Contracting*. Cambridge, Mass.: Harvard University Press, 1993.

Snow, David A., E. Burke Rochford Jr., Steven K. Worden, and Robert D. Benford. "Frame Alignment Processes, Micromobilization, and Movement Participation." *American Sociological Review* 51 (August 1986):464–81.

Squires, Gregory D. "Community Reinvestment: An Emerging Social Movement." In *From Redlining to Reinvestment: Community Responses to Urban Disinvestment*, ed. Gregory D. Squires, 1–37. Philadelphia: Temple University Press, 1992.

Stoecker, Randy. "Community Organizing and Community-Based Redevelopment in Cedar-Riverside and East Toledo: A Comparative Study." *Journal of Community Practice* 2, no. 3 (1995):1–24.

———. "The Myth of Community Empowerment: Rethinking the Community Development Corporation Model of Urban Redevelopment." Draft Manuscript. 1995.

———. "The CDC Model of Urban Redevelopment: A Critique and an Alternative." *Journal of Urban Affairs* 19, no. 1 (1997):1–22.

Suchman, Diane R., D. Scott Middleton, and Susan L. Giles. *Public/private Housing Partnerships*. Washington, D.C.: Urban Land Institute, 1990.

Sullivan, Mercer L. *More Than Housing: How Community Development Corporations Go about Changing Lives and Neighborhoods.* New York: Community Development Research Center Graduate School of Management and Urban Policy New School for Social Research, 1993.

Tarrow, Sidney. *Power in Movement: Social Movements, Collective Action and Politics.* New York: Cambridge University Press, 1994.

TeamWorks. *An Interim Assessment of the Community Initiatives Program's Public Policy Initiative.* A Report to the John D. and Catherine T. MacArthur Foundation. Arlington, Va., 1991.

Throgmorton, James A. *Planning as Persuasive Storytelling: The Rhetorical Construction of Chicago's Electric Future.* Chicago: University of Chicago Press, 1996.

Tittle, Diana. *Rebuilding Cleveland; the Cleveland Foundation and Its Evolving Urban Strategy.* Columbus, Ohio: Ohio State University Press, 1992.

Vidal, Avis C., Principal Investigator. *Community Economic Development Assessment: A National Study or Urban Community Development Corporations—Preliminary Findings.* New York: Community Development Research Center, Graduate School of Management and Urban Professions, New School for Social Research, 1989.

———. *Rebuilding Communities: A National Study of Urban Community Development Corporations.* New York: Community Development Research Center, Graduate School of Management and Urban Policy, New School for Social Research, 1992.

Vidal, Avis C., Arnold M. Howitt, and Kathleen P. Foster. *Stimulating Community Development: An Assessment of the Local Initiatives Support Corporation.* A report submitted to the Local Initiatives Support Corporation, June 1986. Cambridge, Mass.: The State, Local and Intergovernmental Center, John F. Kennedy School of Government, Harvard University, 1986.

Wiewel, Wim, and Lauri Alpern. "Decentralization of Policy-making." In *Social Justice and Local Development Policy,* eds. Robert Mier, Robert Giloth, J. Kari Moe, and associates, 115–34. Newbury Park, Calif.: Sage, 1993.

Wiewel, Wim, and Pierre Clavel. "Conclusion." In *Harold Washington and the Neigbhborhoods: Progressive City Government in Chicago, 1983–1987,* eds. Pierre Clavel and Wim Wiewel, 270–93. New Brunswick, N.J.: Rutgers University Press, 1991.

Williams, Rhys. "Constructing the Public Good: Social Movements and Cultural Resources." *Social Problems* 42 (February 1995):124–44.

Wright, David J. "Comprehensive Strategies for Community Renewal." *Rockefeller Institute Bulletin* (1998):48–66.

Yin, Jordan. "The Transformation of the Community Development Corporation: A Case Study of Politics and Institutions in Cleveland, 1967–1993." M.S. thesis Graduate School of Cornell University, 1994.

Zdenek, Robert. "Community Development Corporations." In *Beyond the Market and the State: New Directions in Community Development*, eds. Severyn T. Bruyn and James Meehan, 112–27. Philadelphia: Temple University Press, 1987.

# Index

Property Research Management Center, 195

Protest campaigns, CRA, 88

Protest, against redlining, 241

Publications, 215; as agenda setting, 195, 215, 216

Public sector, non-cash contributions to projects, 170

Public-private partnerships, 72

*Qualitative Interviewing: The Art of Hearing Data*, 276

Racial concerns, 11, 16, 57, 76, 77, 97, 185

Rapoza, Inc., 195

Ratner, W.S., 38

Reagan, cutback of CBDO Support, 81

Redlining, 243

Rehab Network, Affordable Housing and Jobs Campaign, 257, 258

Relationships, developing, 155

Renewing hope, x, 136, 140, 153, 158, 233, 259, 273, 274

Rental housing, costs in managing, 64

Rental income, 63

Reports, as advocacy and ideological documents, 194

Research design, ix, 274–275, 280

Respect, lack of by funders, 160, 161

Revolving loan funds, 12, 61

Richardson, Laurel, 279

Rich, Michael, 88

Risky projects, funding for, 166

Robert, Benson, 246

Rutgers Evaluation Study, 94, 97

Salamon, Lester, 40

Sample, 277, 278

SBA (Small Business Administration), 68, 70

Scott, W. Richard, xii, 35, 37

Section 8 Housing, 2, 10, 29, 69, 71, 78, 82, 83, 170, 175; complementing LIHTC, 169

Seed money, 107, 176

Service fees, 170, 171

Set-asides, 174

SHAC (State Housing Action Coalition), 194, 198; Housing Trust Fund Campaign, 198, 240

Shell coalitions, 244

*Shelterforce*, 216

Sherradan, Michael, 147

Shiffman, Ronald, 216

Shore Bank Advisory Services, 195

Sidney, Myra, 58, 91, 95, 96, 97, 238

Show projects, 119, 120

Simmons, Adele (president of MacArthur Foundation), 223

Single Room Occupancy projects, 209, 210

Slumlords, 78

Smith, Steven, 2

Snow, David, 38, 263, 272

Social agendas, pressures against, 114

Social Assets, 12, 142, 149

Social capital, 155, 227

Social change, 137, 230

Social cost accounting, 209

Social costs, 24, 110, 111, 159, 160

Social equity, 149, 251

Social leveraging, 13, 16, 82, 164

Social mission, 2, 53

Social movement, creating a sense of belonging, 230

Social networks, 155, 156

Social service grants, community-based development organizations as eligible recipients, 71

Social service agencies, providing space for, 165, 181

Social services, 53, 54, 60; dangers in providing, 53

Socialization of poor youth, 153

Societal sector, 35, 132, 261, 262, 263, 266, 268; influenced by issue framing, 265, 269

Soft costs, 170

Soft money, 184

Soup kitchen project, 182

South East Community Organization, 47

Special districts, 175

Speciation, 265